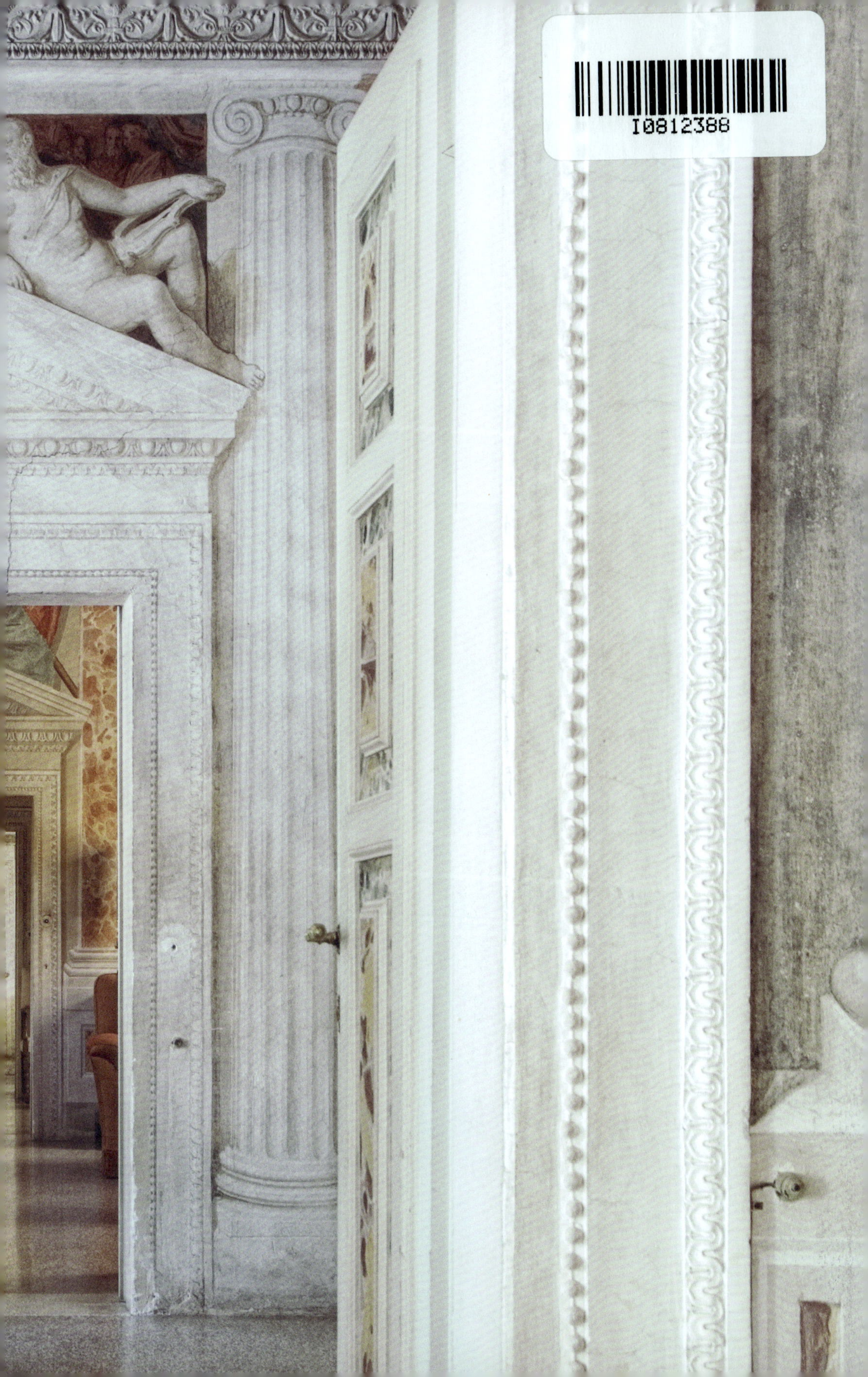

PROSECCO & SPRITZ

DISCOVERING THIS GLAMOROUS WINE AND ITS APERITIFS

Text

Elisa Giraud

Cocktails

Leonardo Cisotto

Photos

Arcangelo Piai & Friends

SIME BOOKS

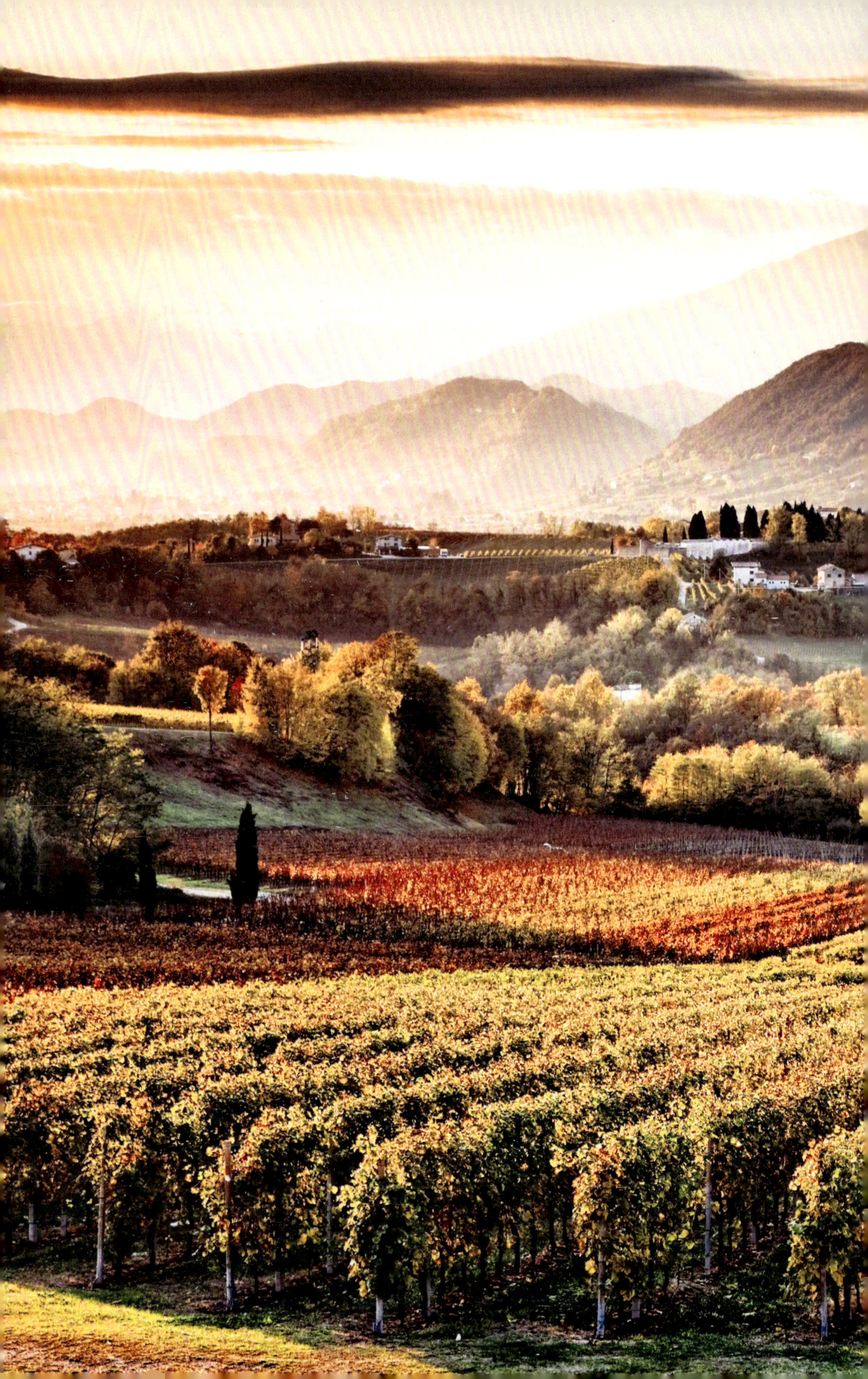

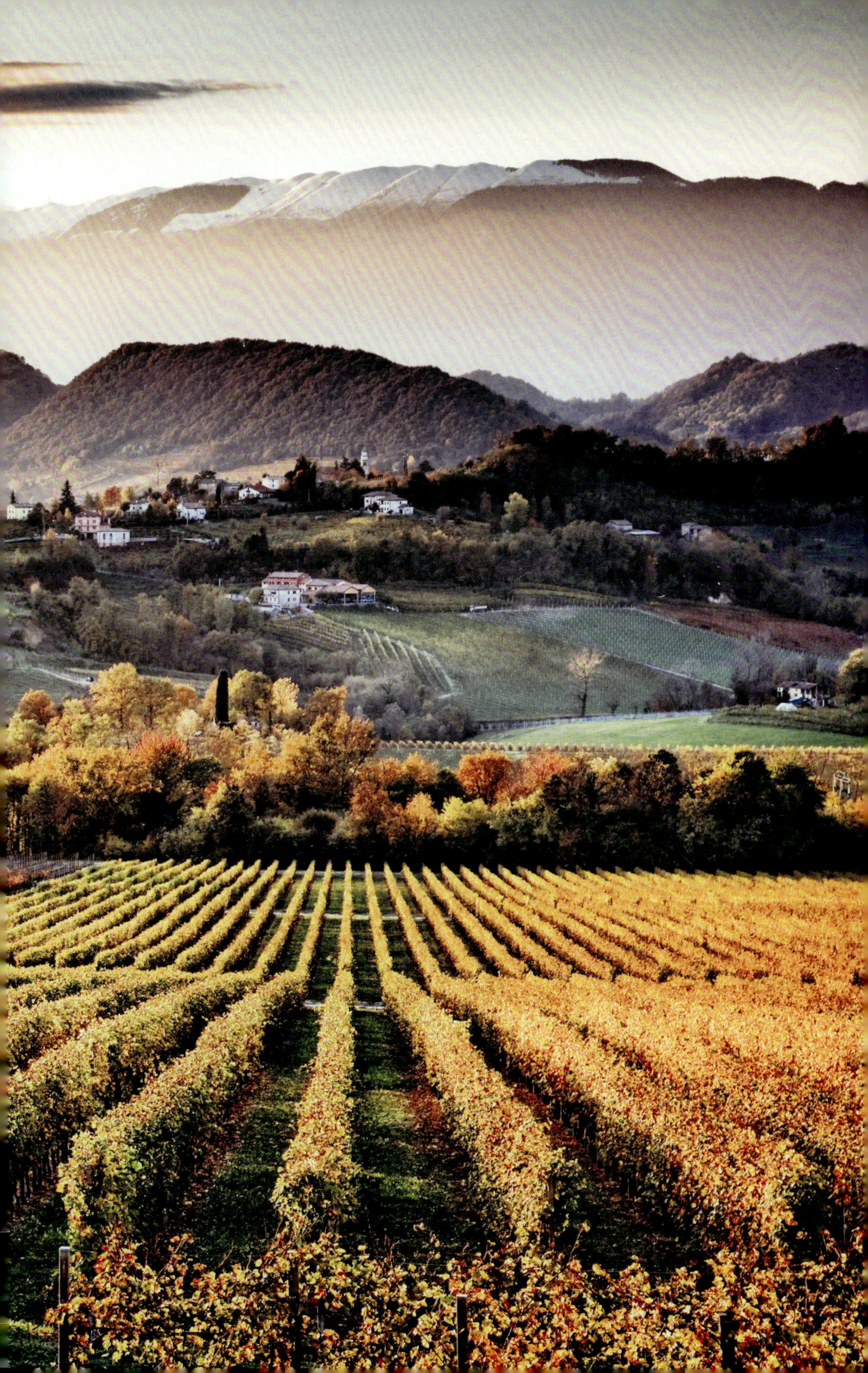

FOREWORD

by ANTONIO PADOVAN

The year zero of Prosecco was 2009, when this grape with its ancient history lost its name. The Prosecco grape became Glera. And Prosecco became that wine made primarily from Glera grapes and produced only in an area comprising part of the Veneto and of Friuli Venezia Giulia. Since then this new Italian wine has become highly fashionable. The hills where it is made have been transformed into effervescent oil wells, mines of straw-colored gold. The area where Prosecco is produced today has a centuries-old peasant tradition, which has developed deep-rooted values among its people, handed down to the present generation from their grandparents and great-grandparents. Such values saved this region, keeping it embedded firmly in the soil during the industrial boom years. At the same time, however, the rural mindset, built around the unpredictable moods of nature, has instilled in the people a plague that today afflicts new wine-growers: their skill in attaining the finest of the vintage is all too often bound up closely with an inability to foresee the state in which we will leave these fragile, beautiful hills to those who come after us. Our wineglasses are filled with the skills of those who for generations have known how to get the most out of the native terroir (a whole made up of soil, tradition and people) but also, unfortunately, the phytopharmaceuticals which the new monoculture increasingly needs to survive, having been deprived of the biodiversity that formerly protected it. The bubbles of this wine enclose all the excellencies and the shadows of the land from which it comes.

A corner of paradise at risk of extinction. Fortunately, ever more frequently enlightened wine-growers arise, who know that the love and labor spent in the vineyards lying on steep hillsides (some of them very rugged), working them by hand and using natural methods, yields a distinctive flavor that will inevitably be found in the wineglass. When I drink the Prosecco that I choose for myself, I breathe in the bouquet of passion, not the chemicals of the new millennium. The Prosecco I enjoy is made by people who understand that the land is not ours, but we hold it as a legacy for our children's children.

< pages 2-3 San Pietro di Feletto

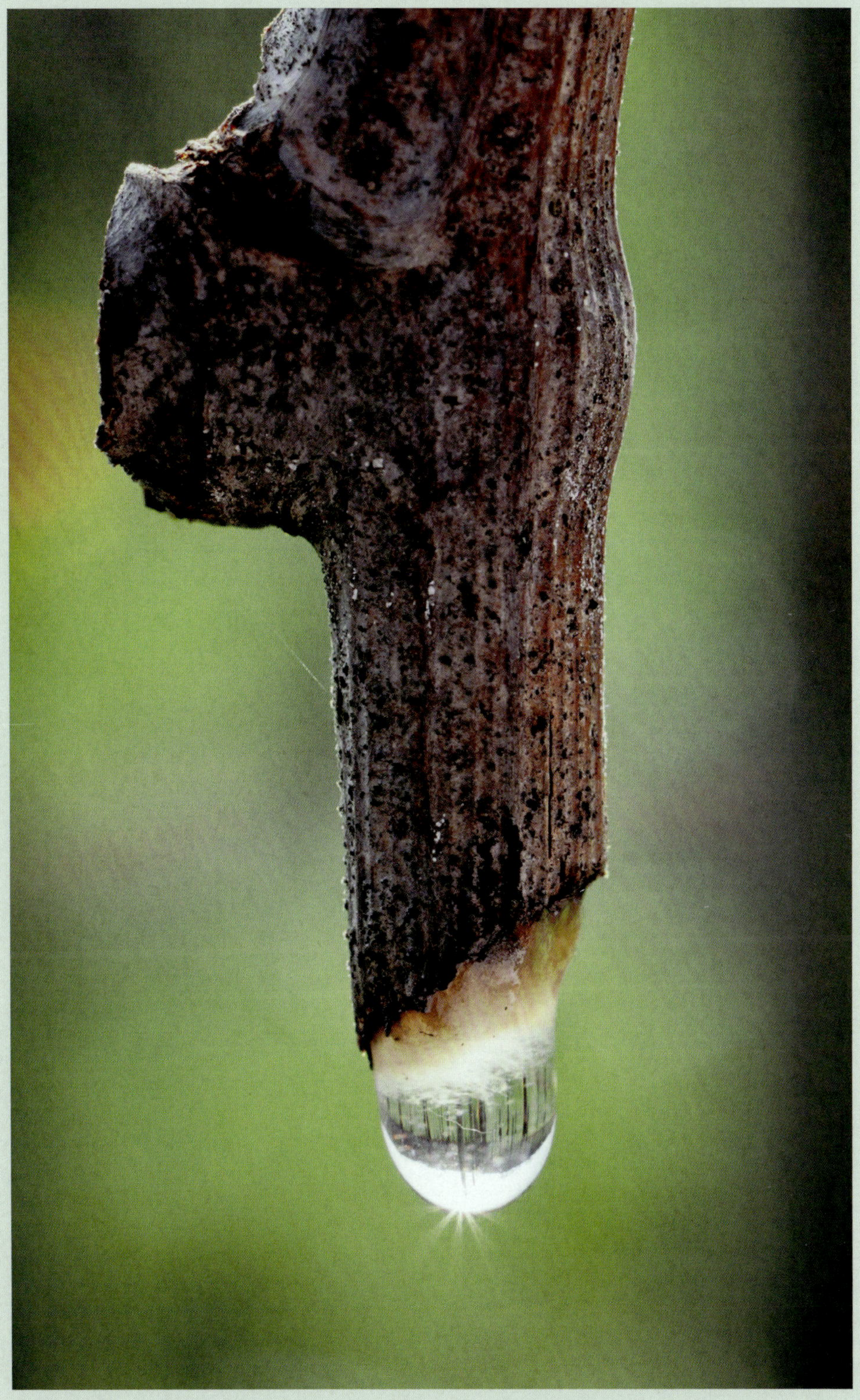

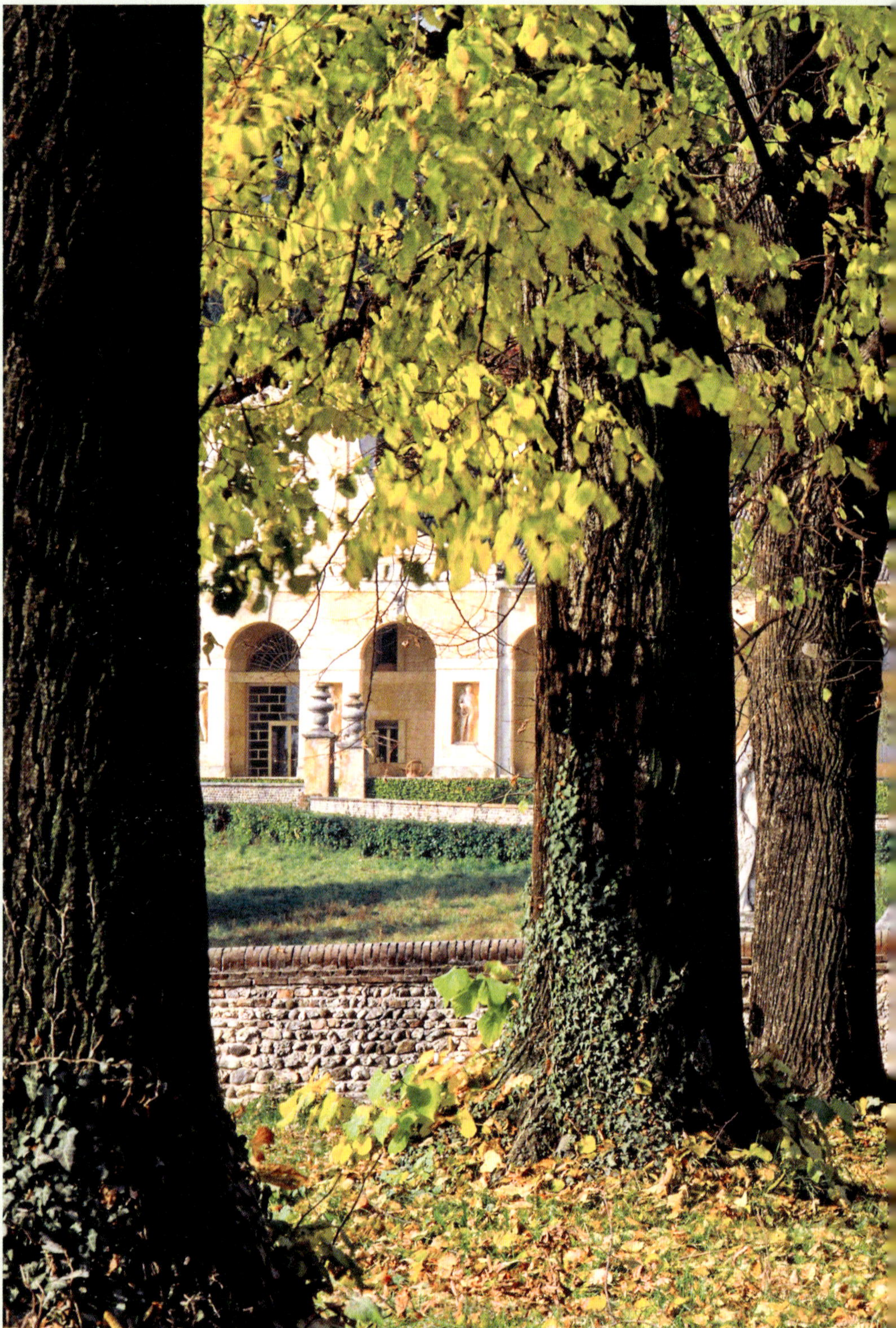

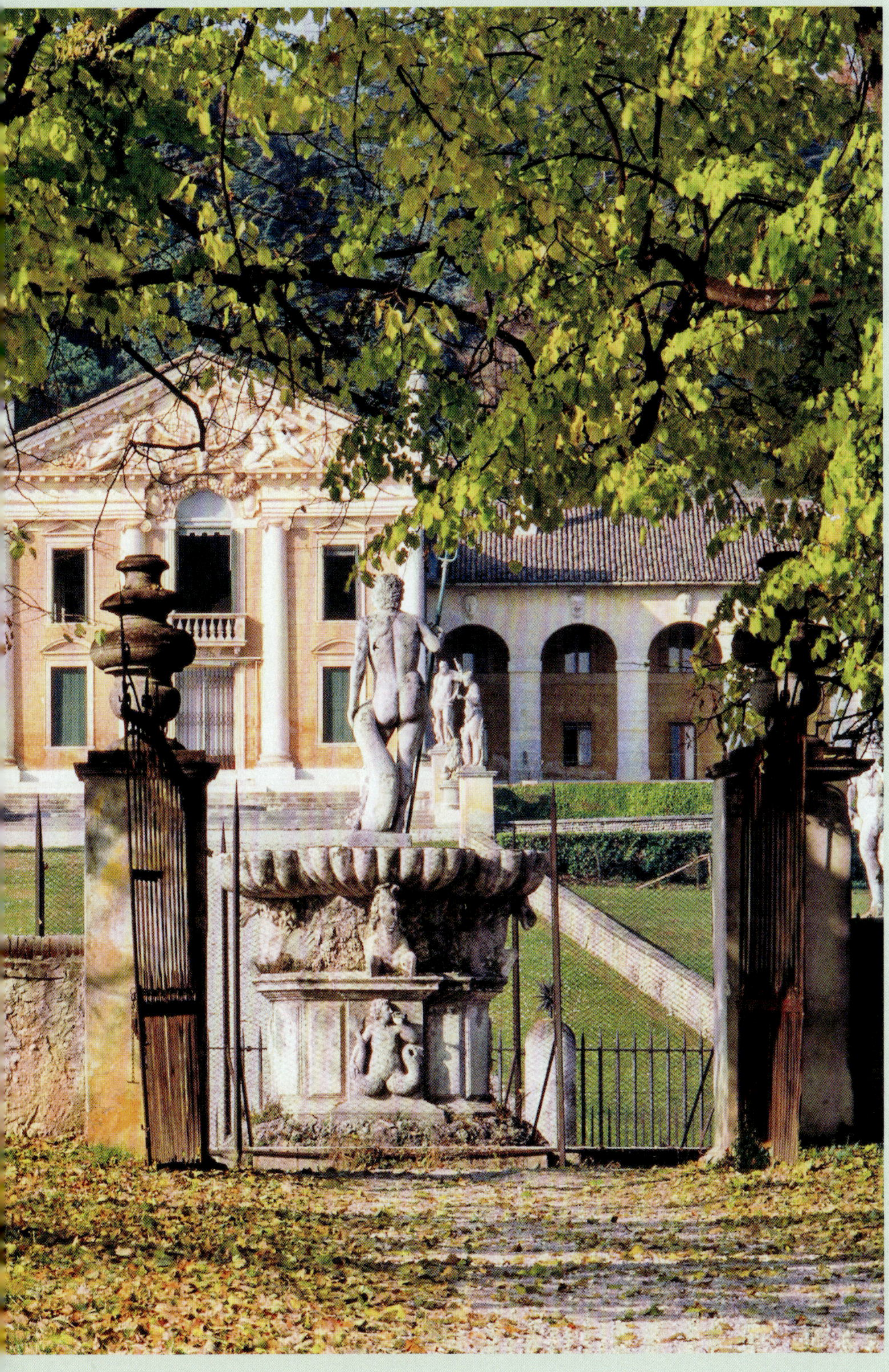

Villa di Maser (Villa Barbaro)

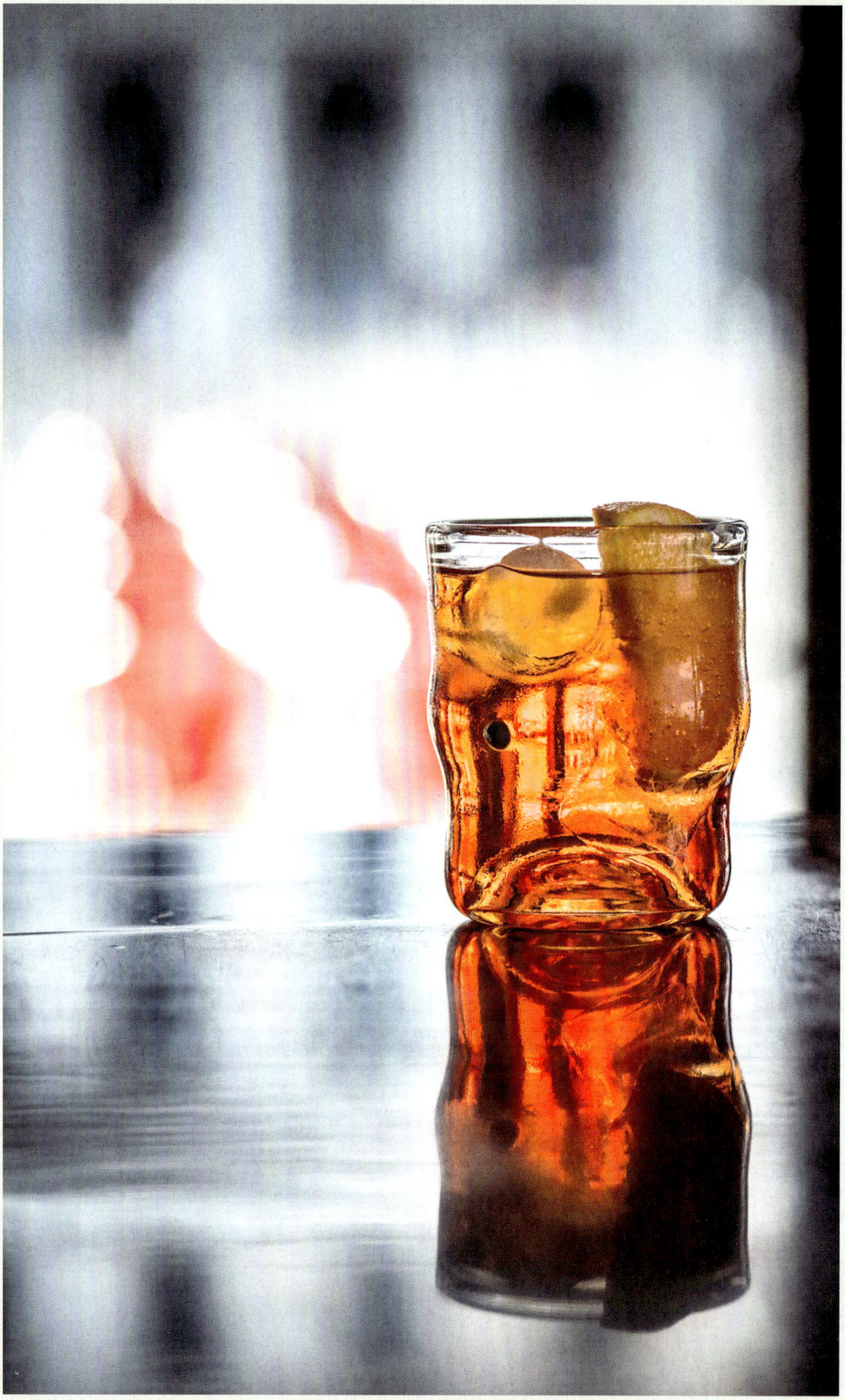

Venice, Grancaffè Quadri

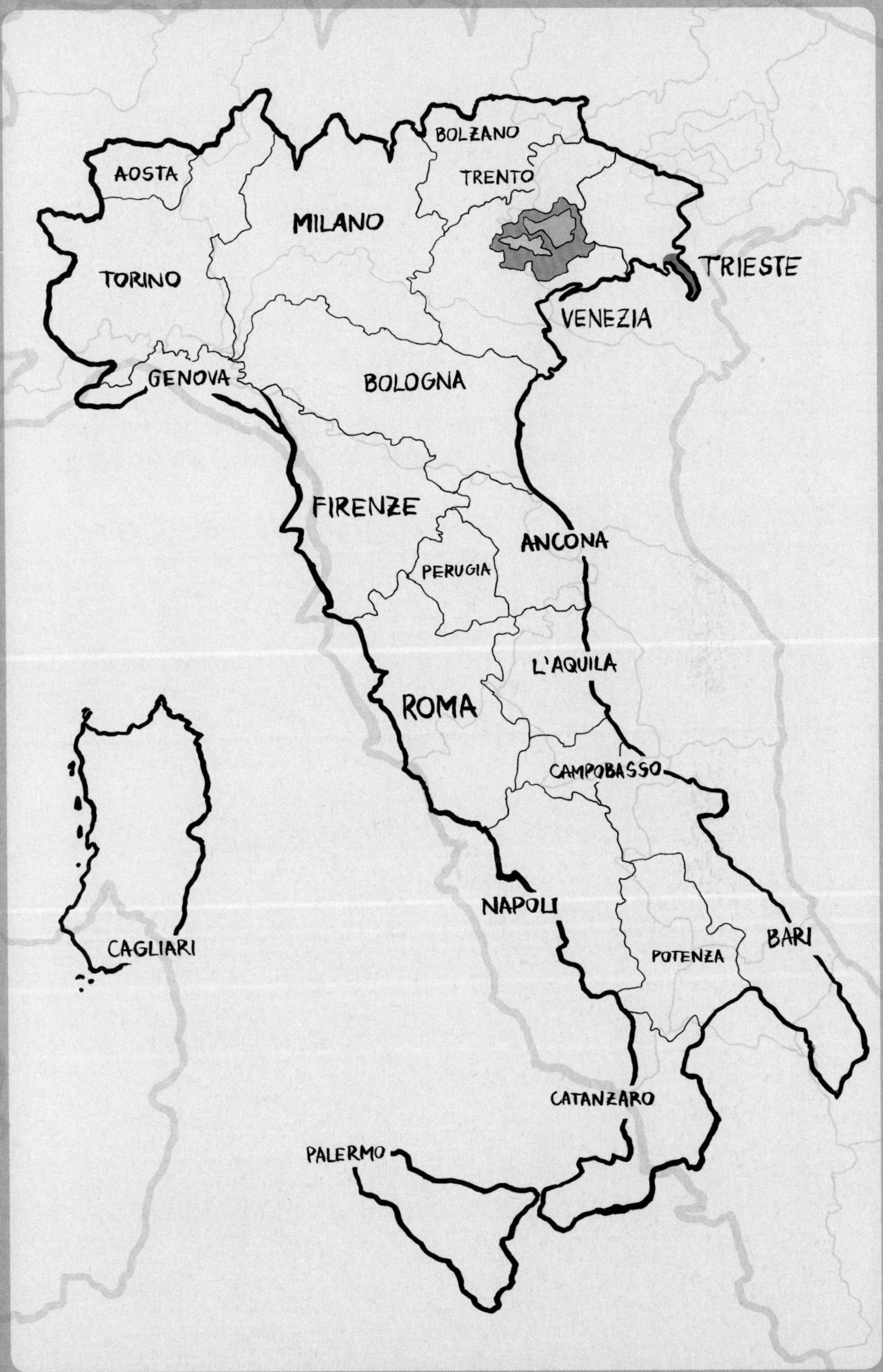
BOLZANO
AOSTA
TRENTO
MILANO
TRIESTE
TORINO
VENEZIA
GENOVA
BOLOGNA
FIRENZE
ANCONA
PERUGIA
L'AQUILA
ROMA
CAMPOBASSO
NAPOLI
CAGLIARI
BARI
POTENZA
CATANZARO
PALERMO

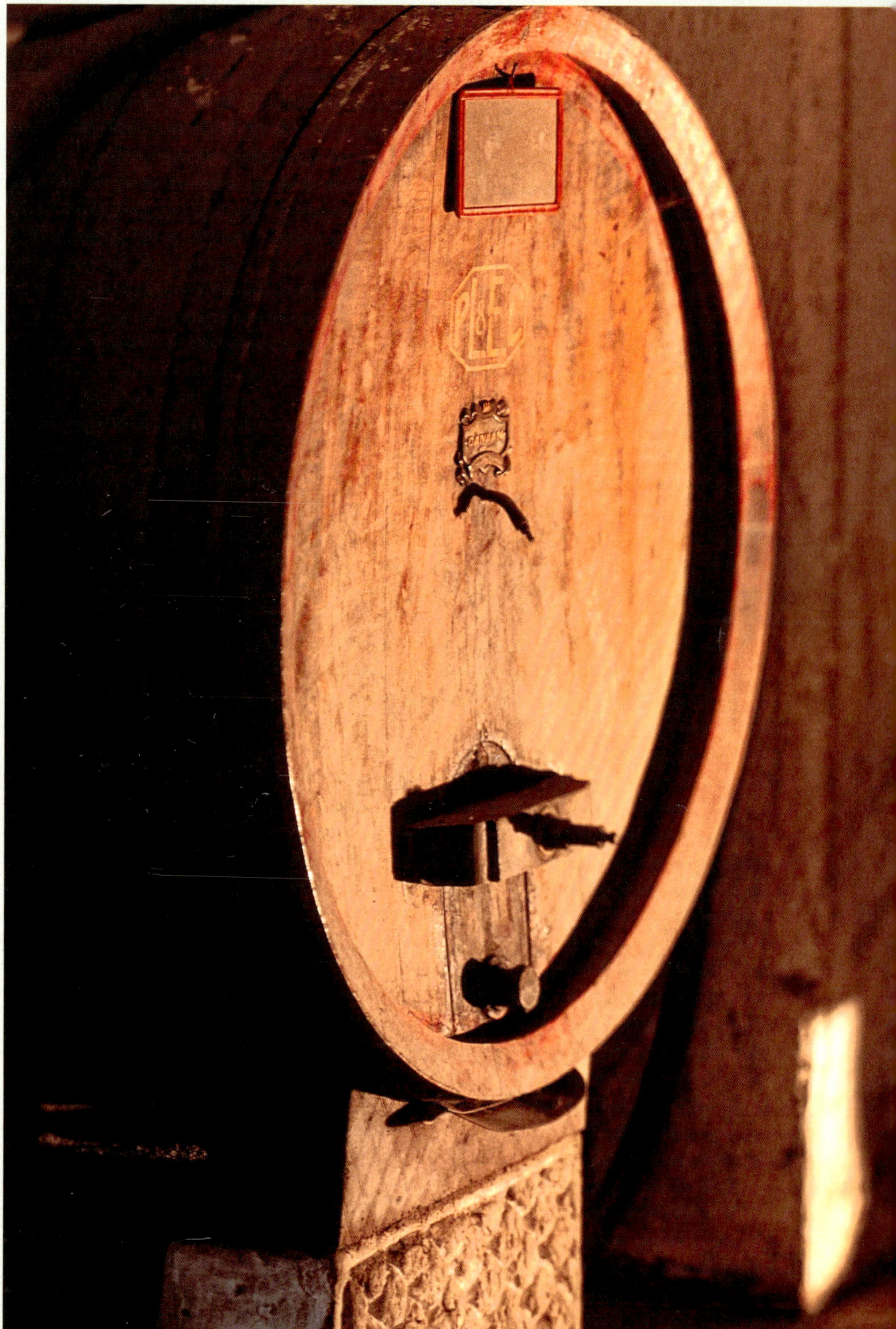

Conegliano

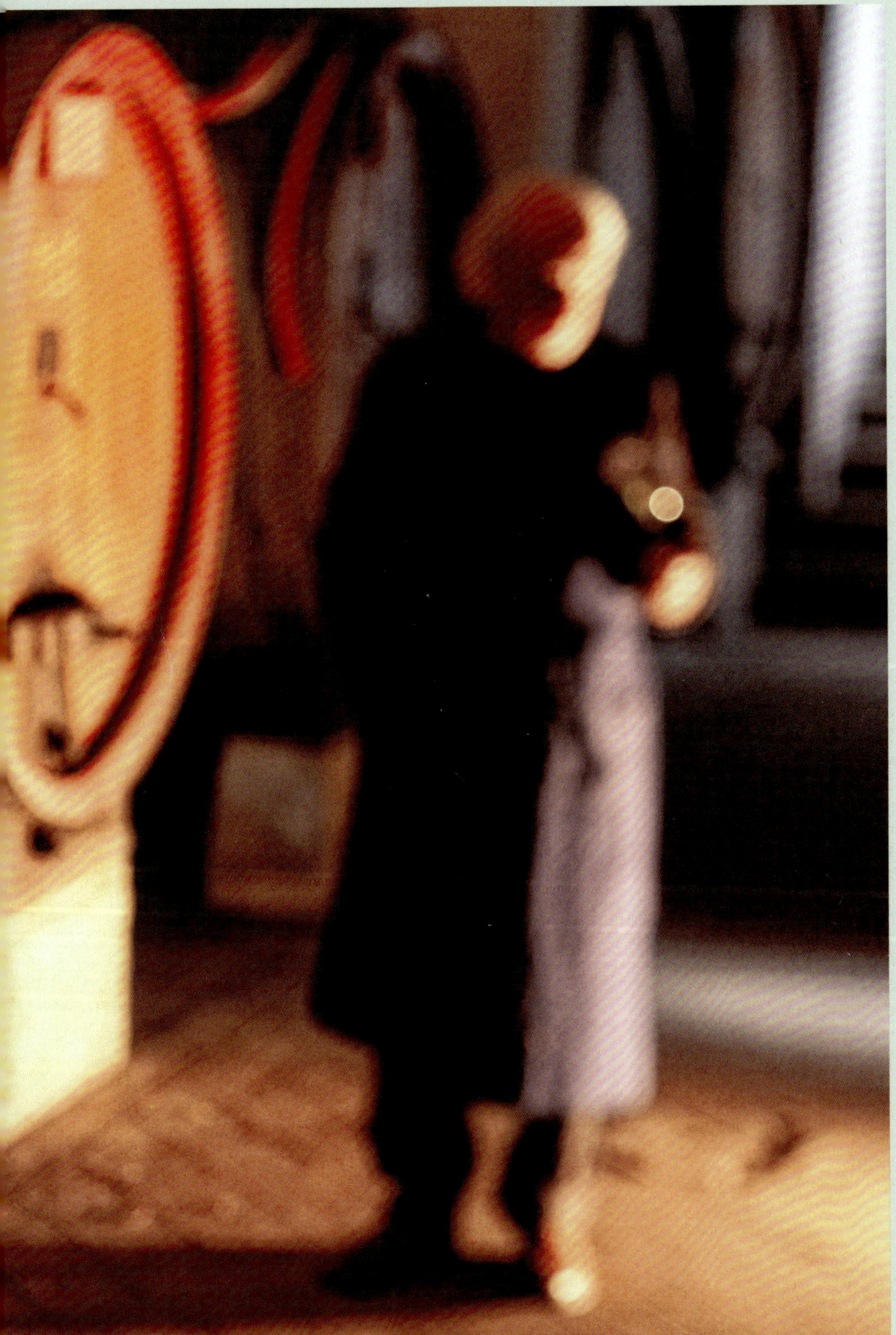

pages 12-13 Collalbrigo >

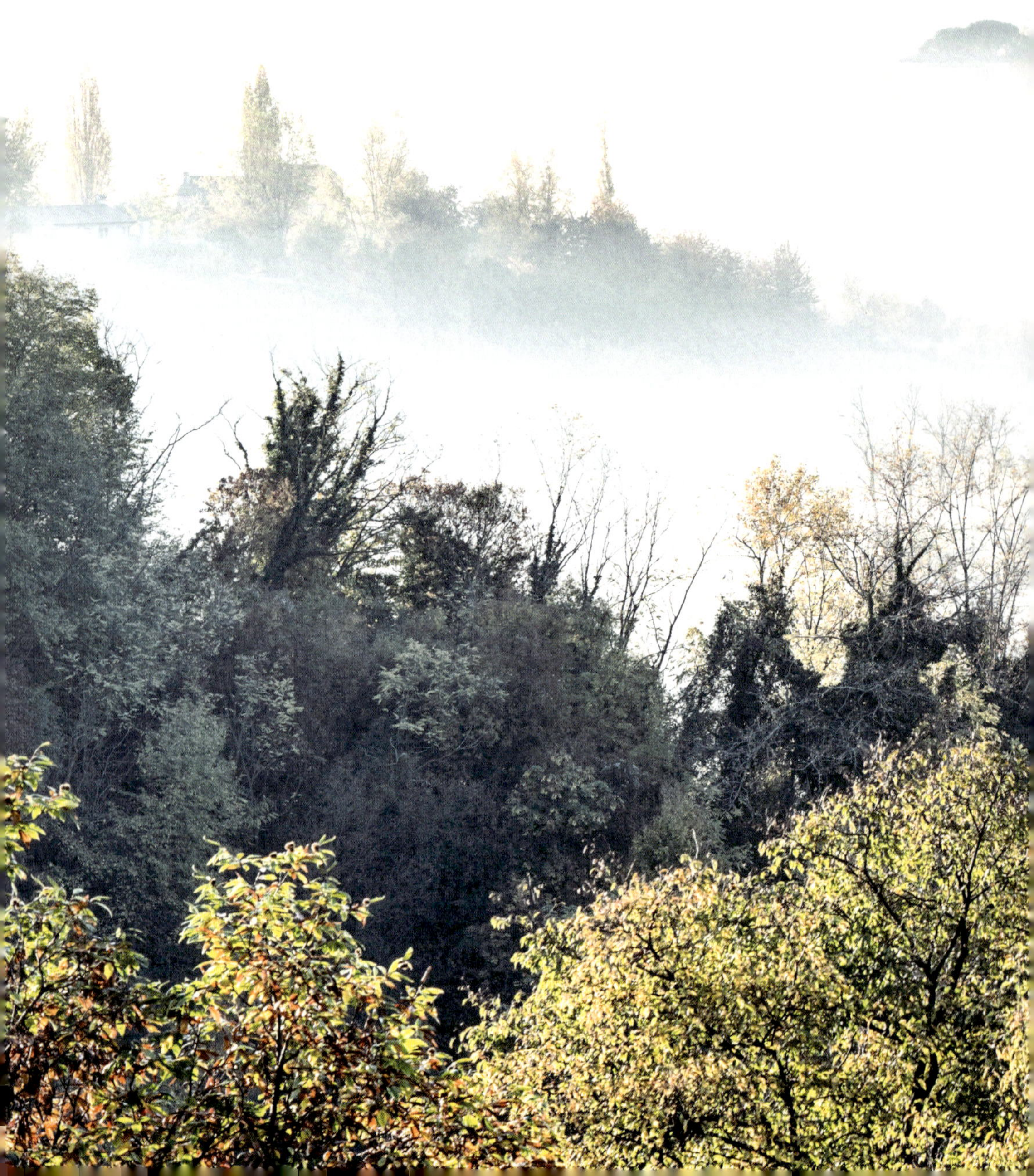

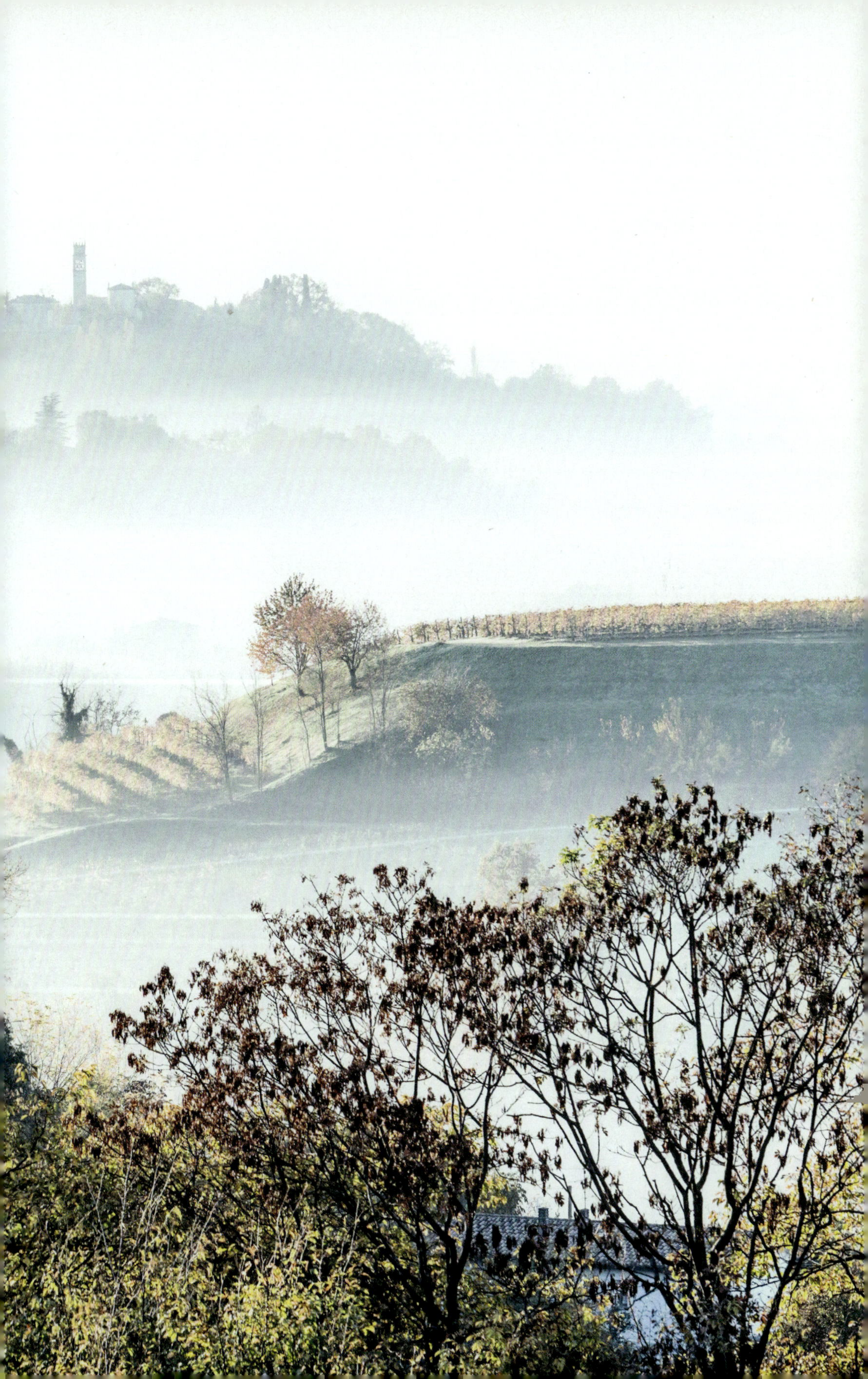

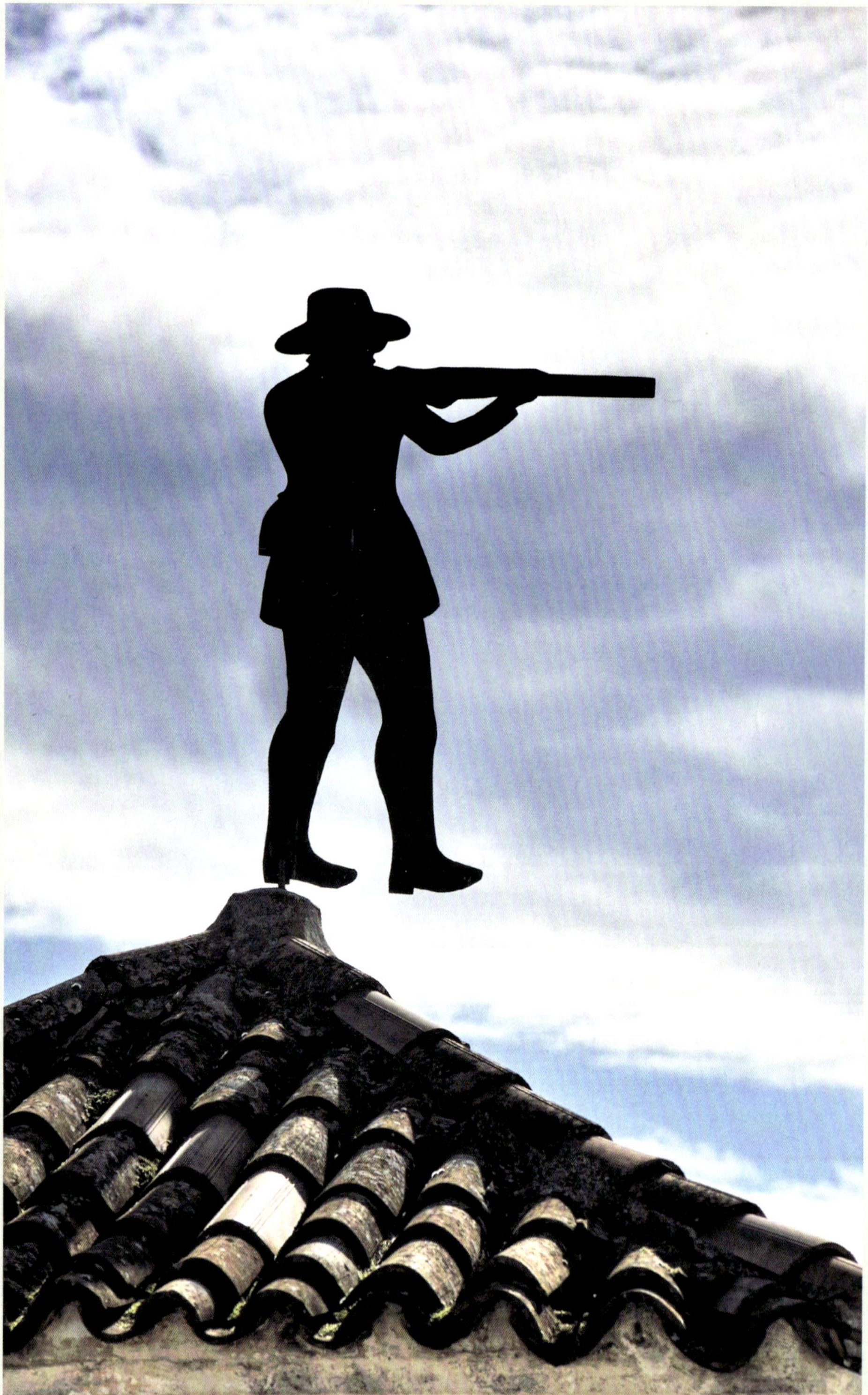

Tezze di Piave

INDEX

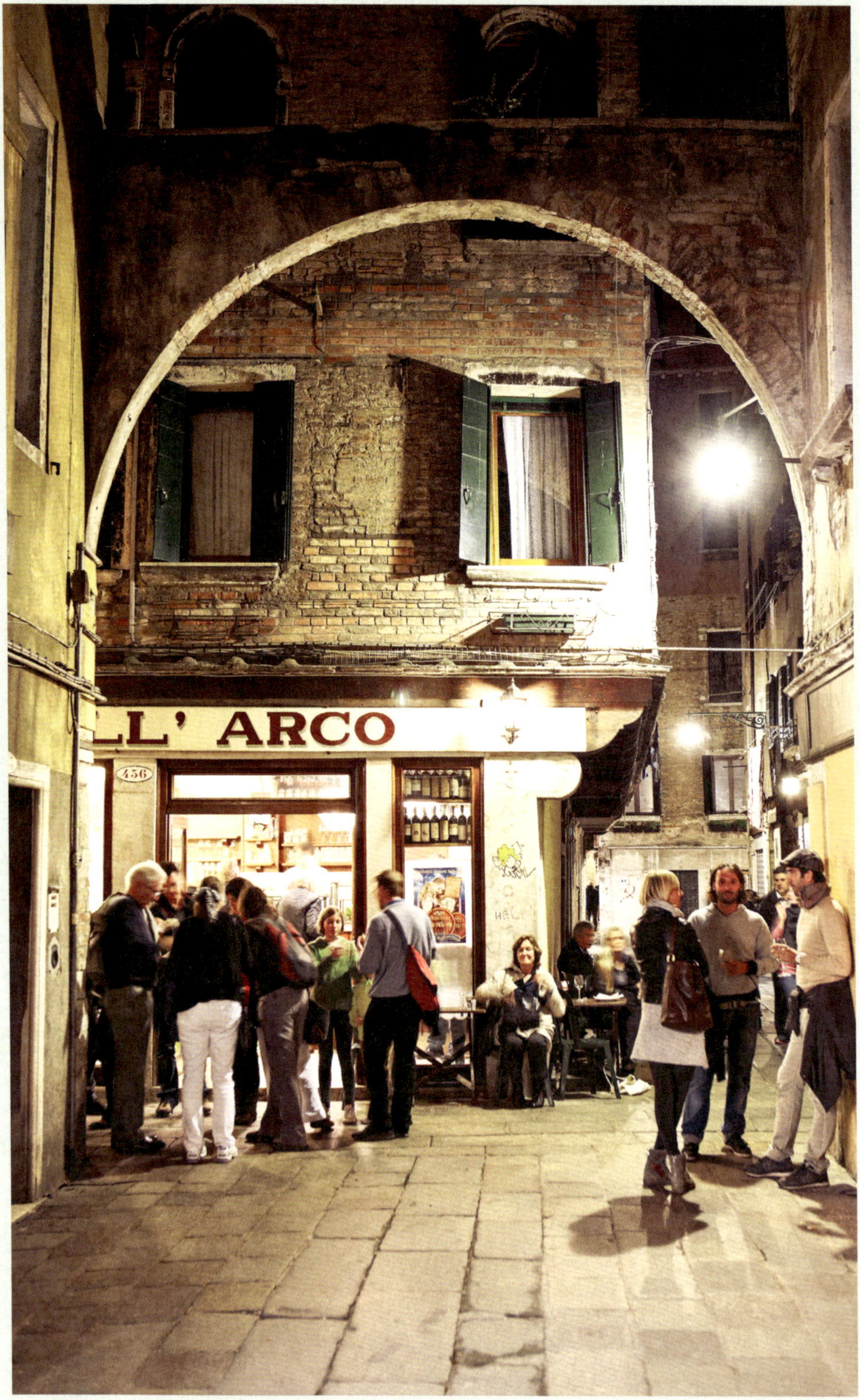

Venezia

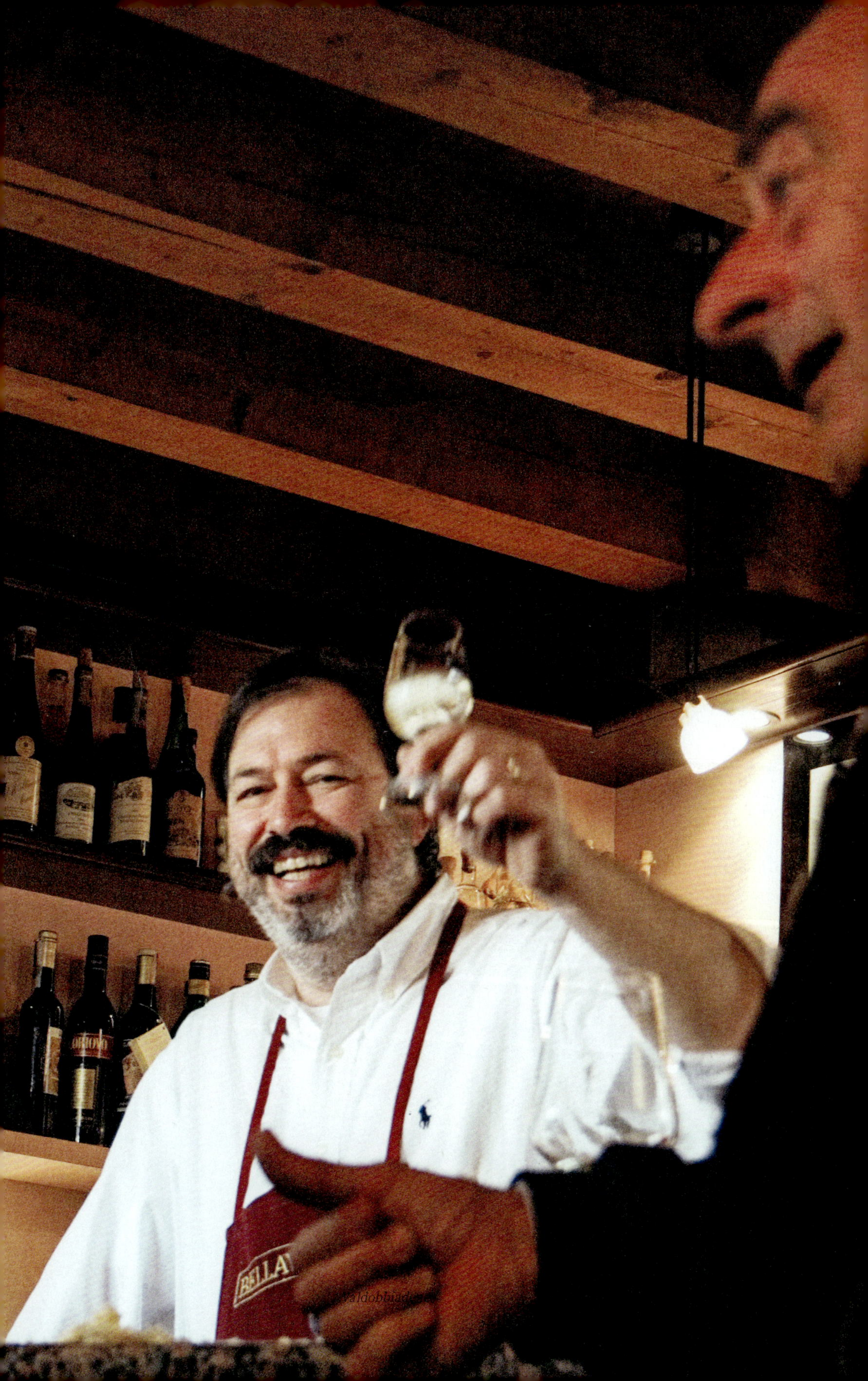

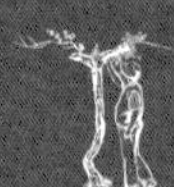

THE HISTORY OF PROSECCO

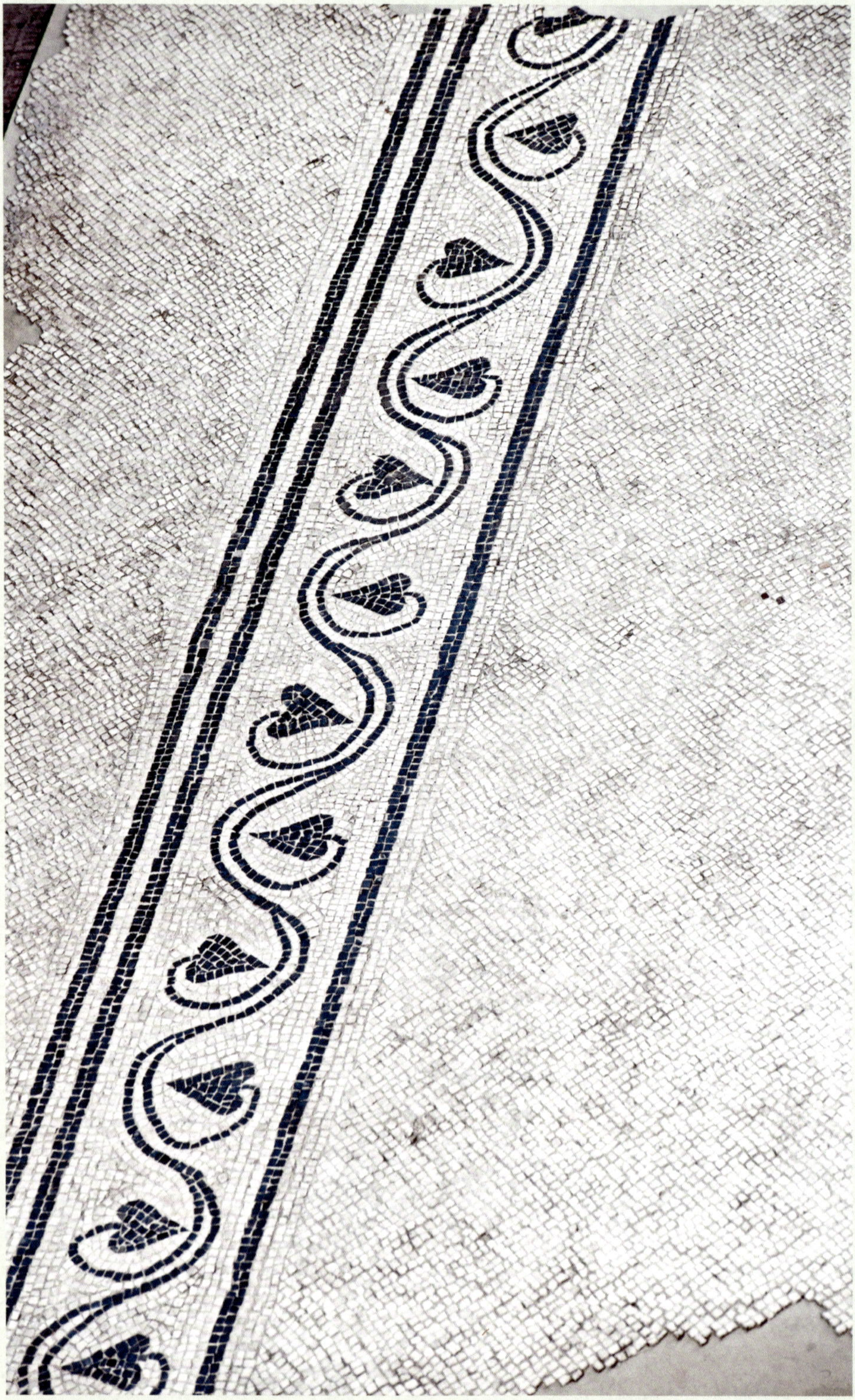

Oderzo, Roman forum

ORIGINS OF THE WINE IN THE NORTH EAST

There is evidence of vines growing wild in the Veneto ever since the Neolithic, as shown by the frequent finds of grapevines in the lakeside villages built on stilts by Lake Garda and Lake Fimon. However, it was not until the 7th century BC that we find the earliest clues to winemaking in the Veneto by the Arusnates, an ancient people who produced Rhaetian wine (from a native grape now extinct) and the raisin wine that is an ancestor of Recioto. Some authors have advanced the idea that wine, after the Greek ènos, gave its name to the population of the Veneto. They were in fact called Enetoi or Hènetoi in Greek. But naturally it was with the Romans that viticulture really developed, starting from the eastern Veneto from the 2nd century BC. Before the Romans, there were only wild vines. Then with the centuriation or subdivision of the territory, starting with Opitergium (the modern Oderzo) and Concordia, the Roman colonists began to grow vines systematically over a large area.

The cultivation of the vine and the production of wine for regular consumption (and not just special festivals or religious rites, as had happened in the past) followed the development of two major roads built by the Romans: the Via Annia (131 BC) and the Via Claudia Augusta (begun in 15 BC and completed in 47 AD, later known as the Via Claudia Augusta Altinate), which ran from Altino and extended as far as Augusta Vindelicum (today's Augsburg). The modern wine routes, the Strada dei Vini del Piave and the Strada del Prosecco, with the winemaking areas of Montello and Colli Asolani are now strung out along the axis of the old Via Claudia Augusta. The Romans concentrated on the production of wine for the legions deployed on the frontiers of the empire. The cultivation of the vine was important, but in 92 AD the Emperor Domitian issued an edict prohibiting planting new vineyards and ordered the vines to be grubbed up to convert the land to tillage for growing wheat. Viticulture came to an abrupt standstill lasting almost two hundred years, until the Emperor Probus abolished Domitian's edict and winemaking returned.

pages 20-21 Farra di Soligo, San Lorenzo church >

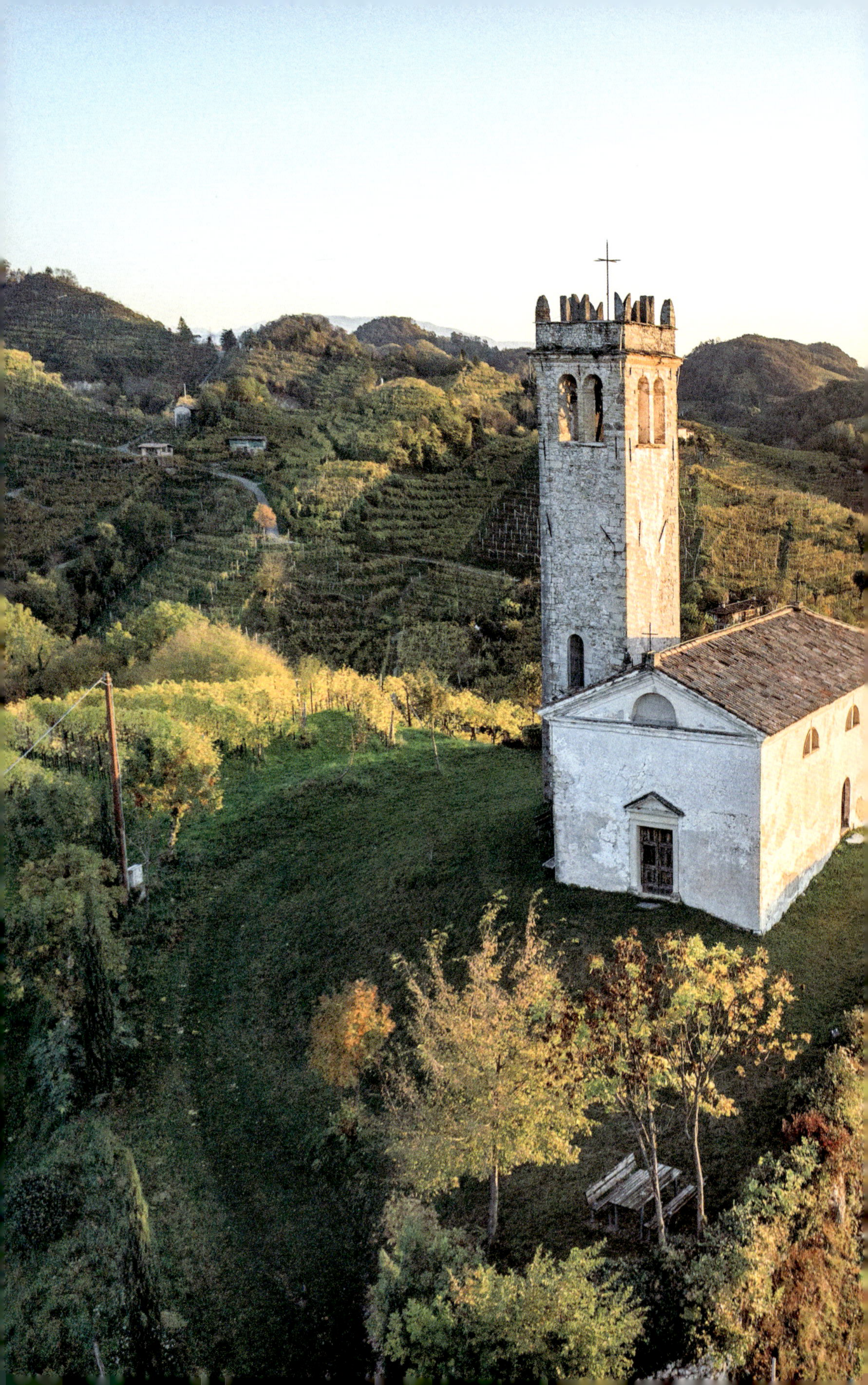

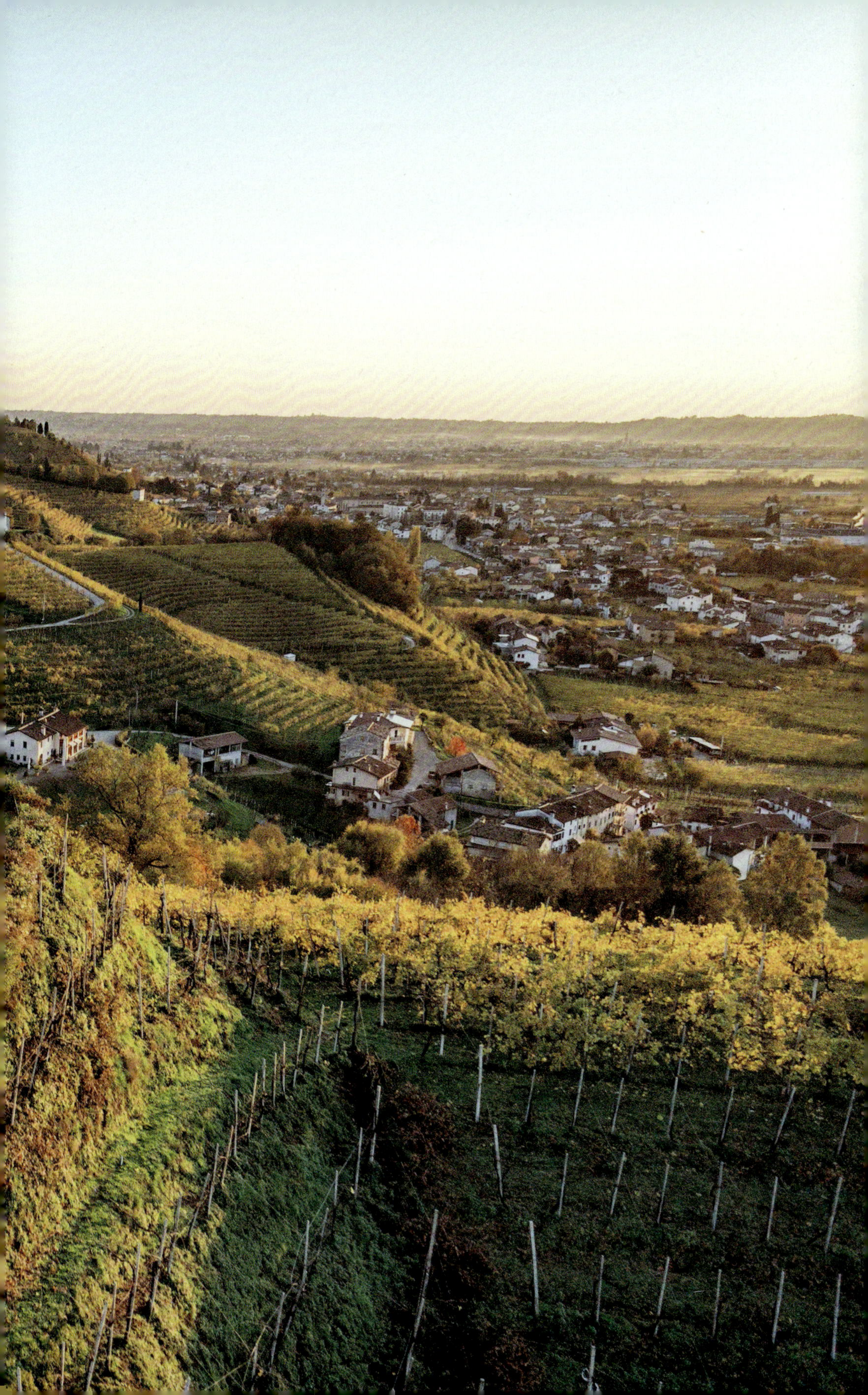

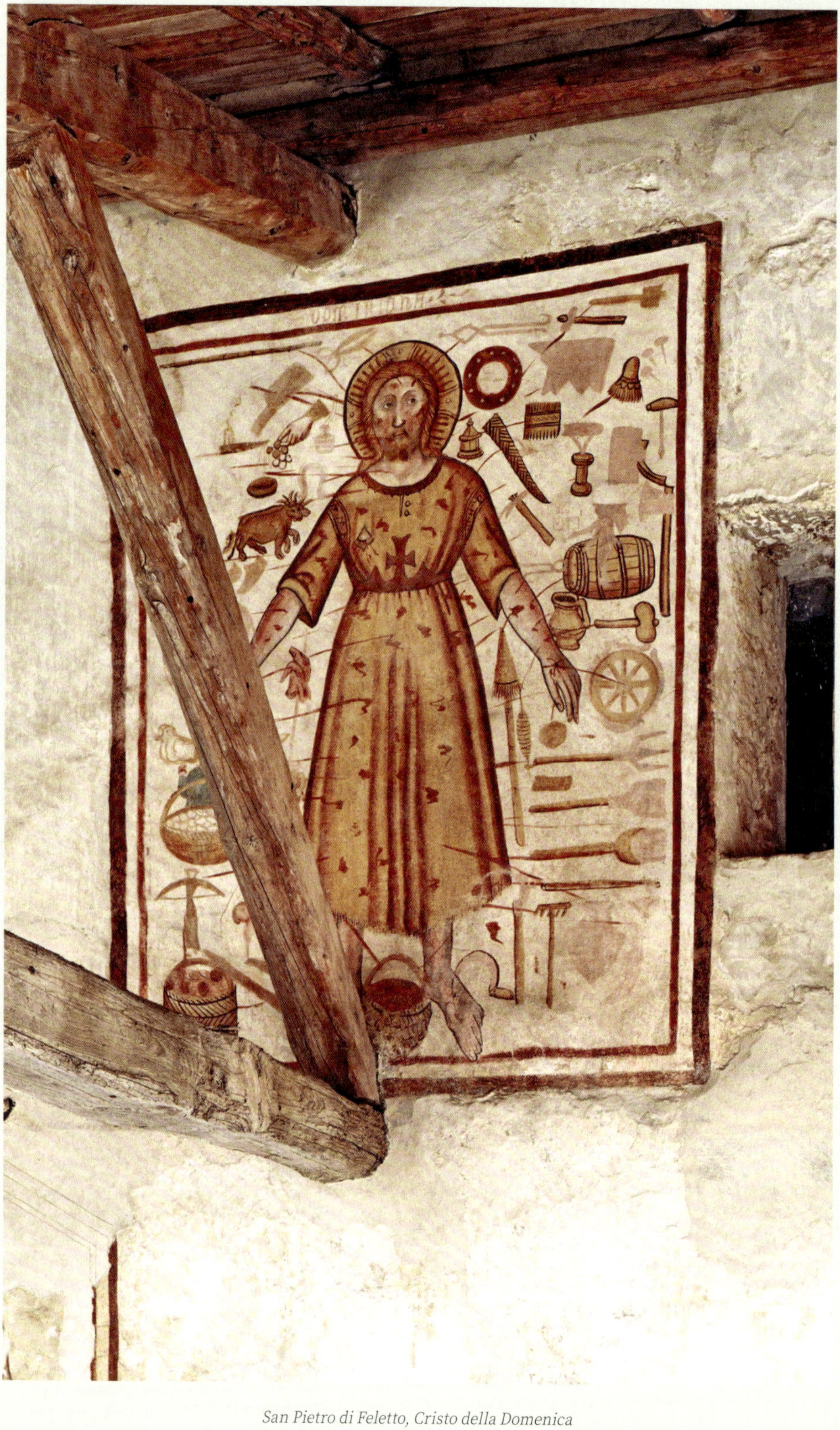

San Pietro di Feletto, Cristo della Domenica

THE ORIGINS OF PROSECCO

As we have seen, in the Veneto, viticulture as the production of wine for consumption and commerce dates back to the Roman centuration (land subdivision). In that period the vineyards of the Karst-Trieste area produced the prized Pucinum wine, Prosecco's ancestor. Some centuries later, viticulture, like agriculture in general, was disrupted by the barbarian hordes that devastated the land. Farming was revived by the monastic orders, especially the Benedictines, who also did much to advance it. After the year 1000, the power of the Serene Republic of Venice was on the rise and the wine trade became one of its most lucrative commercial activities. Venice's slow decline began in 1492, with the discovery of America, and continued through the centuries, finally becoming irreversible in the 1700s. Like the barbarian invasions, 1709 was another critical year in the history of viticulture. A great frost ravaged the vineyards and most of the native varieties were lost. Historians and researchers have failed to discover exactly when and how Prosecco spread from the Karst region to the hills of Conegliano and Valdobbiadene, but the name Prosecco appears in documents dating from the second half of the 18th century. So scholars see Prosecco as reaching the Venetian hills in the closing decades of the Venetian Republic. In the hills of Conegliano and Valdobbiadene, the Prosecco vine found an ideal habitat, producing an even finer wine than in its home range and becoming much in demand among the Venetian nobility. The presence of a number of Venetian villas is a testament to how many noble families in the Serenissima Republic chose this area to engage in winegrowing. The fall of the Venetian Republic in 1797 did not put an end to viticulture and winemaking. In fact after the Congress of Vienna in 1815, a catalogue of the vines cultivated was produced, in which the name Prosecco appears, though this was a very different wine from what it is today. After the middle years of the 19th century, Prosecco gradually began to acquire the qualities associated with it now.

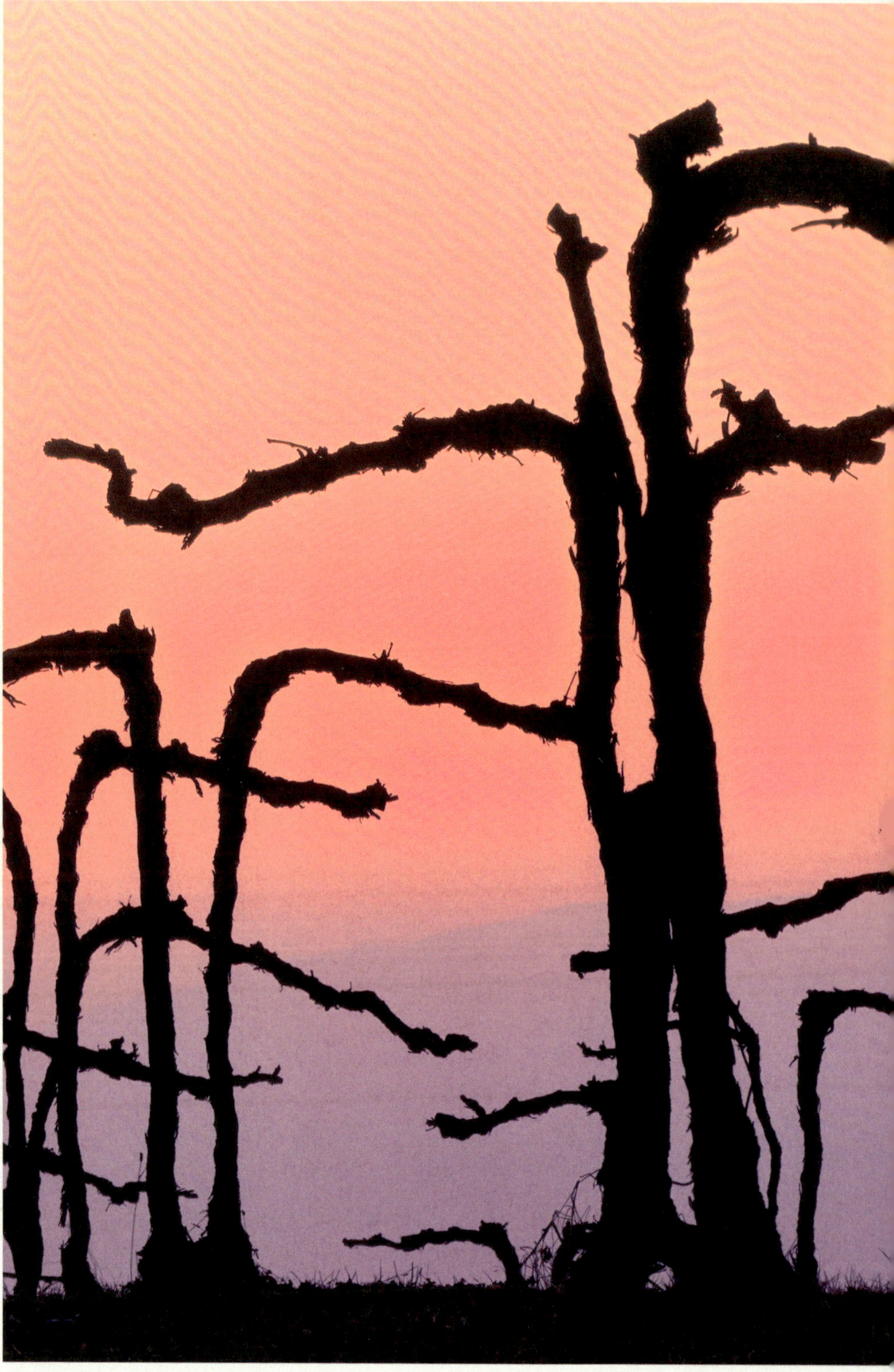

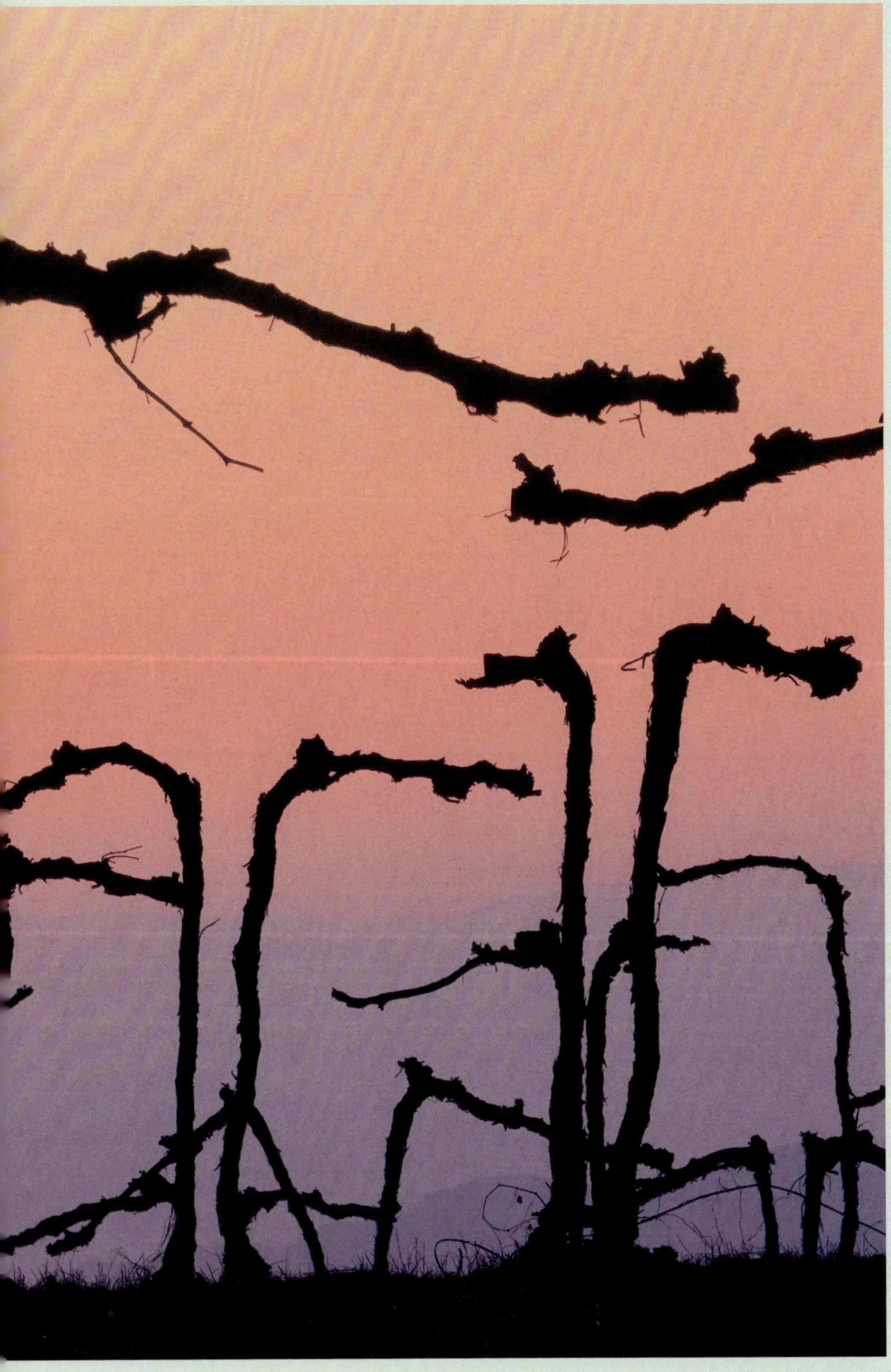

Collalto

PROSECCO ASCENDS TO THE OLYMPUS OF WINES

The spadework for the rise of Prosecco was done in the later 19th century. In 1868 Professor Antonio Carpenè and the *abbé* Felice Benedetti, president of the local Agricultural Consortium, founded the Società Enologica Trevigiana. Before this Prosecco grapes were grown mixed with other varieties, but they now began to be grown on their own. In same year a little book was published titled *Per le auspicatissime nozze Bianchini-Dubois*. Its author was Count Marco Giulio Balbi Valier, who a few years earlier, in 1850, had isolated and selected a Prosecco clone that seemed more promising than the others (and subsequently termed Prosecco Balbi). In his booklet, Balbi writes that he has planted only Prosecco vines that were "more reliable and fruitful than all other varieties, and made a refined white wine full of grace and strength." Prosecco started to make a name for itself in those years. 1876 was a historic date for winegrowing and the science of wine in the Trevigiano and Veneto. On July 9, 1876, by royal decree, King Victor Emmanuel II instituted the Oenological School of Conegliano, the first of its kind in Italy. The project was fostered by Professors Antonio Carpenè and Giovanni Battista Cerletti. Apart from being one of the founders, the latter was its first director, and the school was named after him on September 16, 1936. The Oenological School is one of the factors, together with the vineyards and local institutions, that have helped create, launch and enhance Prosecco's reputation worldwide. With a university approach, laying great stress on research, the Oenological School has always innovated scientifically, modernizing the technology used in viticulture and winemaking. It was only after World War II that the wine-growing area of Conegliano-Valdobbiadene began to fulfil its potential.

The winegrowers were confident they had a quality product on their hands. In 1945 they formed the Confraternità dei Cavalieri del Prosecco and in 1962 the a consortium for the protection of Prosecco wine from Conegliano-Valdobbiadene. Fifty years on, thanks to the winegrowers' tenacity, the arc of hills from Conegliano to Valdobbiadene has become like a liquid, sparkling goldmine, the driving force for the whole the Prosecco District, particularly the Treviso plain and Asolani hills.

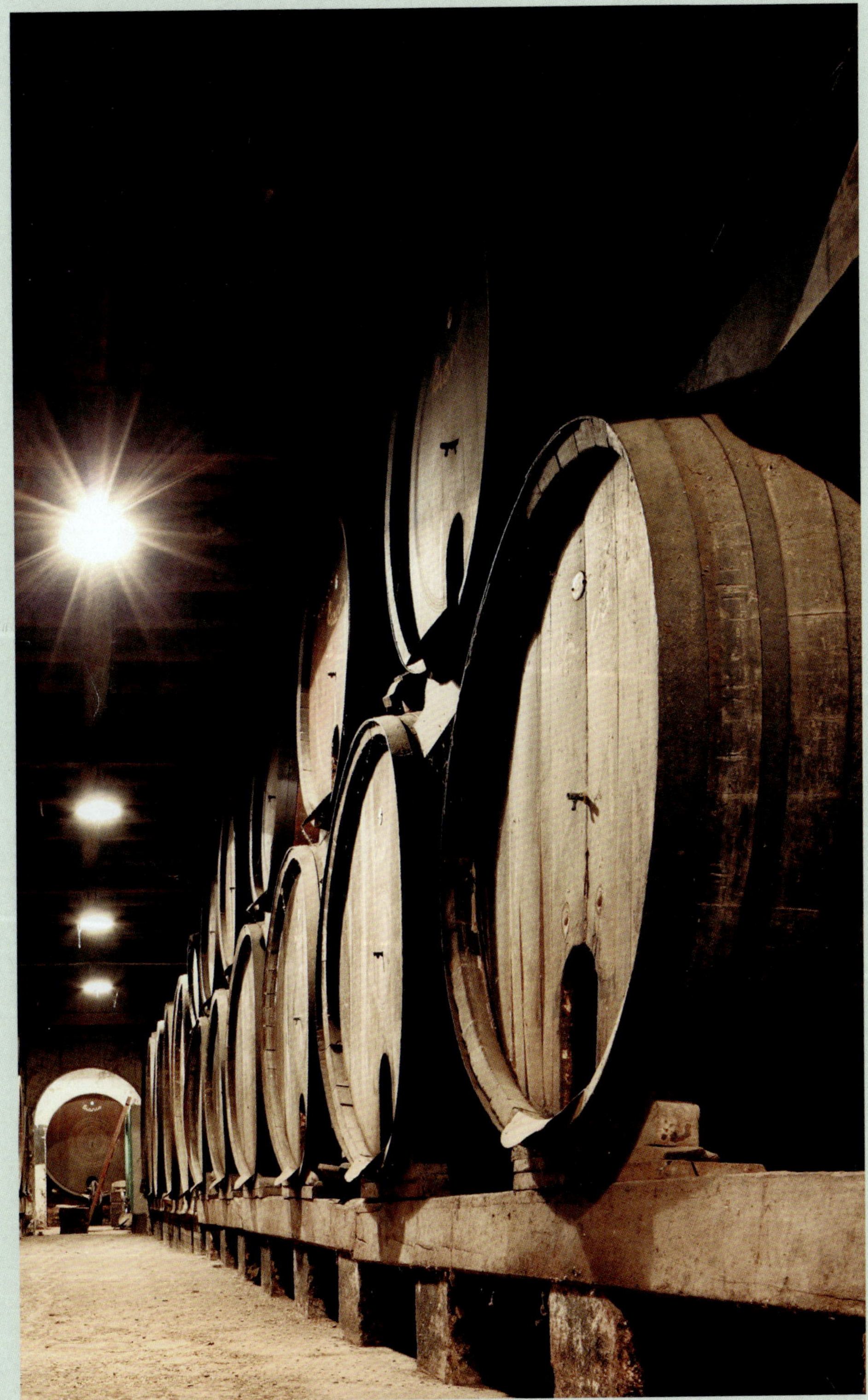

Mareno di Piave, Villa Montalbano Balbi Valier Paoletti

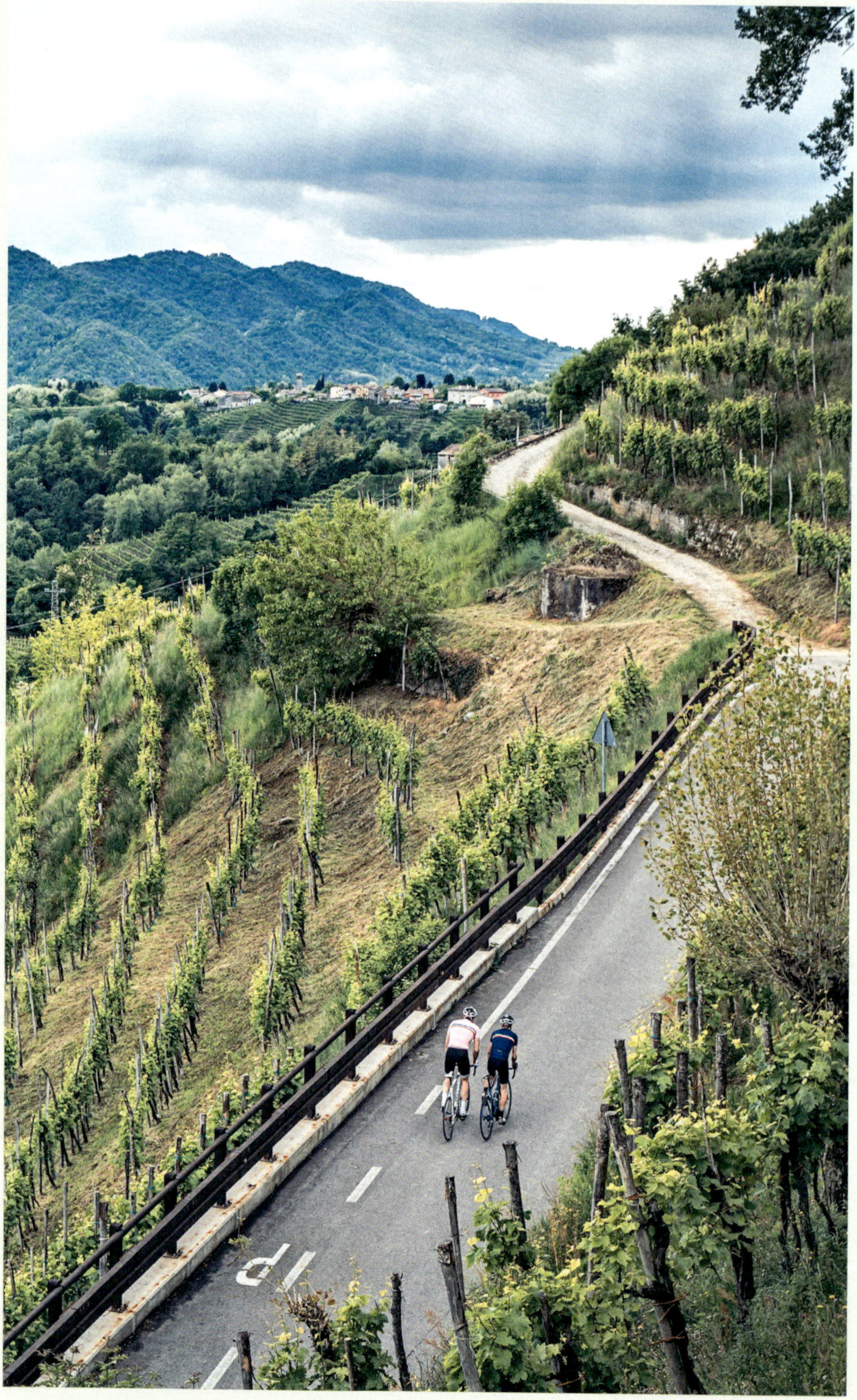

Rolle, the Prosecco route

THE PROSECCO ROUTE

From town to town, up and down the winding curves of the hills, amid a labyrinth of rows of vines, where getting lost is not a bother but a pleasure, runs the Route of Prosecco and the Wines of the Conegliano Hills and Valdobbiadene. When it was originally laid out in 1966, it was the first wine route in Italy. A ring-shaped itinerary that you can follow however you like best: by car, motorcycle or bike, on foot or on horseback. A circuit stretching 120 kilometers, along which you will find hospitality in the wineries and discover how Prosecco is made. You can taste traditional products and dishes in the many inns, farmhouses and restaurants you come across, and visit medieval hermitages, churches and villages, enjoying not only the fine food and wine, but also the landscape, history and art treasures.

In 2003, the Route was renewed and three themed routes were added to the historical route. The main itinerary is the one that combines the two capitals of Prosecco Superiore DOCG, ideally starting from Conegliano and reaching Valdobbiadene. This joins up with the ring of "The feud of the Collalto," winding through the lands of the family of the same name in Susegana, the town with two castles. "History and culture between Serravalle and Follina" comprises visits to some of the area's most significant architectural works. "The Torchiato di Fregona" is the region's oenological pearl.

Not far away there is another itinerary that passes through hills covered with vineyards, ancient forests and localities associated with the Great War. This is the Wine Route of Montello and the Colli Asolani, which snakes past Mount Grappa and the River Piave. It starts from Nervesa della Battaglia and arrives at Montebelluna, passing through Possagno, Asolo, Maser, and crossing Montello. The hill, the destination of the journey, was covered until the nineteenth century with an oak forest. It timber was much sought after by the Republic of Venice, which drew many of its supplies from here to build military ships and cargo vessels.

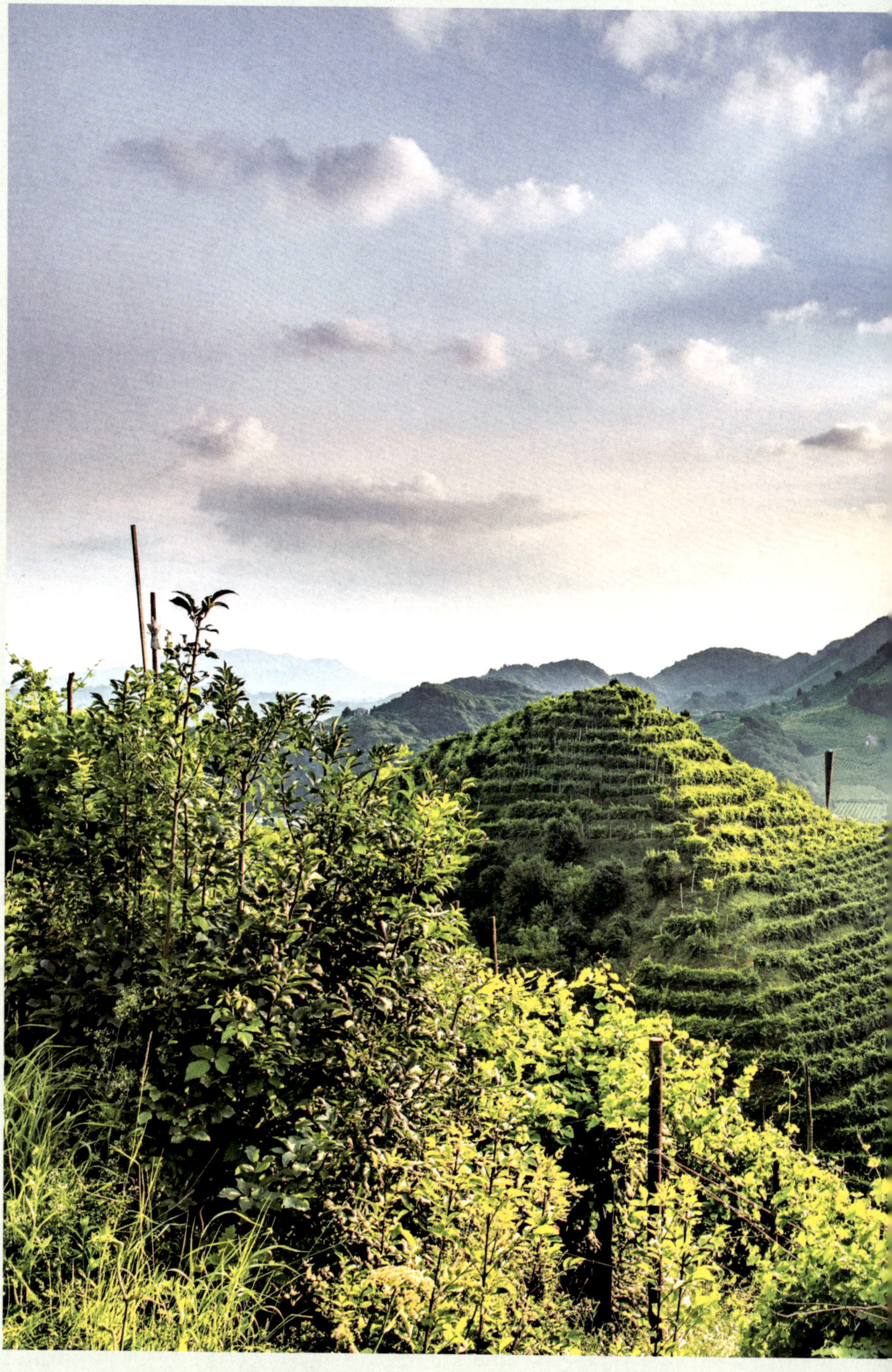

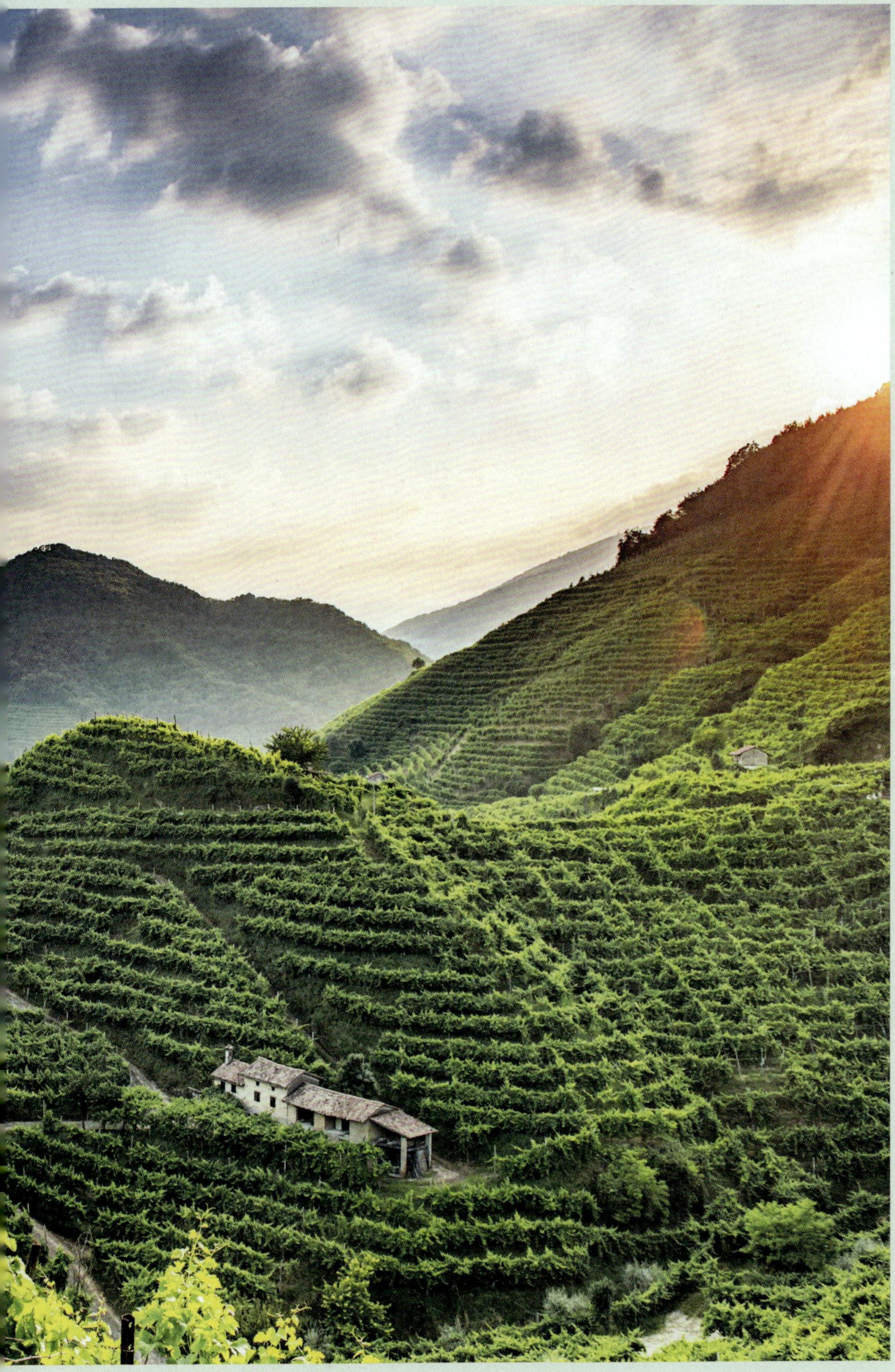

Hills between Col San Martino and Colbertaldo di Vidor

WINE AND VINIFICATION

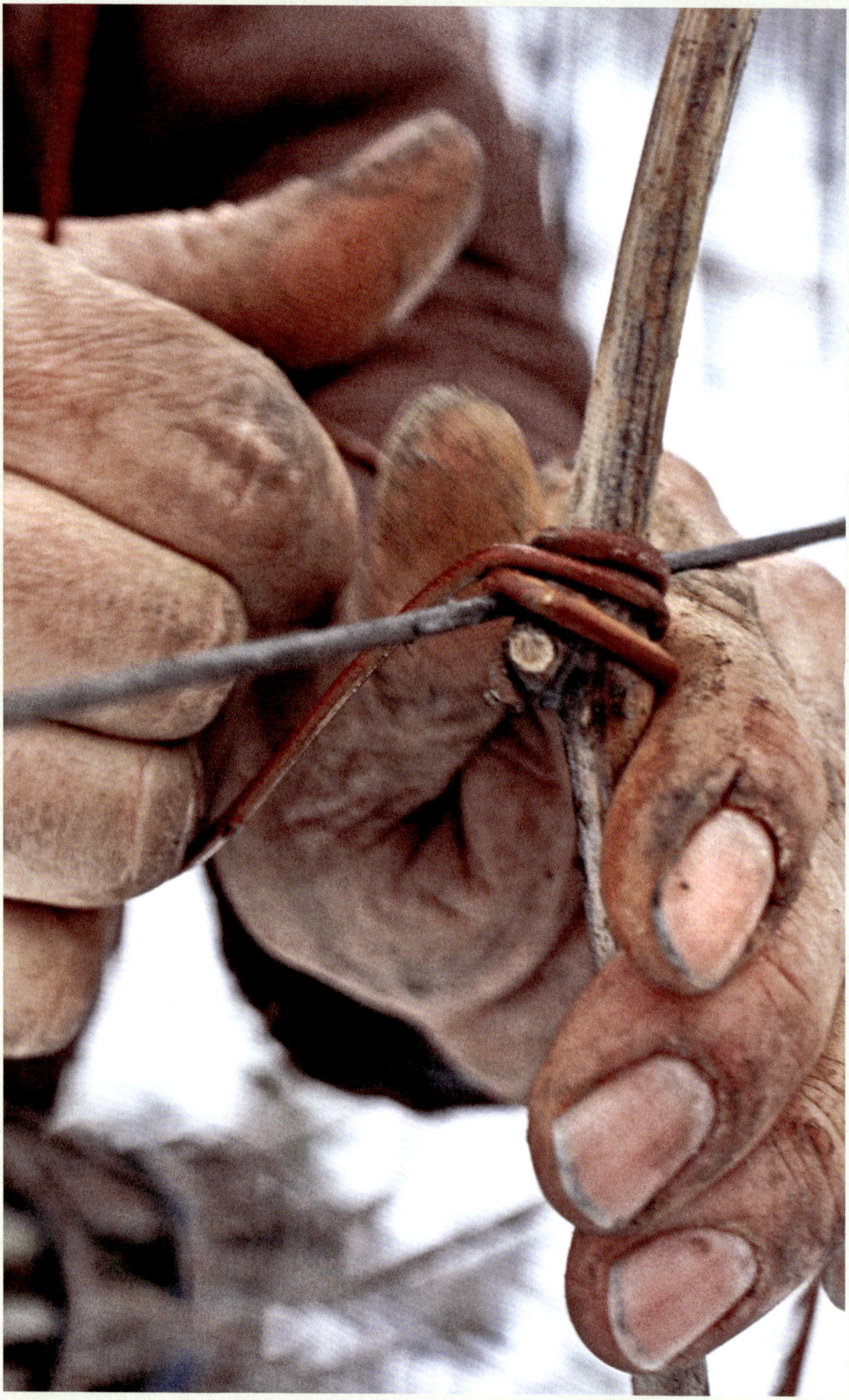

Valdobbiadene

TERROIR

Cultivating talent. A common expression usually applied to people. But the vignerons who grow Glera vines also cultivate talents. Just like humans, vines express their genetic potential differently depending on the environment in which they are grown. Glera's worldwide success confirms it is a talented vine, but it is scientifically proven that if it were grown in other parts of the world it would not develop the same qualities. Soil and climate in synergy with man determine the quality and typicality of wine.
This is what is meant by terroir. In the case of Prosecco, the hilly landscape appears homogeneous, like the plain, yet appearance are deceptive. Climatic factors and above all the soil vary and determine the aromatic nuances of wine. These differences, together with the anthropic factor, form the terroir and determine the colors, bouquet and flavors of wine.
In the hills, harvesting the grapes for Prosecco Superiore is a heroic task, because the vineyards cling to steep slopes where the grapes can only be picked by hand. The landforms of these hills and those of Asolo DOCG have ancient origins, dating back to the rising of the sea beds and lake beds. One part of the hills was shaped by glaciers descending from the Dolomites and bearing various sediments down the valleys. The traces left by centuries of transformation have resulted in the coexistence of different soils and landforms. Some slopes are steeper, others gentler. The different elements that make up the soil and the different exposure to climatic factors determine the scents and perfumes that characterize Prosecco DOCG.
The soils of the plain where Prosecco DOC is produced are more homogeneous, as the climate is generally temperate, although various areas have features that determine certain nuances of the wine. The soil is of alluvial origin, so mainly made up of clay and silt; hence it is rich in minerals and microelements and favors grapes that well suited for producing sparkling and semi-sparkling wines.

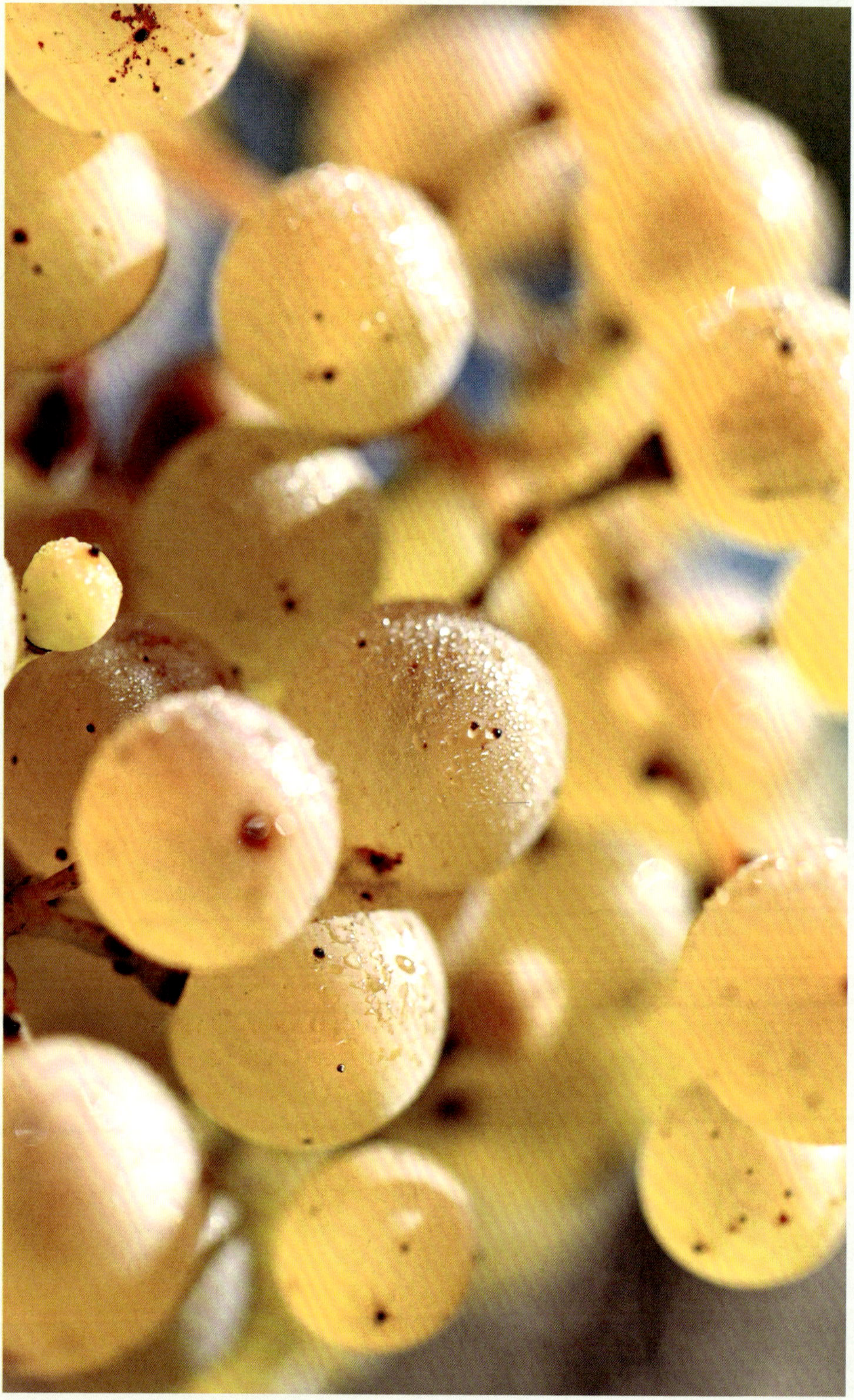

CULTIVAR

Cultivar, vine, vineyard, wine. The cultivar is the variety of vine grown in a vineyard and from which wine is produced. Prosecco is made from the Glera grape cultivar, a white grape variety. It has hazel-colored shoots and produces long, large bunches with yellow grapes touched with gold at peak ripeness. Until 2009, the vine was commonly called "Prosecco."

With the establishment of the DOCG Conegliano Valdobbiadene, which requires special protection, the synonym "Glera" was officially adopted so as not to confuse the vine and the wine. Together with Glera, to produce all the denominations of Prosecco (DOC, DOCG Conegliano Valdobbiadene, Asolo), historically other varieties are also used, up to a maximum of 15%, such as Verdiso, Bianchetta Trevigiana, Perera, Glera lunga, Chardonnay, Pinot Blanc, Pinot Gris and Pinot Noir, vinified in white.

Of these vines, five are also vinified in purity and have their own market (Verdiso, Chardonnay, Pinot Blanc, Pinot Gris and Pinot Noir). Among them Verdiso stands out as an ancient vine, native to the Altamarca Trevigiana and now being promoted by a group of local vintners. It is a vigorous vine, steady in production and adaptable to different types of soil. As a wine, Verdiso is straw-colored, light, with greenish reflections, a tenuous, spicy bouquet, delicately fruity with a distinctive hint of green. The taste is dry, lively, tart, with mild apple overtones, a medium body and with a bitter aftertaste. With these qualities, it is used in the composition of Conegliano Valdobbiadene Prosecco Superiore DOCG and in the making of sparkling wines. The Verdiso grapes also produce a raisin wine that is rare, because of the difficulty of drying the grapes.

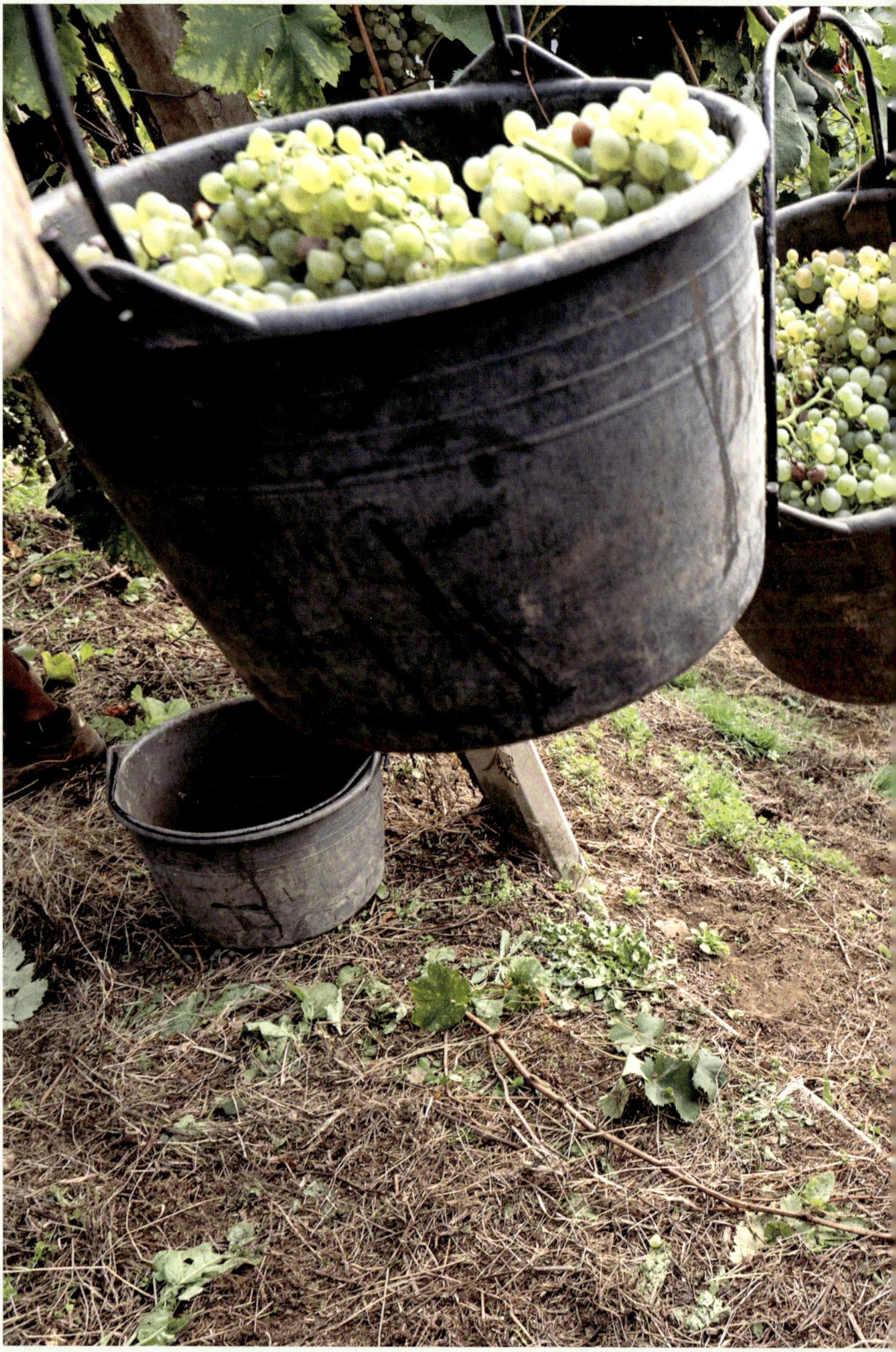

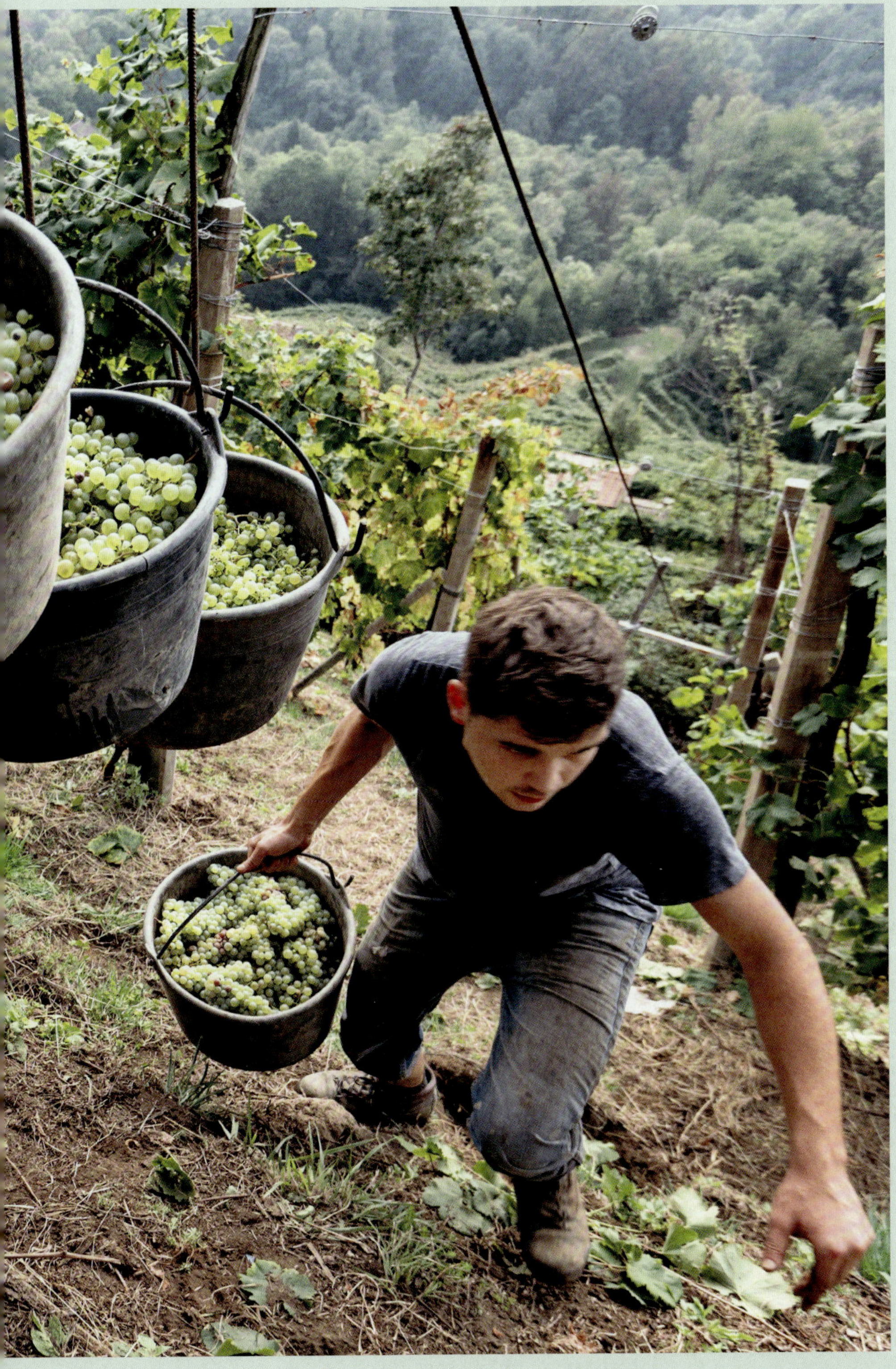

Miane, Combai locality, heroic harvest

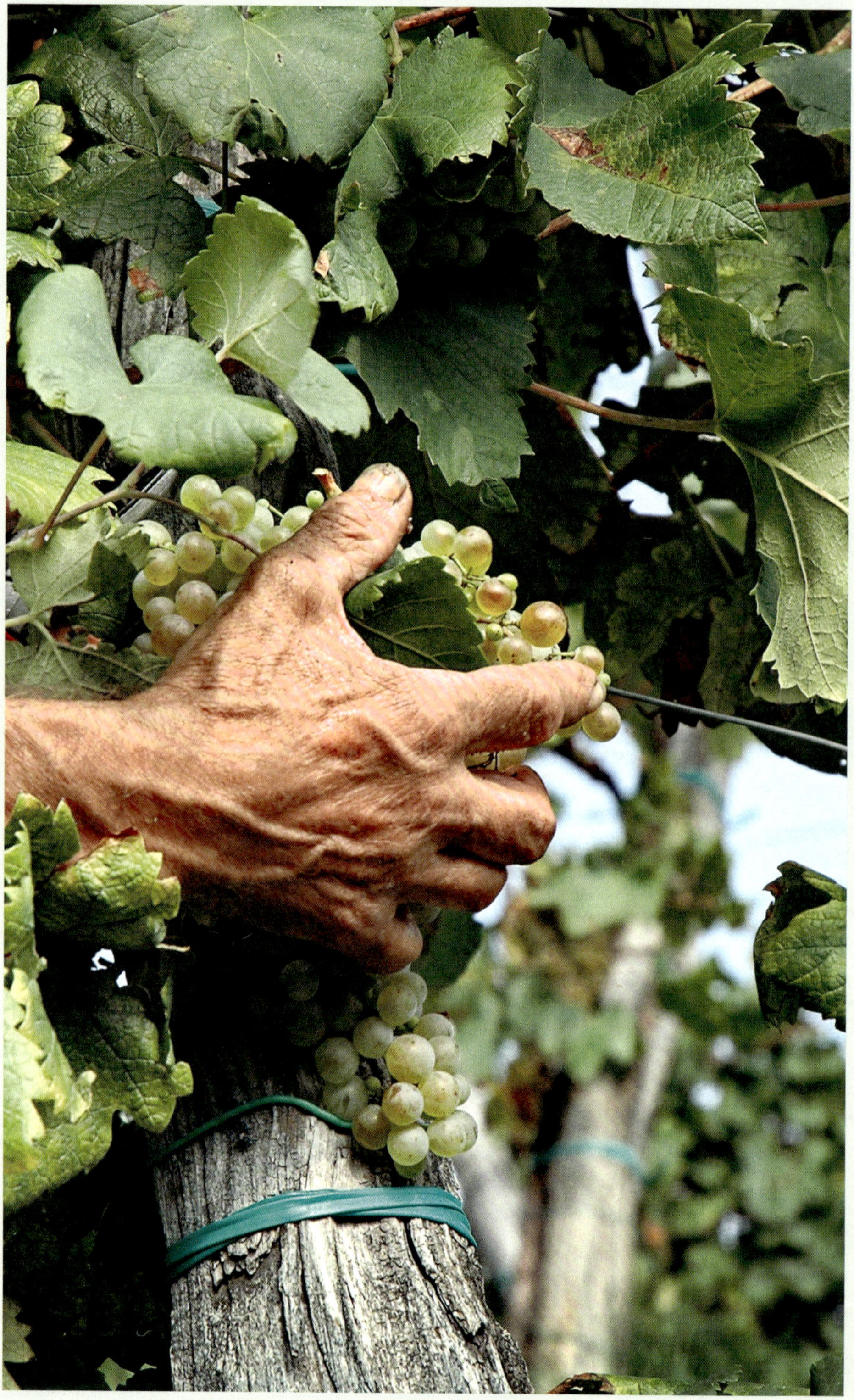

GRAPE HARVEST

The grape harvest is an ancestral rite that evokes periods of effort, but also the happiness of being together and joy because the fruits of a year's work are being gathered in. In the most impervious areas of Conegliano Valdobbiadene, where the hills are steep, the grapes can only be harvested by hand. The machinery is unable to cope with the hillsides and so wine growing is termed "heroic" here. Traditionally September is the month for harvesting Glera grapes, but the period varies from zone to zone. Climatic factors determine the ripeness of the grapes and consequently the right time for harvesting, when the organoleptic maturity (sugars, acidity and aromatic substances) is optimal for wine production. Grape harvesting is a delicate operation because it is important to preserve the integrity of the grapes and avoid spontaneous fermentation. After harvesting the grapes, the first operation is pressing.

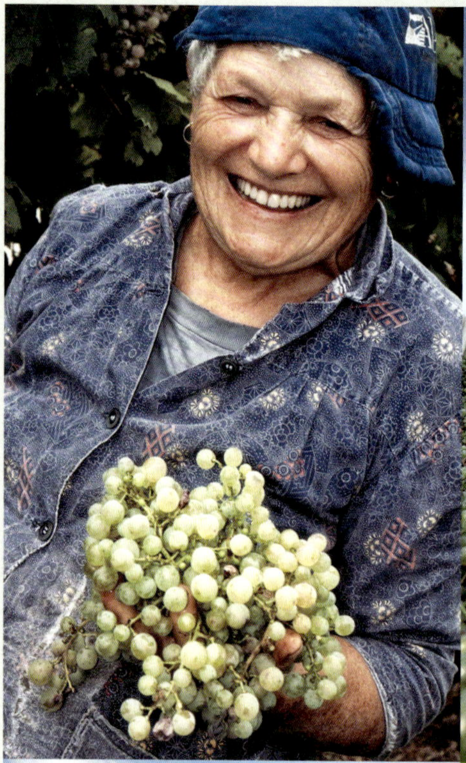
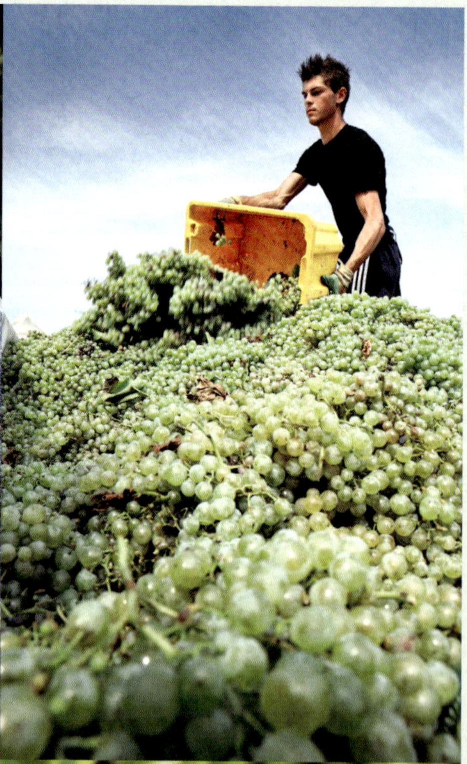
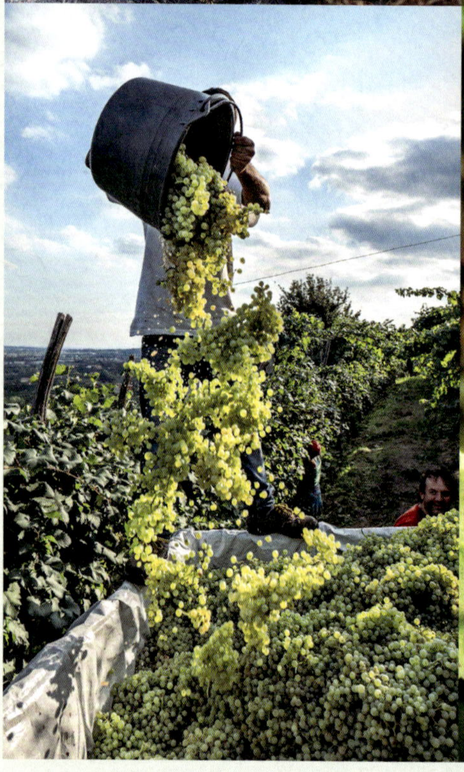
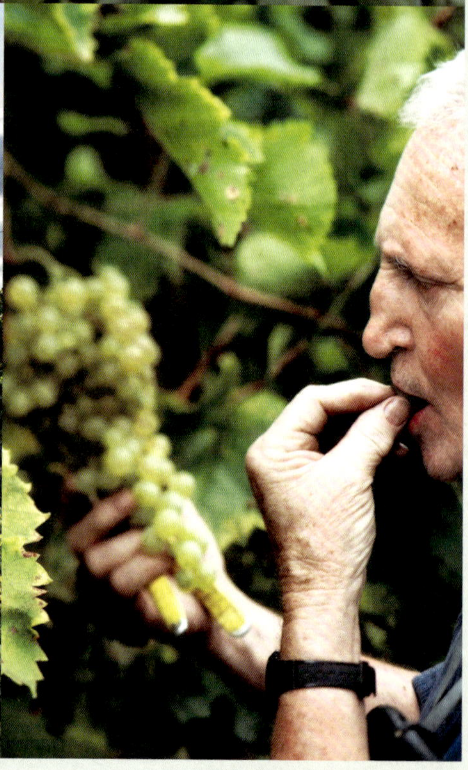

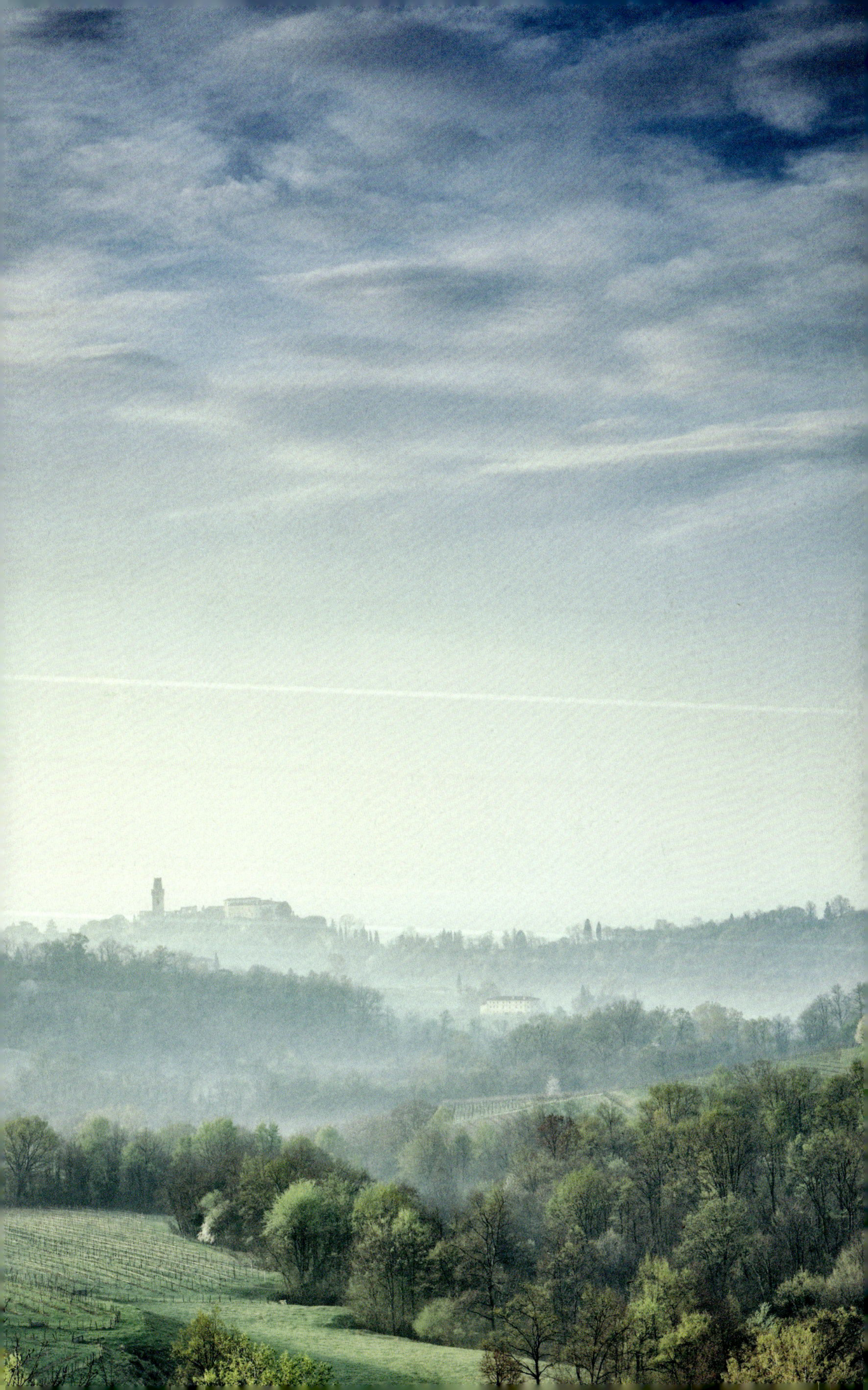

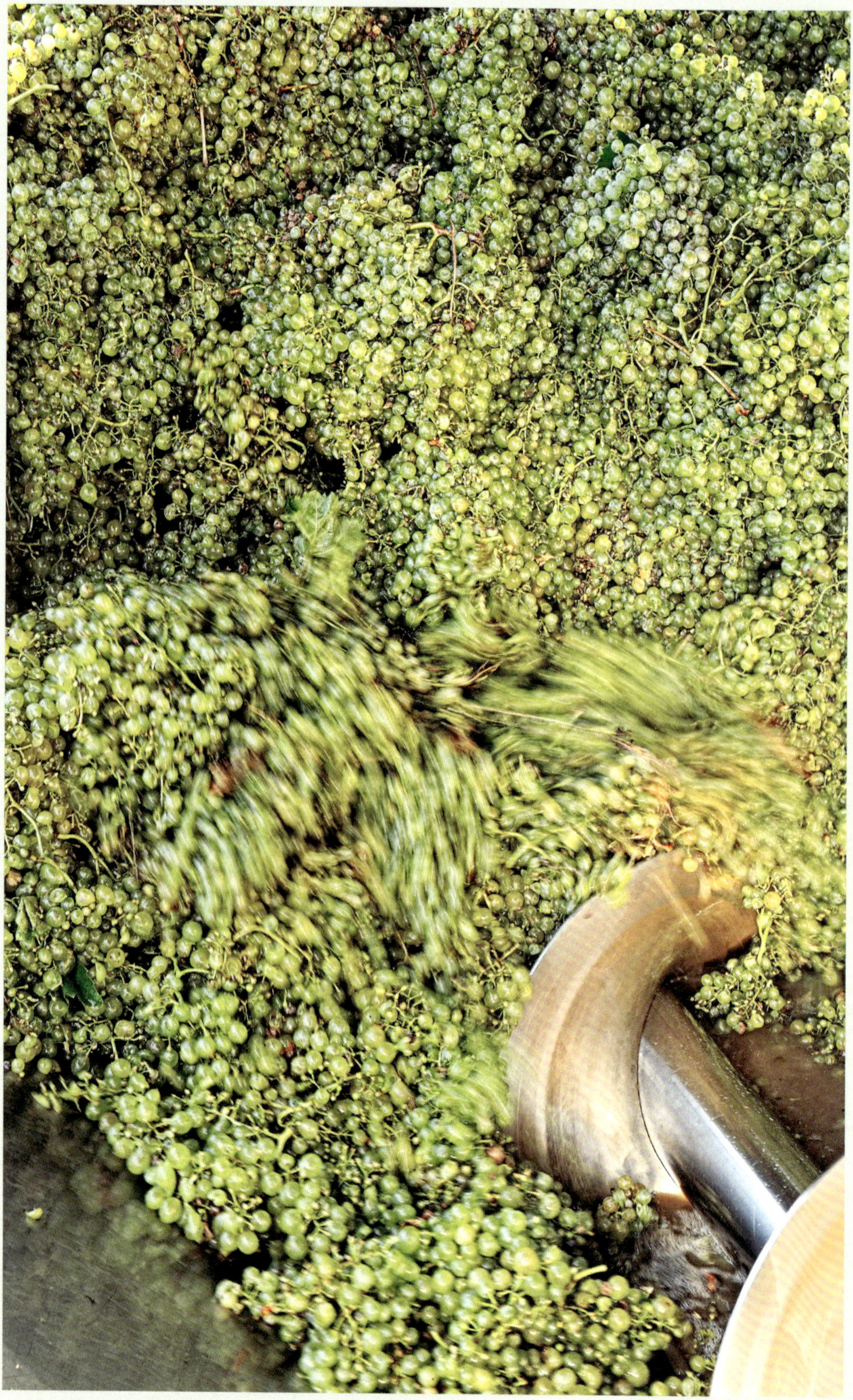

Vittorio Veneto, Carpesica locality

VINIFICATION

Vinification begins with pressing. The grapes are separated from the stalks and ready for pressing. Grapes, pulp, peel and seeds all go into the torchio (basket press or batch press). In spite of the name, which sounds rather harsh, it gently separates the must from everything else. From the heart of the grape comes only the freshest, the finest juice, kept at low temperatures in stainless steel tanks to purify. After a few hours, the impurities are deposited at the bottom of the tank. Then selected yeasts are added to the purified must and transform the sugar naturally present in the grapes into alcohol and carbon dioxide. The activity of the yeast is called fermentation and lasts about twenty days. It is important for it to take place at a temperature between 18 and 22°C, so as to preserve the delicate fragrances of the grapes. After the fermentation comes the period of maturation, when the operations of decanting and filtering produce a limpid wine.
Prosecco Tranquillo is bottled, while Prosecco Frizzante and Prosecco Spumante pass on to one last stage, with natural fermentation.
The wine that is made into spumante is entrusted to the care of the cellarer. He tastes the wines in the different vats and blends it, combining different wines by origin, vintage and organoleptic characteristics. Blending balances the wine, making it richer and more complete, defining its structure, scents and aromas. With regard to vinification, the grapes from which Prosecco is made, mainly Glera (not less than 85%), must be vinified white.
This is specified in the production rules. This means that if you ever came across a bottle of Prosecco Rosé, it could mean only one thing: that wine is not Prosecco, because Prosecco Rosé does not exist.

pages 48-49 Valdobbiadene >

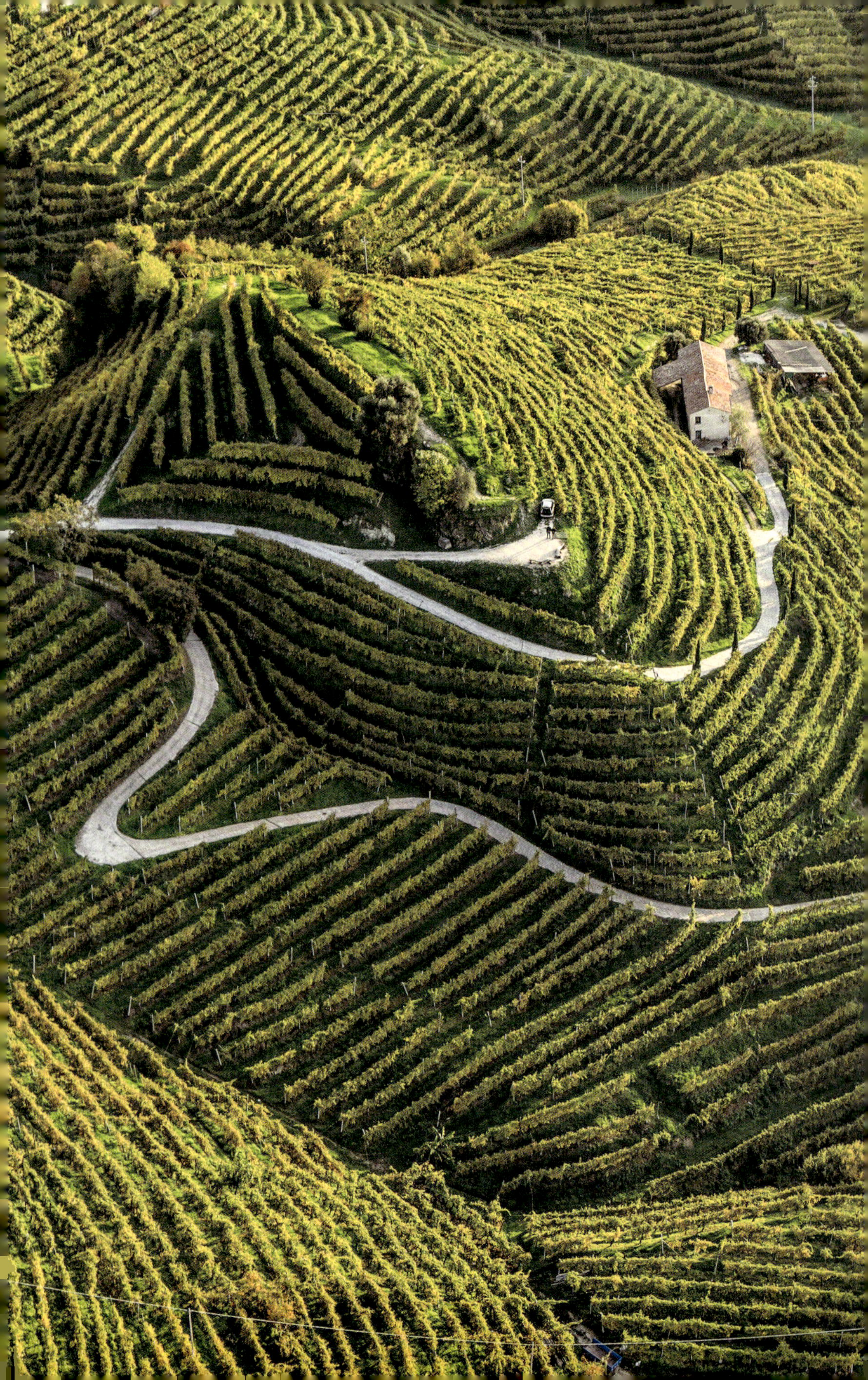

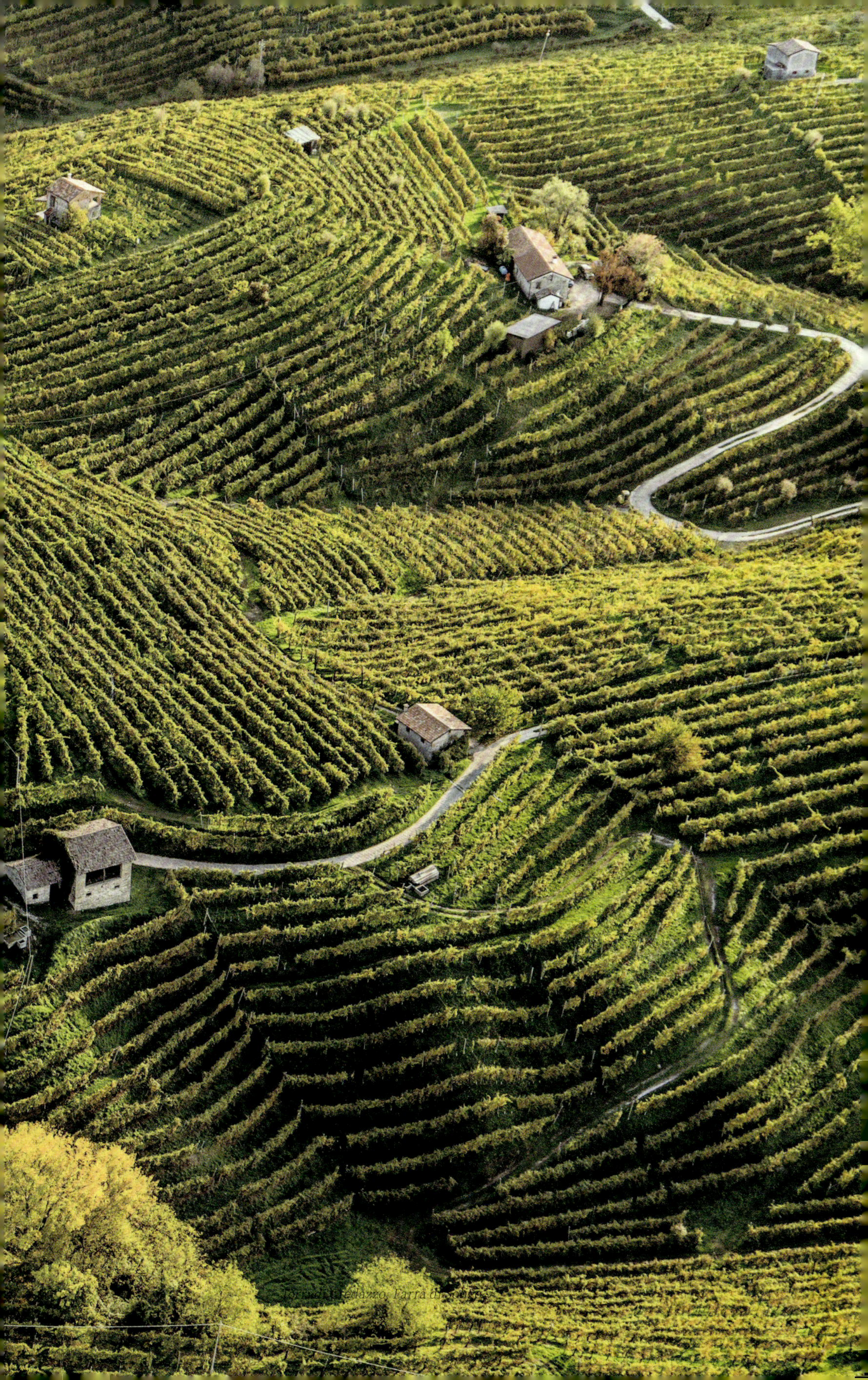

[illegible] Credazzo, Farra di [illegible]

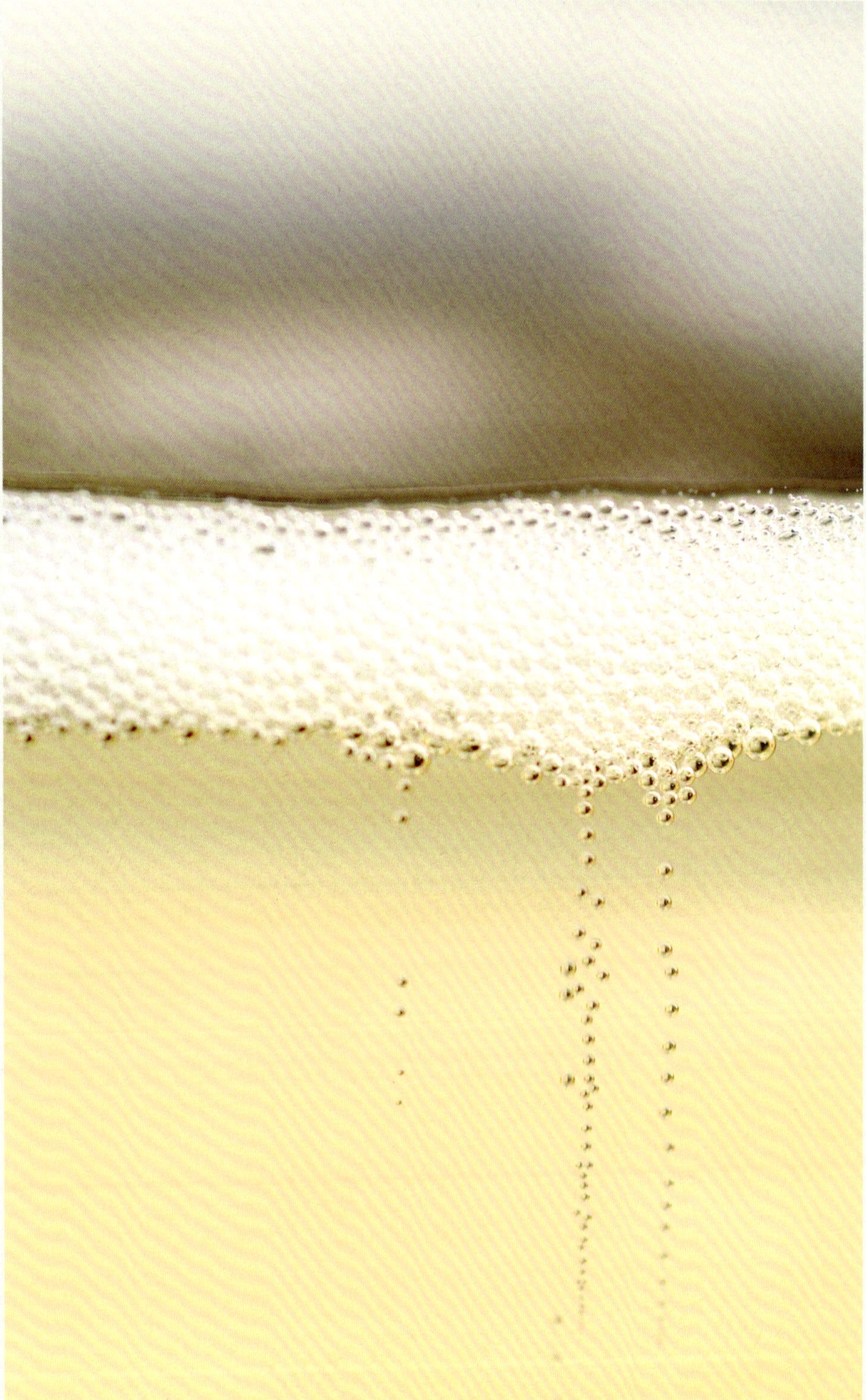

MAKING SPUMANTE

Pearls, as is well known, are precious. The tiny ones that tickle your palate whenever you quaff a glass of spumante are impalpable, but the most sought-after. The bubbles are what make a wine sparkle.

The father of sparkling wine in the Conegliano Valdobbiadene zone was Antonio Carpenè. In the early twentieth century, the method of making sparkling wine was perfected by the winery of the same name, one of the first great Italian spumante wineries. Then the laboratories of the Conegliano Enological School developed the process further. Sparkling wine made by the Italian or Martinotti method is produced under pressure in large stainless steel autoclaves. It is here that the wine, thanks to the second fermentation, acquires its bubbles and becomes spumante. Toward the end of the process, which lasts for at least thirty days, when the temperature is lowered, the fermentation stops, leaving a sugary residue to ensure balance and harmony.

The Italian or Martinotti or Charmat method: fermentation in autoclave. In 1895, Federico Martinotti, director of the Asti Institute of Experimental Oenology, invented and patented the method of controlled fermentation in large containers, then adopted in France around 1910 by Eugène Charmat, who built and patented the equipment. The method involves a second fermentation of wine in large pressurized containers, called autoclaves. This creates wines with fruity notes.

The Classical or Champenoise Method: fermentation in the bottle. This consists of initiating bottle fermentation through the introduction of selected sugars and yeasts. In this way the wine acquires the traditional pressure. After a period of rest, the bottles are placed on special racks (*pupitres*), which ensure the neck is lower than the bottom of the bottle. Turning the bottle at regular intervals (*remuage*) leads the residue of the exhausted yeasts to settle on the cap. The last stage is called *dégorgement* and consists of freezing the neck of the bottle and removing the pellet of yeast, so that the lees are driven out under pressure. Then the traditional mushroom-shaped cork is inserted.

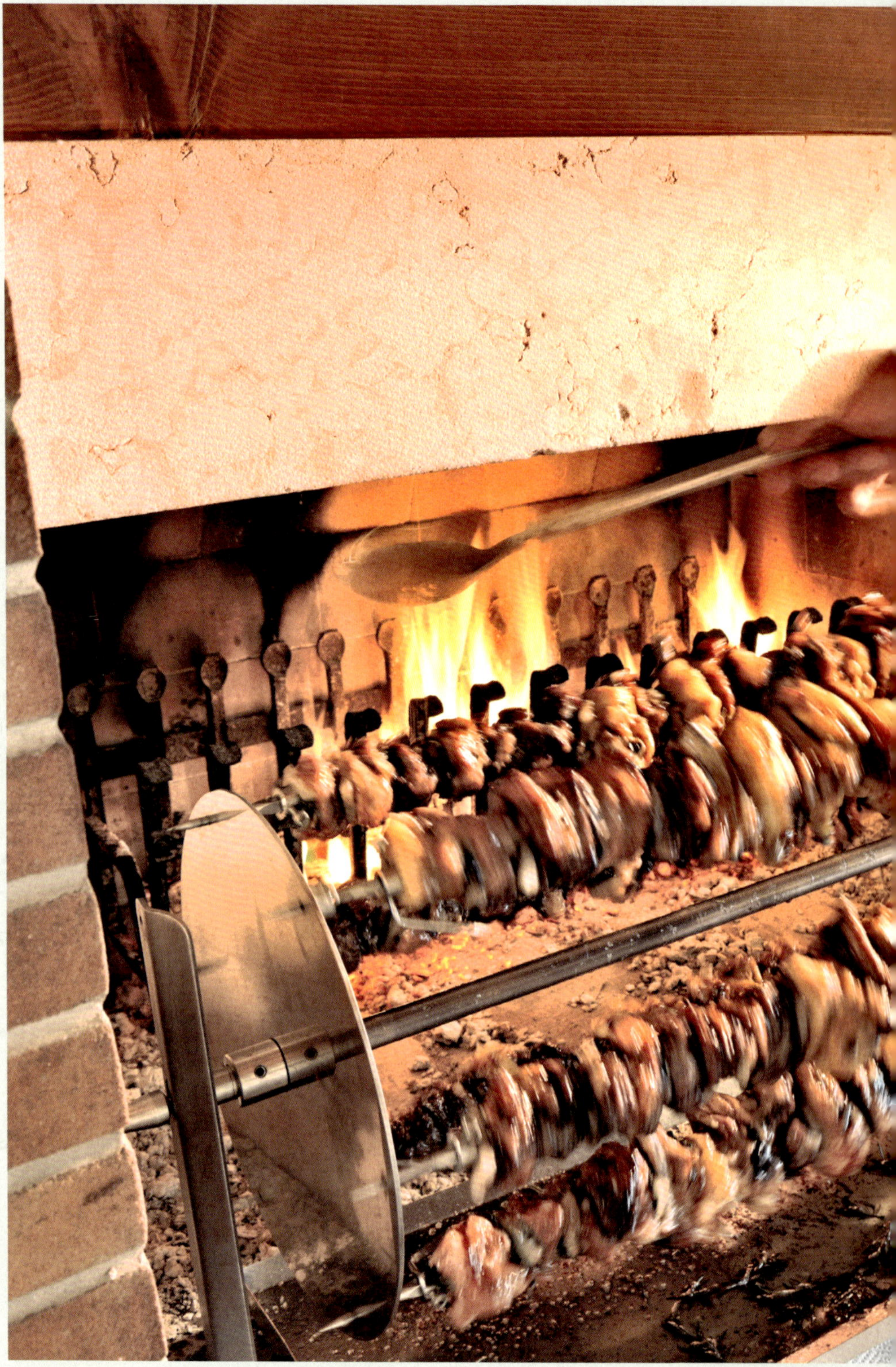

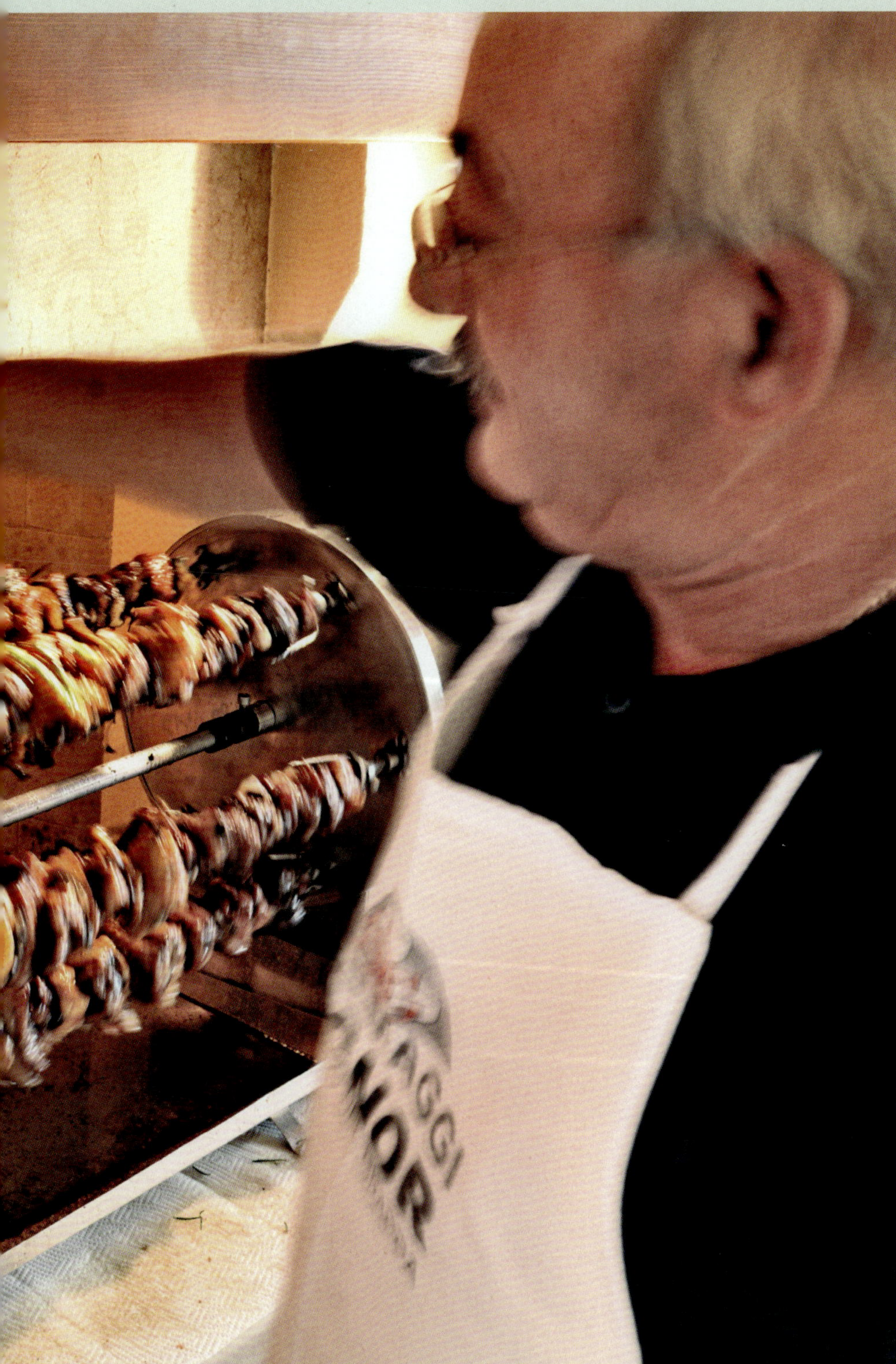

Tezze di Piave

TYPES

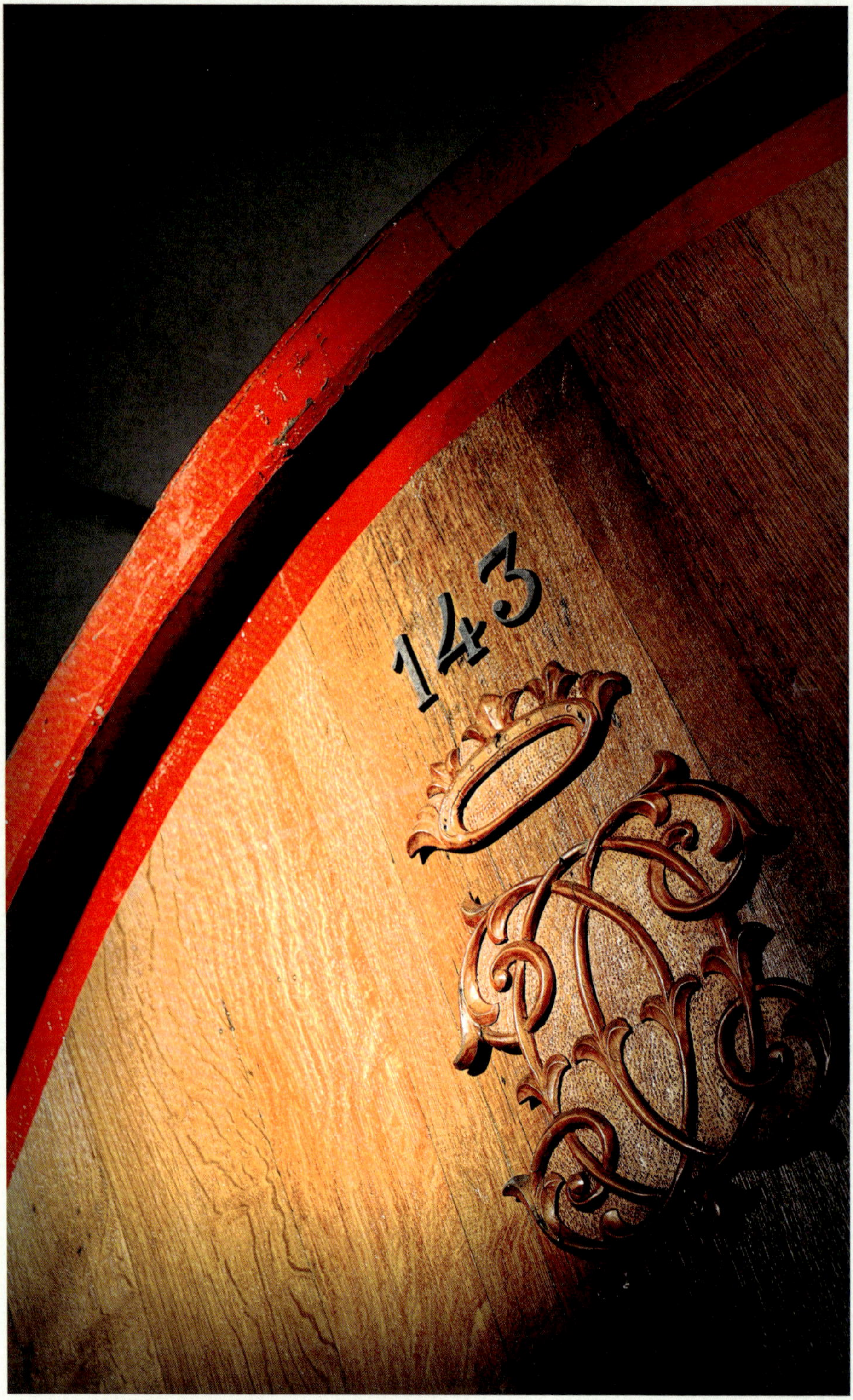

Susegana, Collalto locality

WHAT KIND OF PROSECCO!

Tranquillo, quiet like an old friend you can confide in at the tavern after a day's work, one you share a laugh with, recalling times past. Frizzante, lively like a young man who looks forward to life with enthusiasm. Spumante, sparkling like a boy overjoyed with life. Whether from plain or hill, DOC (*Denominazione di Origine Controllata*) or DOCG (*Denominazione di Origine Controllata e Garantita*), Prosecco is presented with one of these main characters. Within each denomination there are other peculiarities that characterize and distinguish it. In technical terms these are called the different types. The main difference is in the bubbles. The three macro-types have in common a light straw color, with a floral and fruity scent and fresh flavor. Prosecco Frizzante can be Secco (dry) or Amabile (semi-sweet). Spumante can be Brut, Extra Brut, Dry, Extra Dry, Demi Sec, Colfondo (Sur lie). DOCG Conegliano Valdobbiadene can also sport the terms Rive and Superiore di Cartizze.

The last of these represents the top quality of the denomination. It comes from a subarea of only 107 hectares of vineyards, including the steepest hills of San Pietro di Barbozza, Santo Stefano and Saccol, in the municipality of Valdobbiadene. It has scents that recall fruits with white pulp, like apple and pear, citrus, intense peach and apricot and hints of rose, with an almond note in the aftertaste. The flavor is harmonious and elegant, with great softness and freshness, supported by a light and fine perlage. It possesses distinctive complexity, persistence, elegance and verticality compared with the other types of the denomination.

Also worth mentioning is Colfondo or Sur lie, produced by refermentation in the bottle. A traditional technique from the late nineteenth century, by refining on the natural grape yeasts it results in a slightly veiled texture that makes the taste softer and fuller.

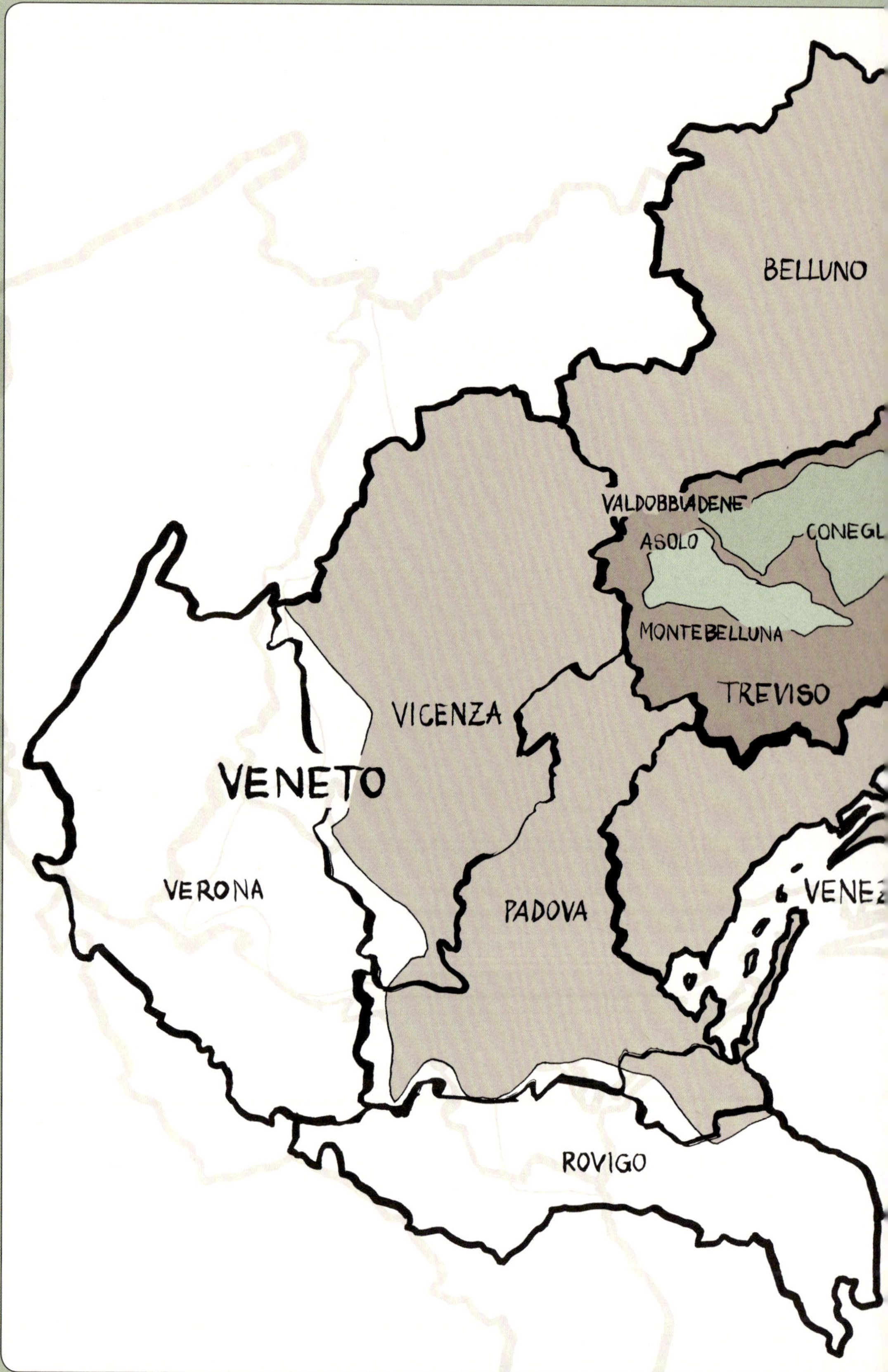
BELLUNO
VALDOBBIADENE
ASOLO
CONEGL
MONTEBELLUNA
TREVISO
VICENZA
VENETO
VERONA
PADOVA
VENEZ
ROVIGO

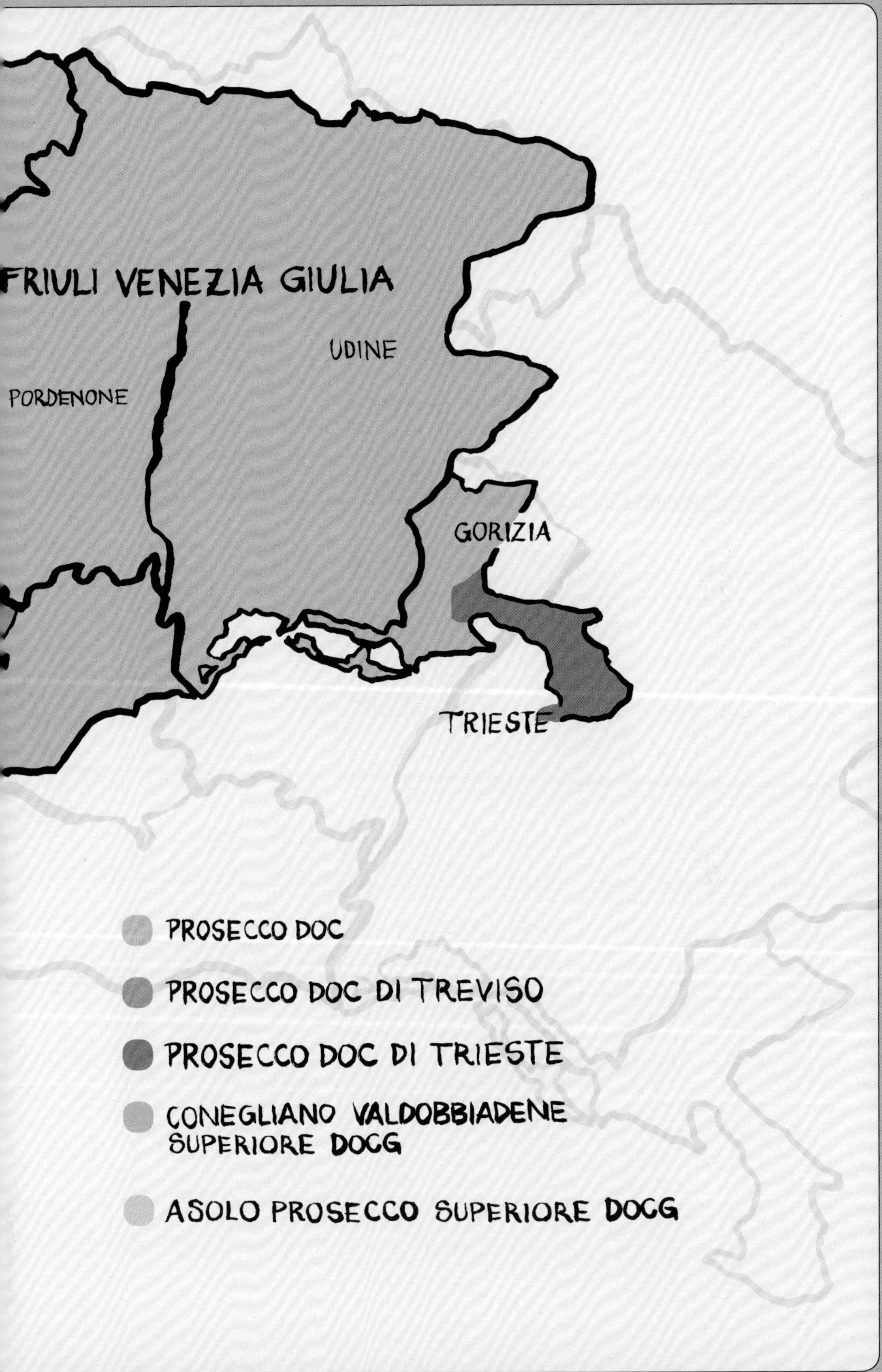
FRIULI VENEZIA GIULIA
UDINE
PORDENONE
GORIZIA
TRIESTE
PROSECCO DOC
PROSECCO DOC DI TREVISO
PROSECCO DOC DI TRIESTE
CONEGLIANO VALDOBBIADENE SUPERIORE DOCG
ASOLO PROSECCO SUPERIORE DOCG

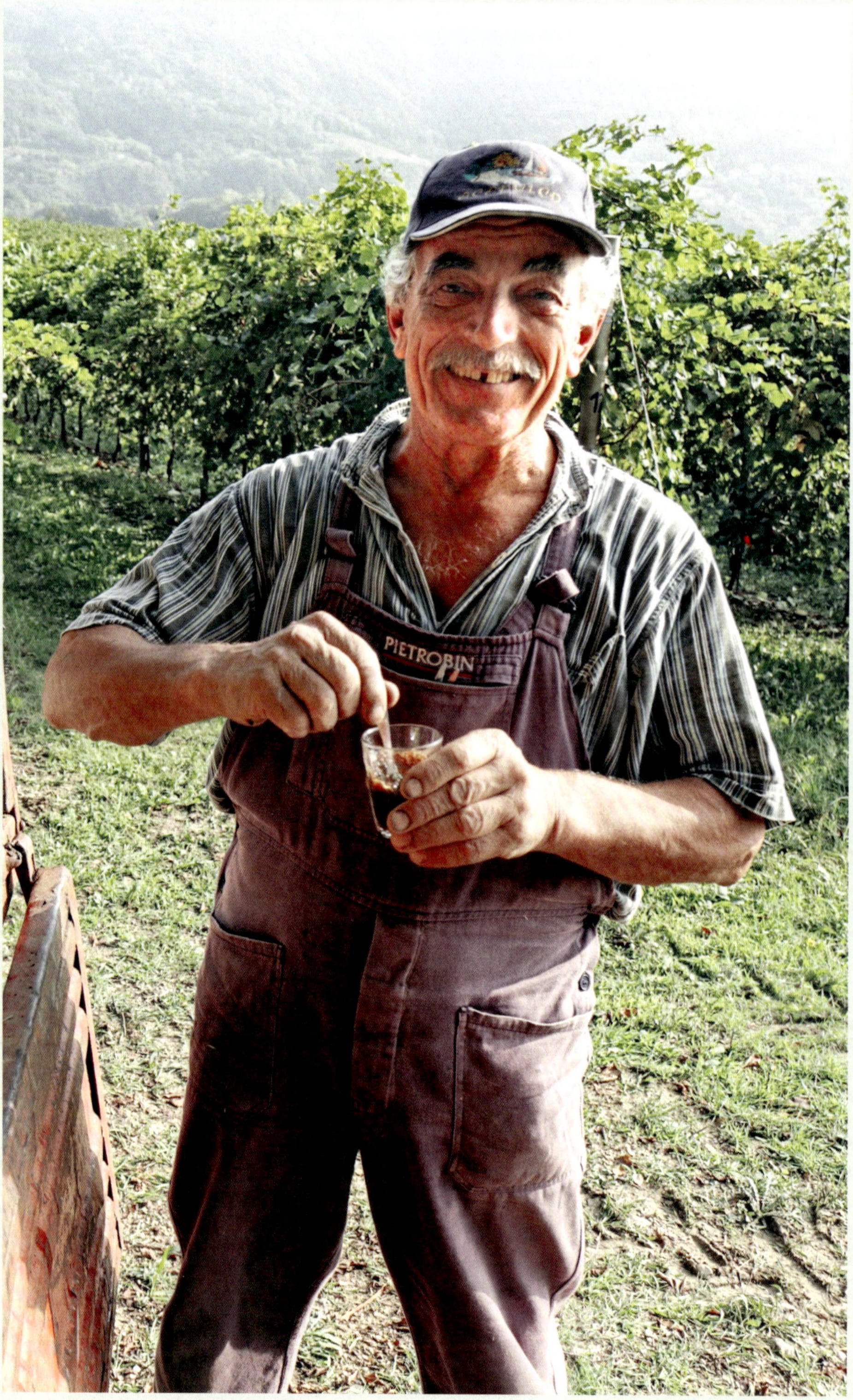

Fregona

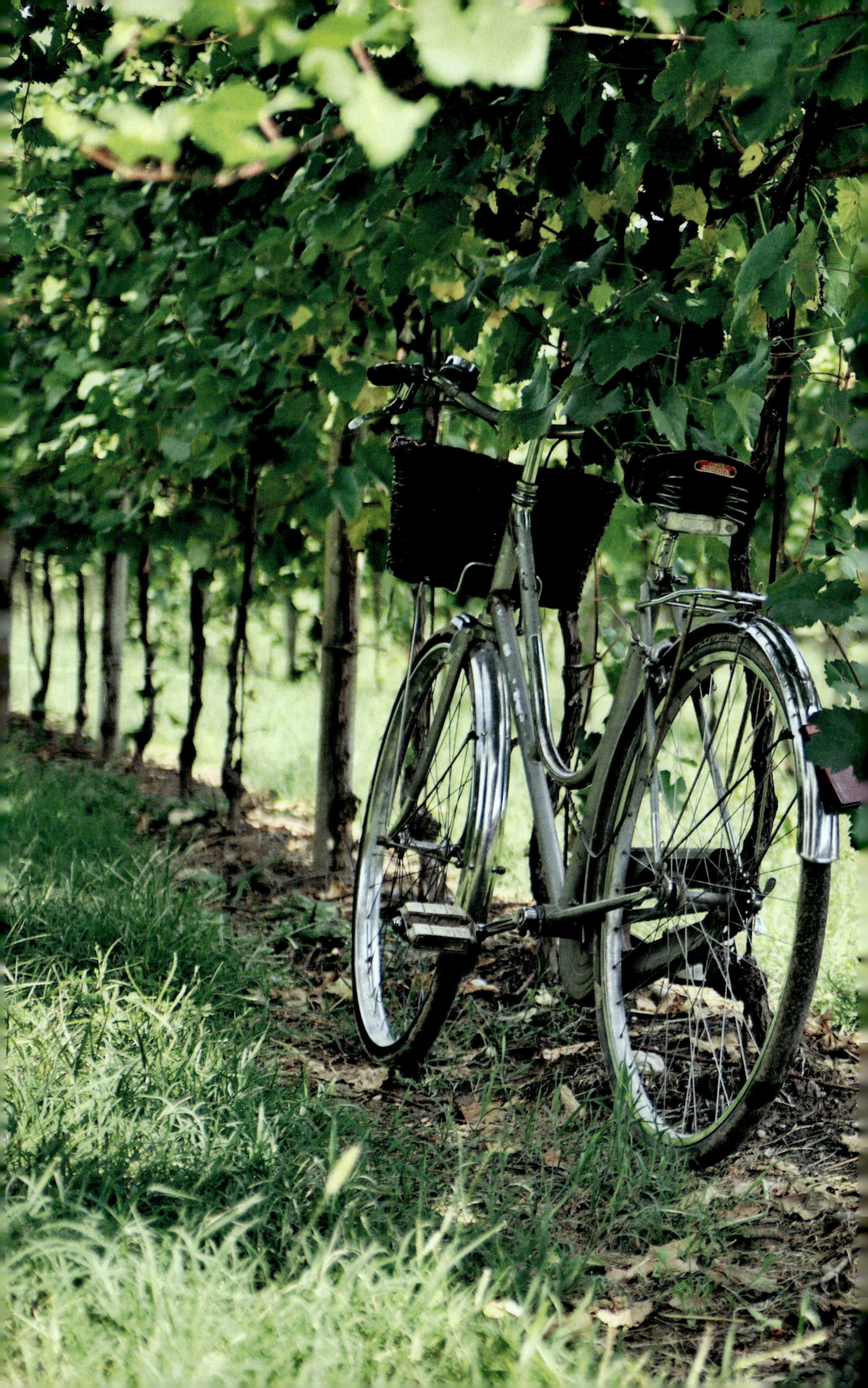

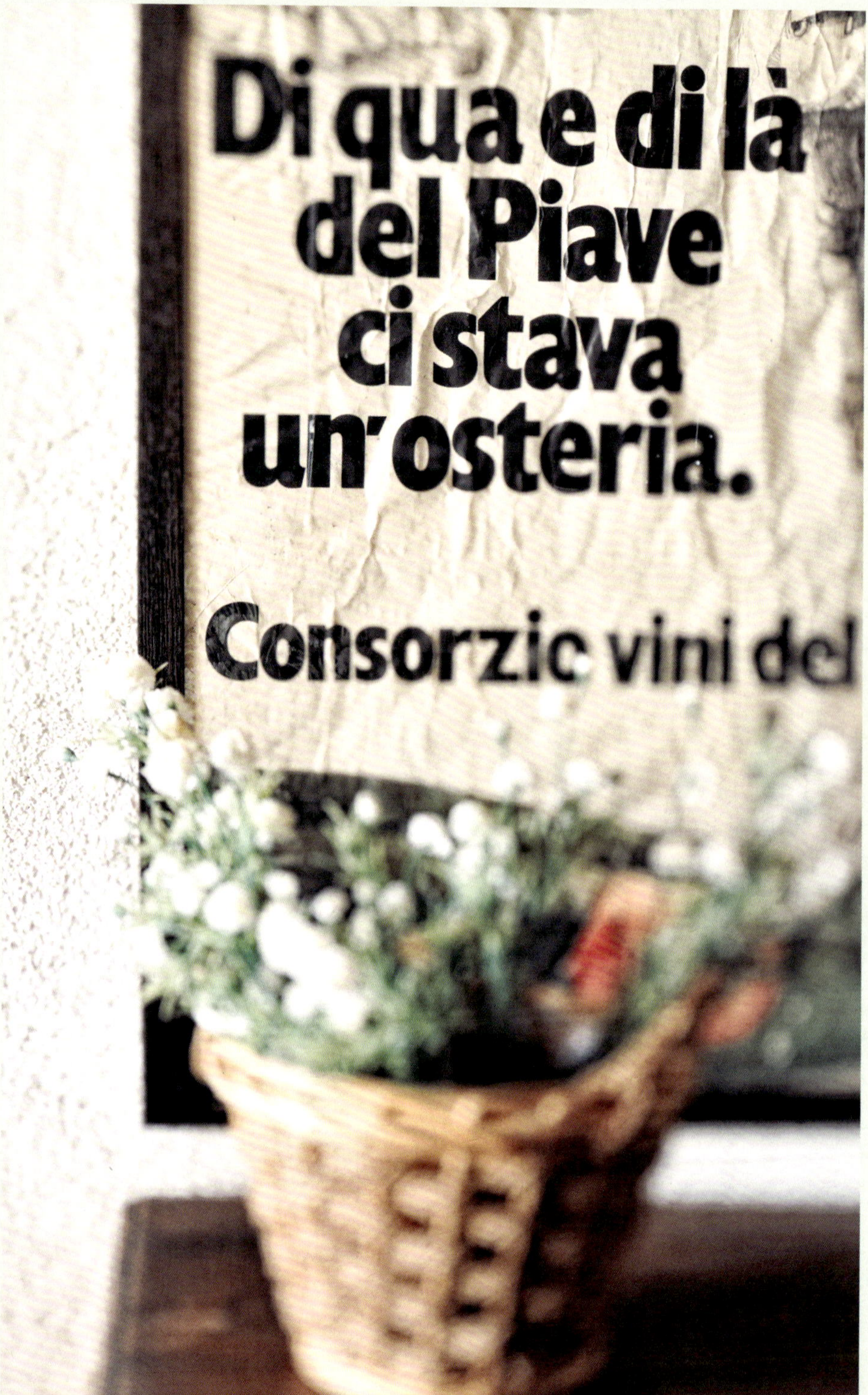

Tezze di Piave

DOC AND DOCG

When it comes to wine, Prosecco in this case, we have to be quite clear about the system of classification and protection, meaning IGT, DOC and DOCG.

The acronym IGT stands for Indicazione Geografica Tipica, DOC for *Denominazione di Origine Controllata* and DOCG for *Denominazione di Origine Controllata e Garantita*. IGT is the base of the pyramid of wine classification, made from Glera grapes. It cannot be called Prosecco, but keeps the name of the varietal. Then there is DOC, a denomination that certifies the origin and specific area of the grapes used for the production of Prosecco. The special names Treviso and Trieste can be used if the grapes, vinification and bottling were all carried out in these two provinces. Prosecco DOC is produced in the provinces of Belluno, Gorizia, Padua, Pordenone, Treviso, Trieste, Udine, Venice and Vicenza. DOCG is reserved for wines already recognized as DOC for at least ten years and which are particularly prized for their intrinsic quality and characteristics due to natural, human and historical factors, and which have gained renown and proved successful on the market in Italy and internationally. Conegliano Valdobbiadene Prosecco Superiore and Asolo Prosecco can sport the letters DOCG on their labels. The former is produced exclusively in 15 municipalities of the hills between Conegliano and Valdobbiadene. The latter in 19 municipalities of the Colli Asolani area.

Each of the classifications, IGT, DOC and DOCG, is restricted to specific regulations of the production code approved by the Italian Ministry of Agriculture. The denomination is indicated on the label.

Since 2010, the DOC and DOCG classifications have been included in the EU's PDO, Protected Designation of Origin, category.

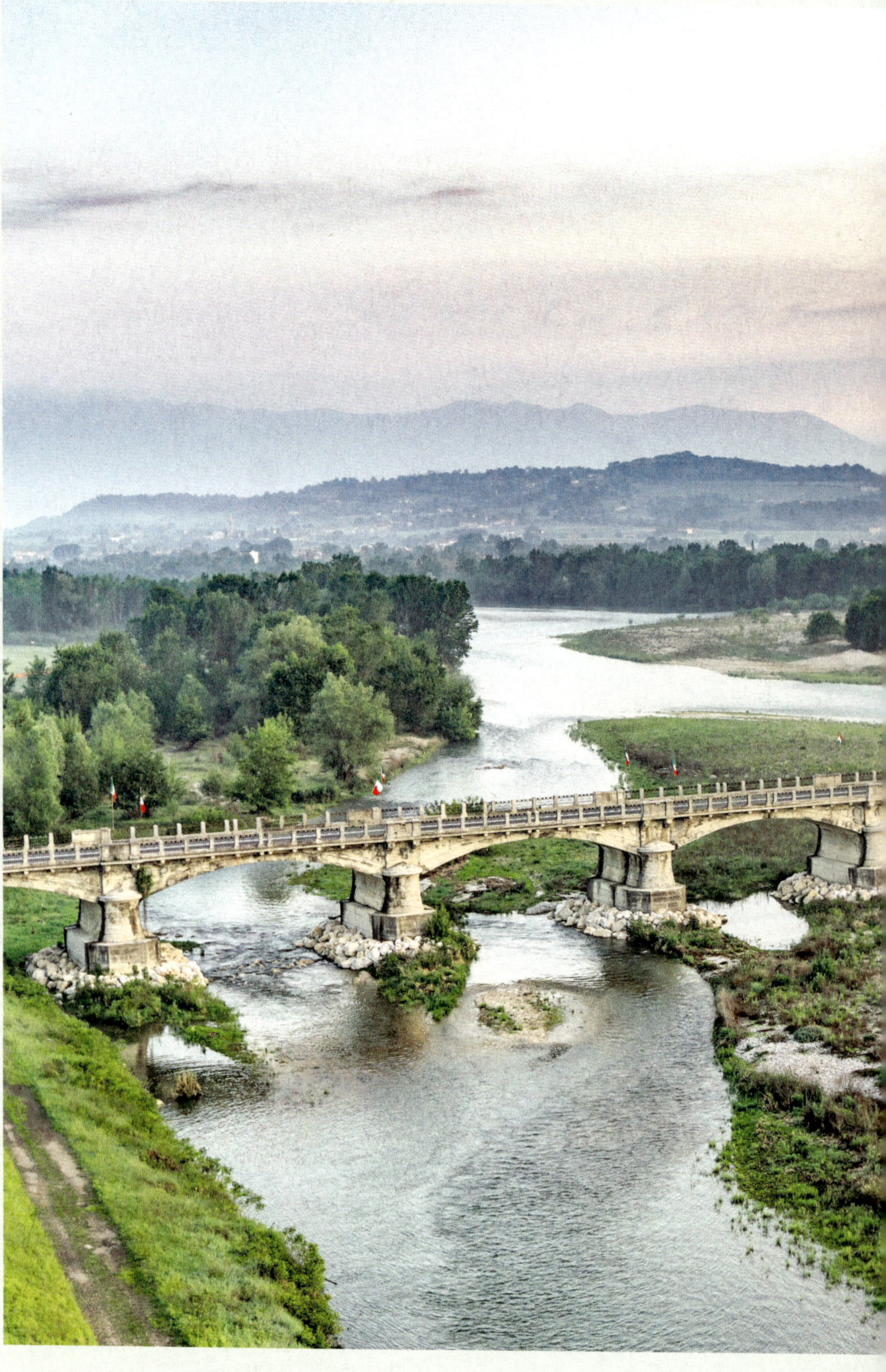

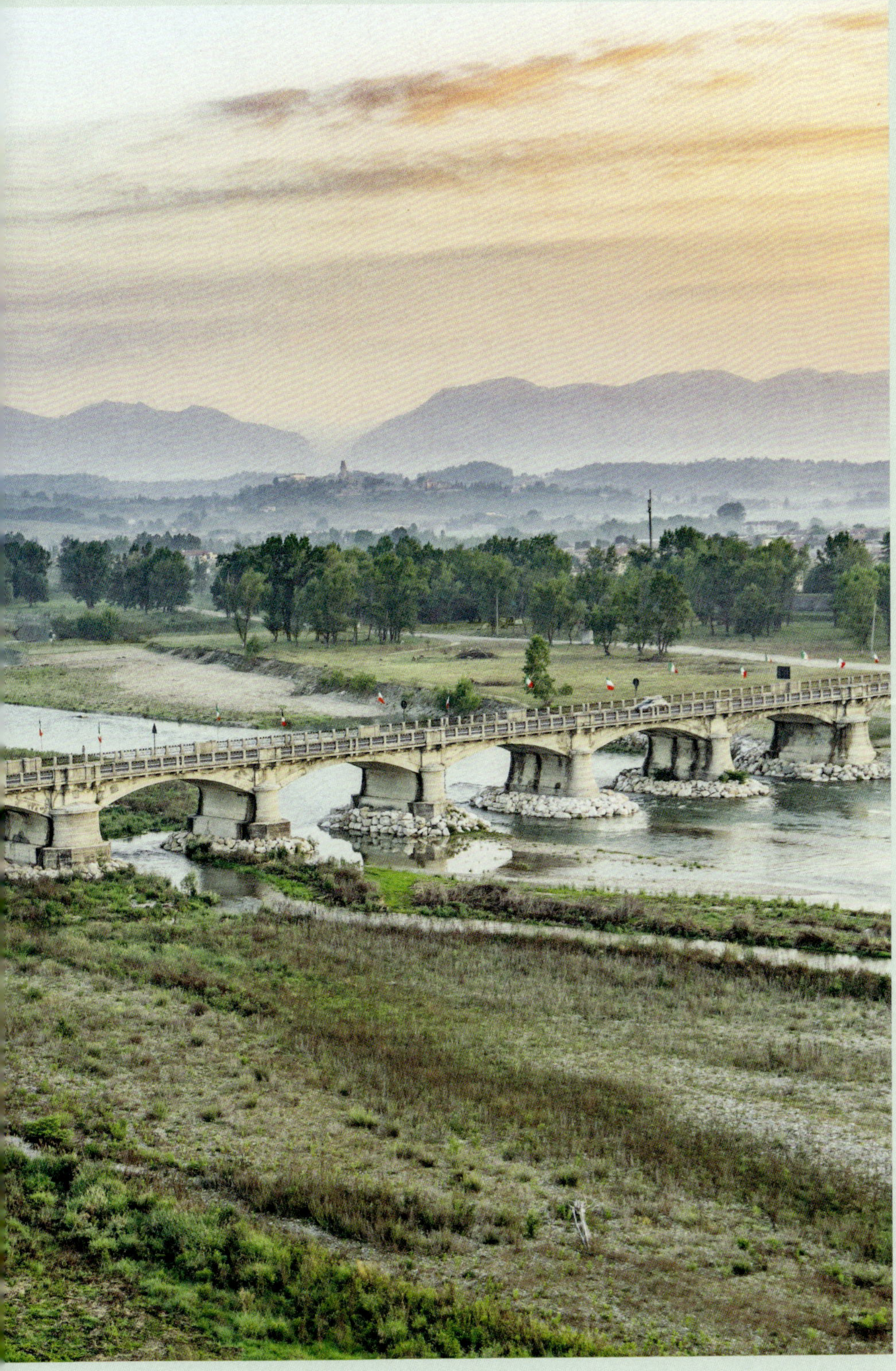

Ponte della Priula, Piave river

TRANQUILLO

Despite being the base version, Prosecco Tranquillo is still the least-known variety. There is no risk of confusing it with the Frizzante or Spumante versions, because the Tranquillo, or still wine, is not bubbly and does not foam. It is a solid wine, but not heavy. It has a full structure, the alcohol content is moderate, and the scents and aromas are typical of the grapes of origin. Its color is like straw glowing in the warm rays of the sun.

FRIZZANTE

Delicately and lightly bubbly, Prosecco Frizzante is the middle brother who comes between Tranquillo and Spumante. Frizzante is usually produced using the Martinotti or Charmat method, placing the base wine Tranquillo in autoclaves, large pressurized steel containers kept at controlled temperatures. Here yeasts and sugars activate the refermentation that generates the bubbles. The wine may be dry or *amabile* (semi-sweet) depending on the residual sugar. It may also be produced by the traditional method of bottle fermentation (ColFondo or Sur lie). This is a late eighteenth-century technique in which, thanks to the refining of the natural grape yeasts, there is a slight veil which makes the flavor softer and fuller.

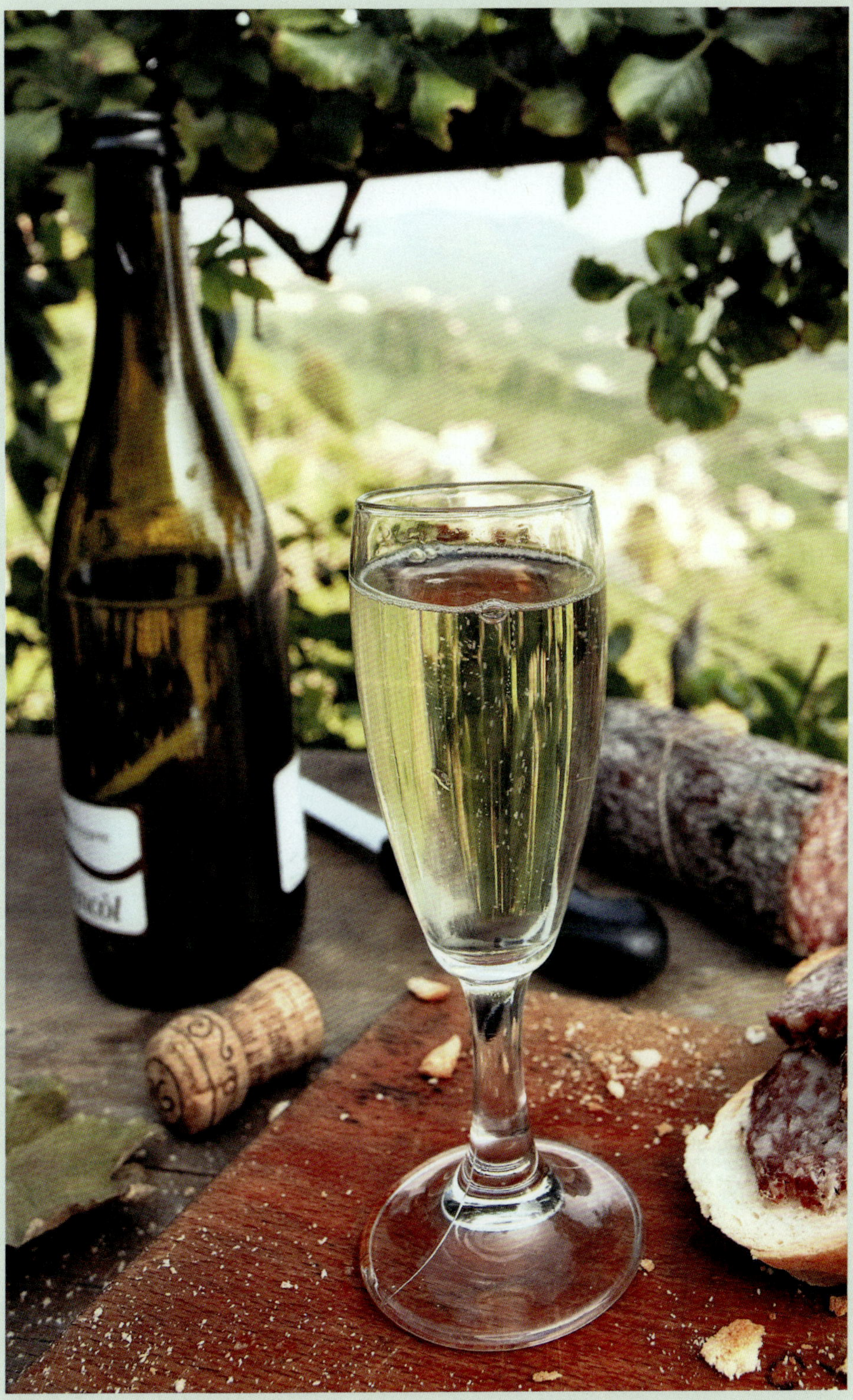

Valdobbiadene

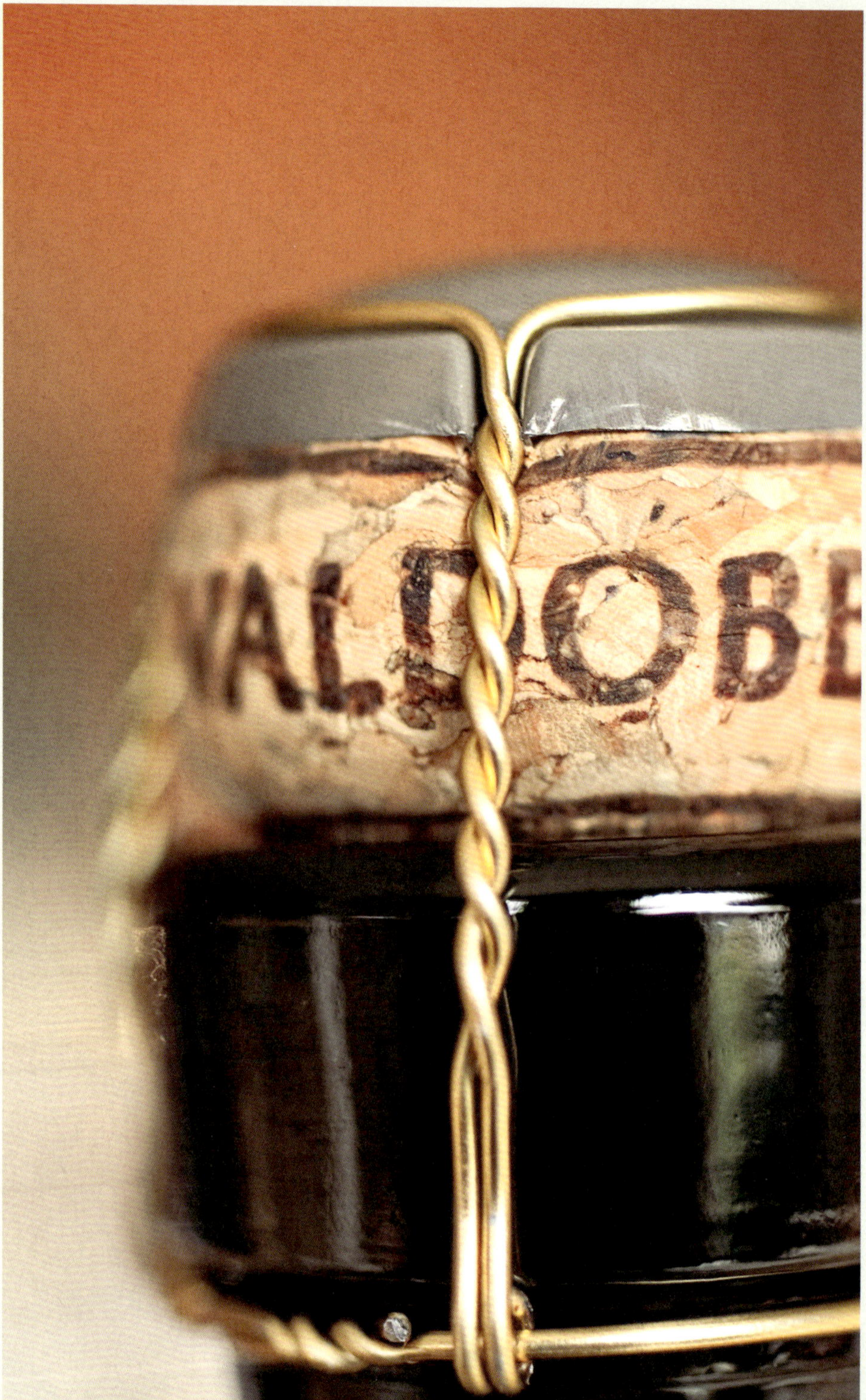
VALDOB

RIVE

The word "Rive" in the local dialect indicates steep hillsides. Docg Conegliano Valdobbiadene Prosecco has 43 different Rive. Each of them expresses a different type of soil, exposure and microclimate. Hence this indication reveals the different facets of Conegliano Valdobbiadene. Spumante Rive are often made in vineyards located in the steepest positions with grapes from a single municipality or village. The name of the locality of the vineyards must be shown on the label, as well as the millesimo or vintage year. For this type, the grapes are harvested strictly by hand.

EXTRA BRUT ASOLO

Asolo is now the only denomination in the whole panorama of Prosecco that can include the words Extra Brut on bottles produced with the Docg label. Extra Brut highlights the prized identity of the hills of Asolo, where the soil is naturally predisposed to produce more highly structured wines. High hills, strong temperature ranges, good ventilation and mineral richness are best expressed in a low-sugar wine. In particular, the large amount of dry residue gives this "secret prosecco" a very elegant and pleasurable structure.

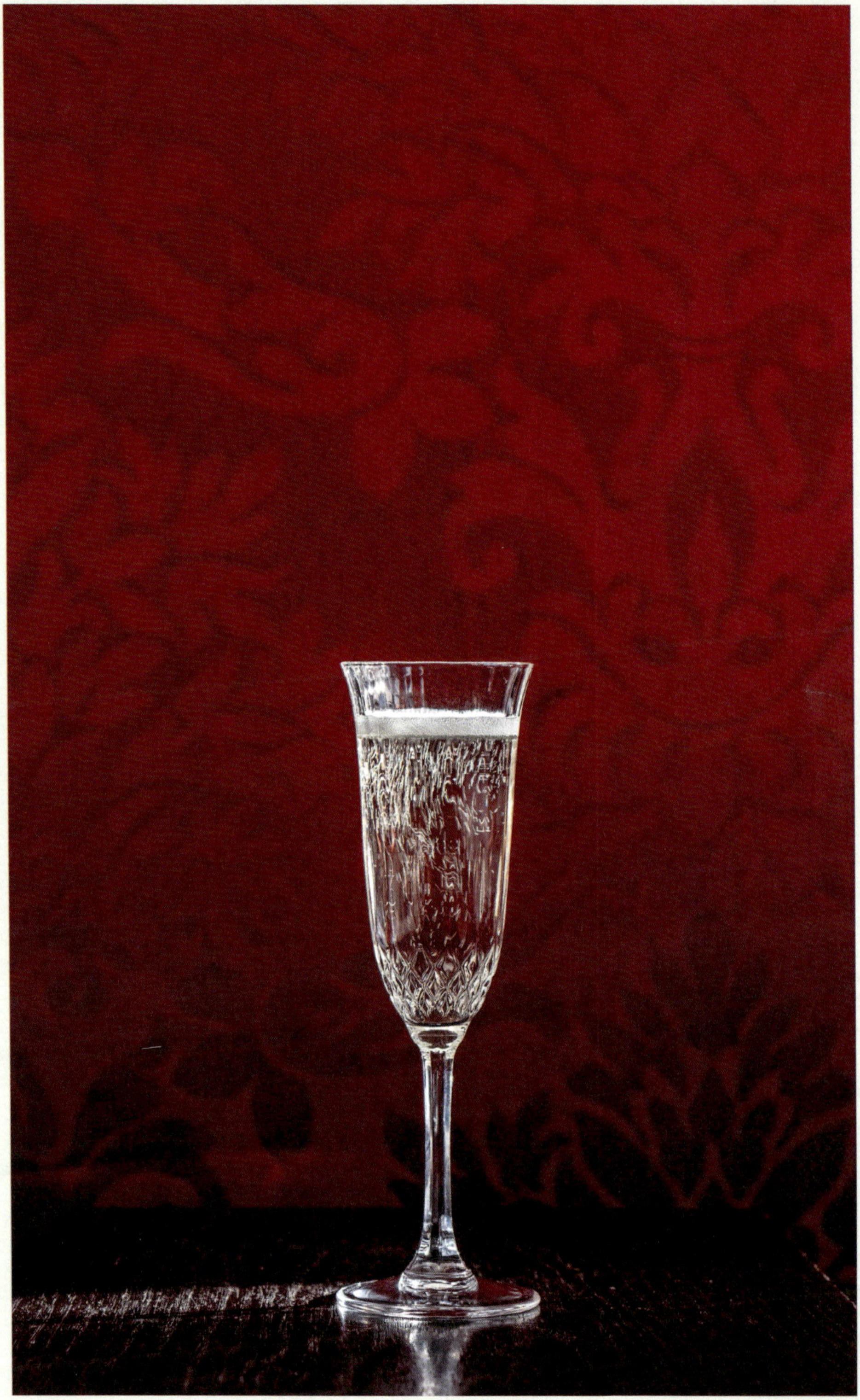

SPUMANTE

The yeasts and sugars turn Prosecco Tranquillo into Spumante. The activity of the yeasts and the energy of the sugars activate fermentation, producing golden bubbles and a whitish foam. This process takes place in large, pressure-sealed steel containers called autoclaves. This technique, known as the Martinotti or Charmat method, is fairly rapid and makes it possible to produce a fine spumante within a few months. It is the perlage, or bubbles, that make the difference from other types.

Spumante is further defined on the basis of the residual sugar it contains. Brut is applied to a wine in which the sugar content is less than 12 grams per liter. This becomes Extra Dry when the sugar content is between 12 and 17 g/liter. Dry when the sugar content is between 17 and 32 g/liter. Demi-Sec when the sugar content is between 32 and 50 g/liter.

The term Millesimato (vintage) is applied to spumante produced with wines from a single year.

CARTIZZE

107 hectares of vineyards forming a pentagon-shaped area, on some of the steepest hillsides of San Pietro di Barbozza, Santo Stefano and Saccol, the hamlets of Valdobbiadene. This is the Cartizze area, the Olympus of Prosecco. The wine is straw-colored with bright reflexes and glints of gold. The harmonious bouquet is a complex cluster of scents that recall fruit with white pulp like apples and pears, citrus fruit, the intensity of peach and apricot, with hints of rose and an almond note in the aftertaste. The flavor is harmonious and elegant, with great softness and freshness. The perlage is light and fine.

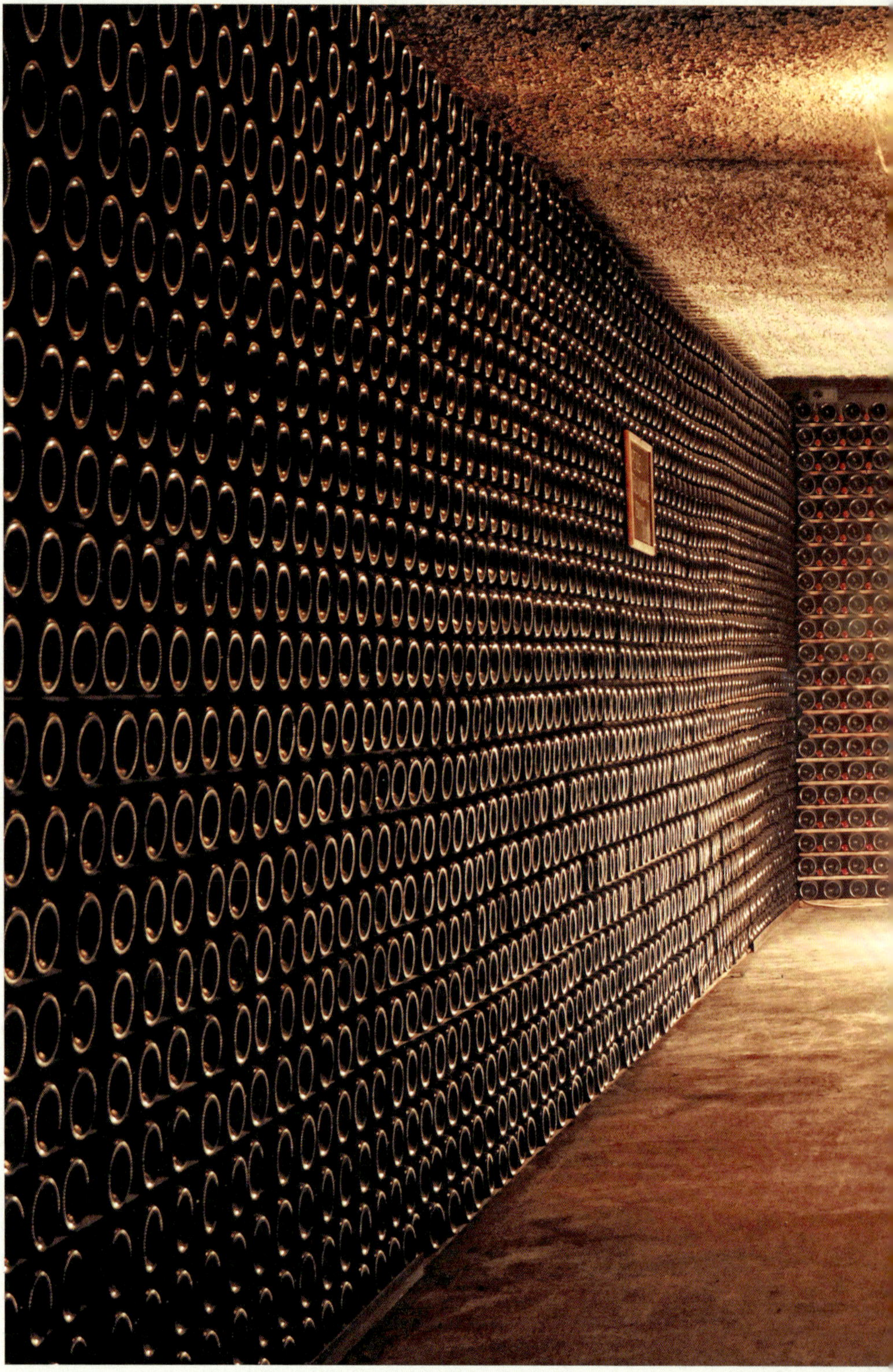

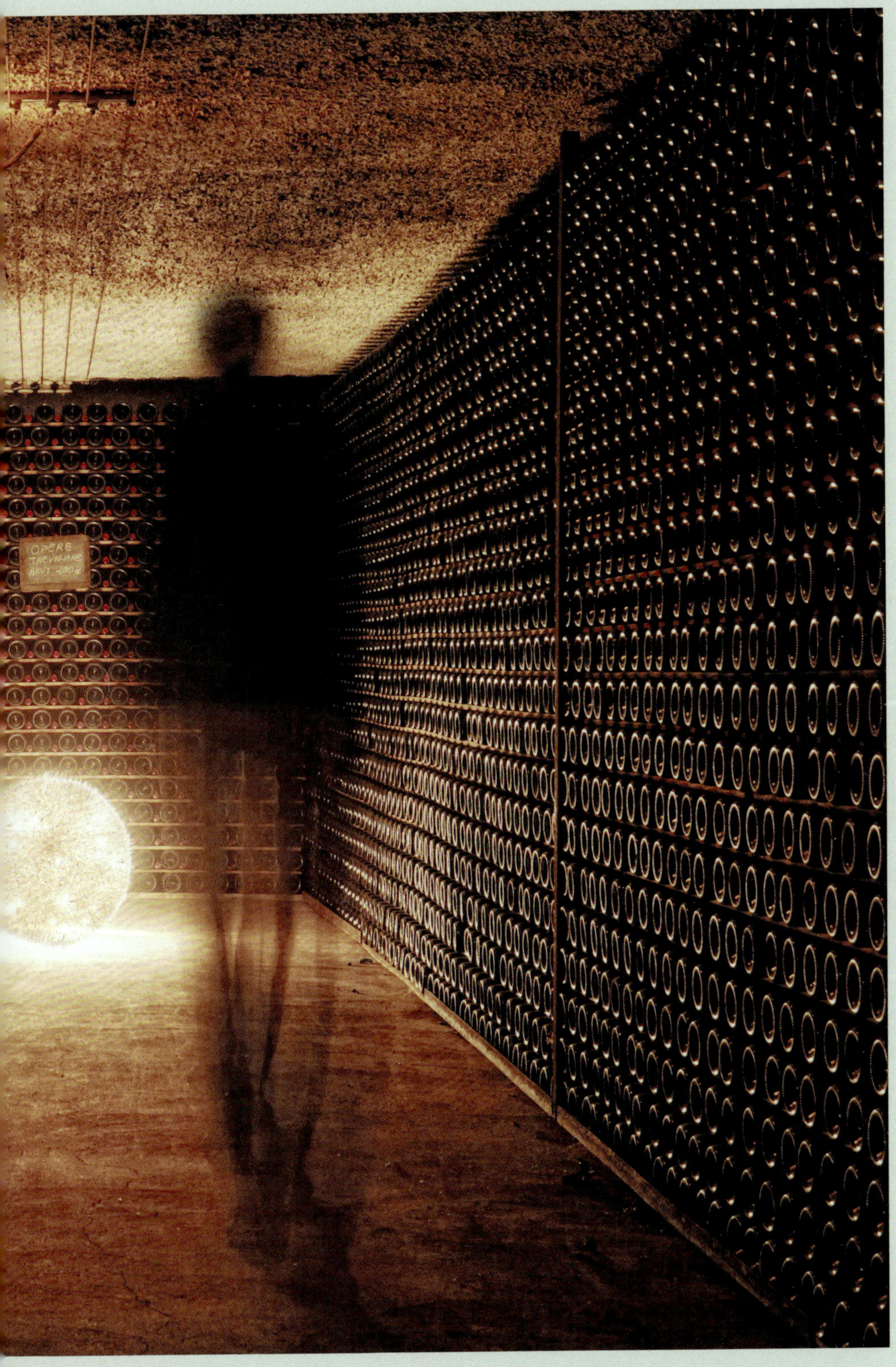

Crocetta del Montello

SUSTAINABILITY

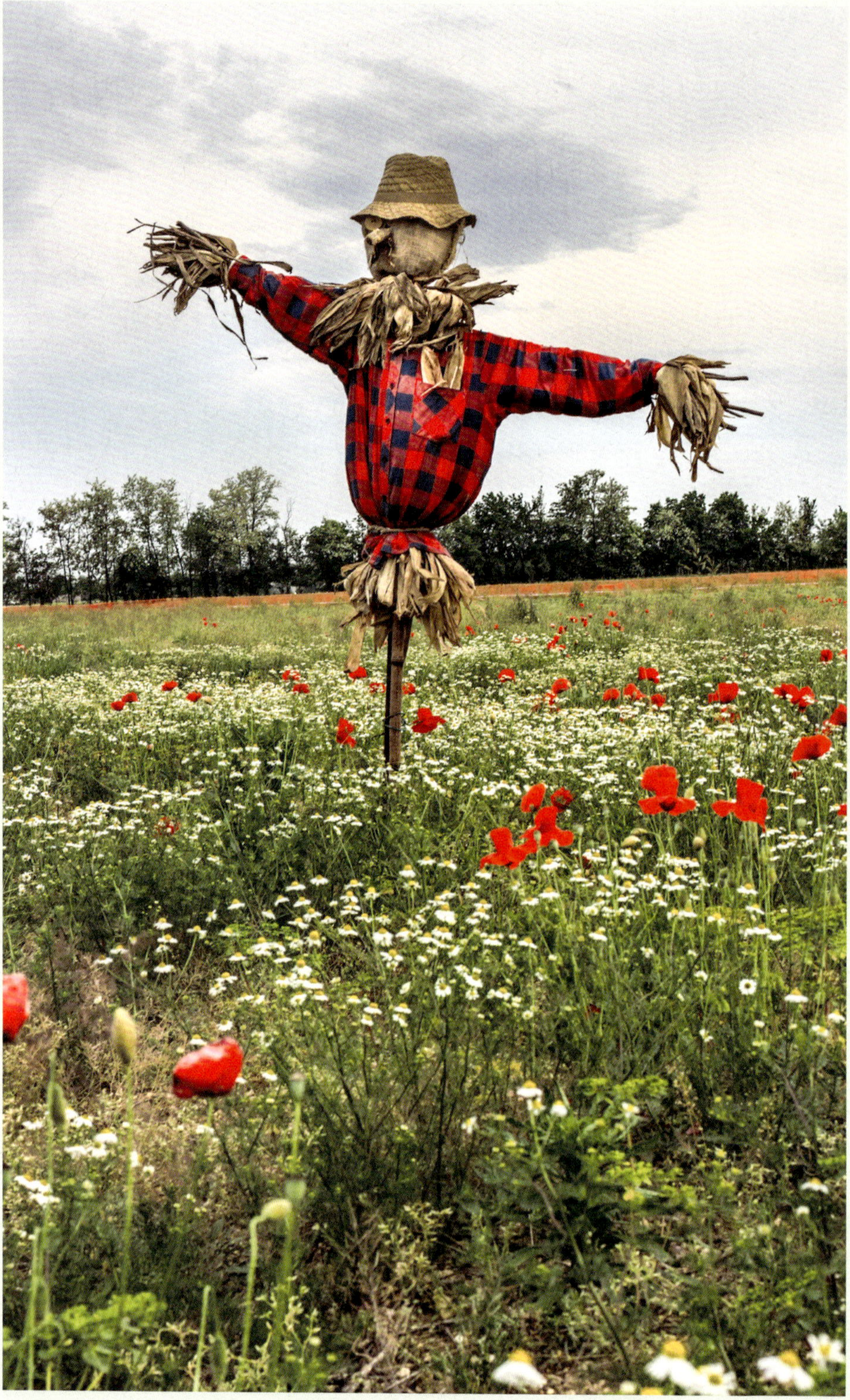

Borso del Grappa

VITICULTURE IN HARMONY BETWEEN PEOPLE AND NATURE

Biodiversity and monoculture are at odds. It is not easy to strike a balance between them. Monoculture is practiced for business reasons; biodiversity is safeguarded out of respect for the environment. It is the eternal dilemma between being and having. Prosecco's success is like a siren song, impossible to resist. In recent years, a large number of forests, cornfields and wheat fields have been replaced by Glera vines and monoculture seems to threaten biodiversity. It is the coexistence of different animal and plant species within the same ecosystem that creates equilibrium through the relations between them. Biodiversity is harmony. If this harmony is diminished, nature rebels, the environment becomes diseased and the landscape impoverished. In the Prosecco district, many people realize that environmental sustainability is a daily challenge to give wine an environmental passport that will increasingly open the doors to global markets. The hilly winegrowing landscape of Conegliano Valdobbiadene is half-cultivated, half wilderness or woodlands, crisscrossed by numerous small streams. The forests, river banks, meadows, as well as the vineyards on steep slopes facing south, are of particular interest for plant biodiversity, hosting species-rich communities, including some typical of dry meadows. Numerous estates are beginning or have already begun converting vineyards. A group of producers of organic Prosecco Superiore is exploring the potential for creating a bio-district within the DOCG zone. Organic viticulture, however, is an agricultural practice that takes a long time to develop and involves all sorts of complications, especially in a land that is impervious because of its specific environmental and working conditions. The hills of Asolo and Montello, the district of Asolo Prosecco DOCG, is an area of woodland and springs where the vines grow between the plains and the hills, in a diversified territory. In addition to the culture and cultivation of the vine, there is room for growing other crops such as potatoes, apples, cherries, peas and beans. The level land of the Prosecco DOC has joined the central-eastern Venezia Bio-district, which seeks to preserve and enhance nature, the landscape and agriculture.

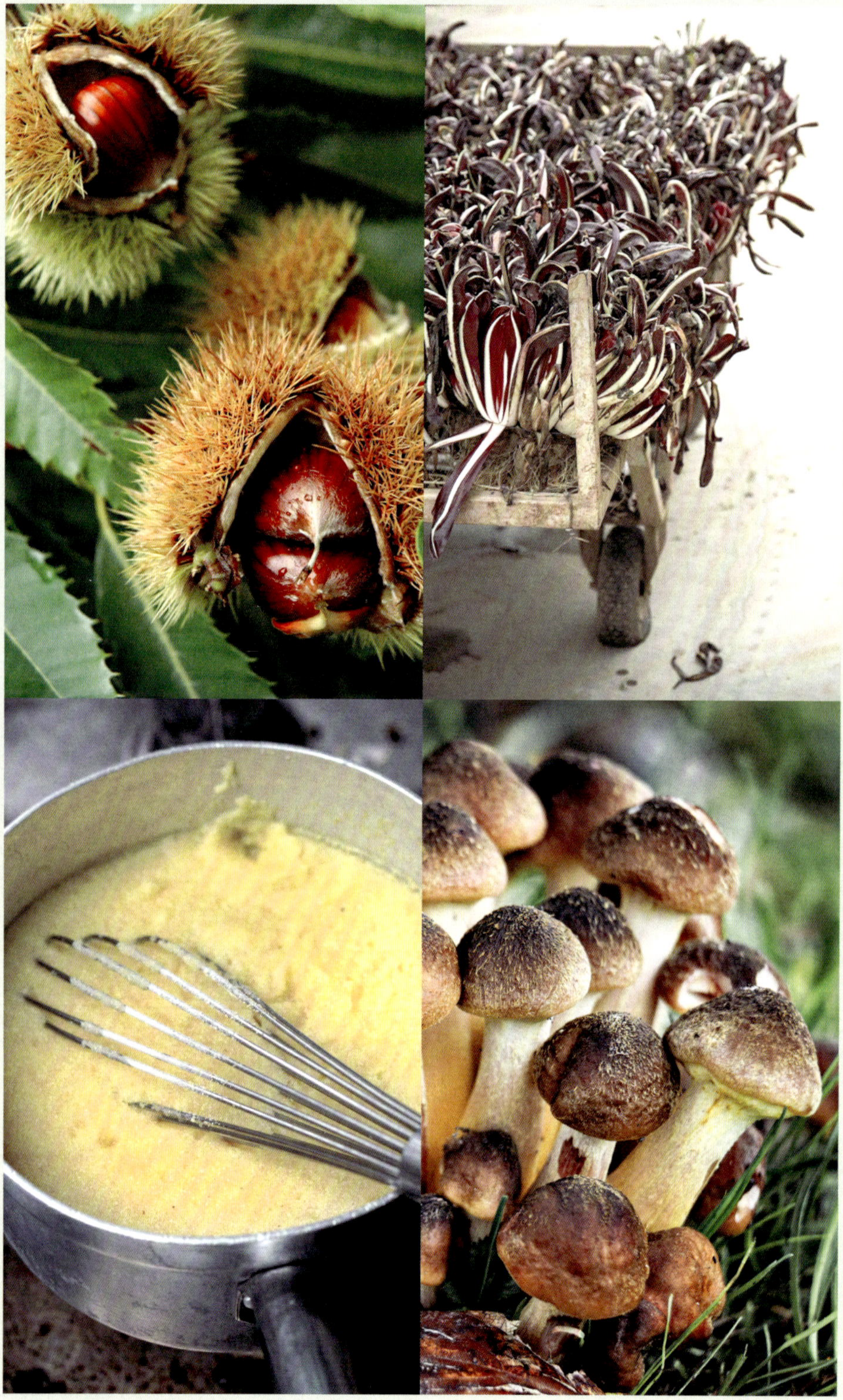

Chestnuts, Treviso chicory, Polenta, Chiodini mushrooms

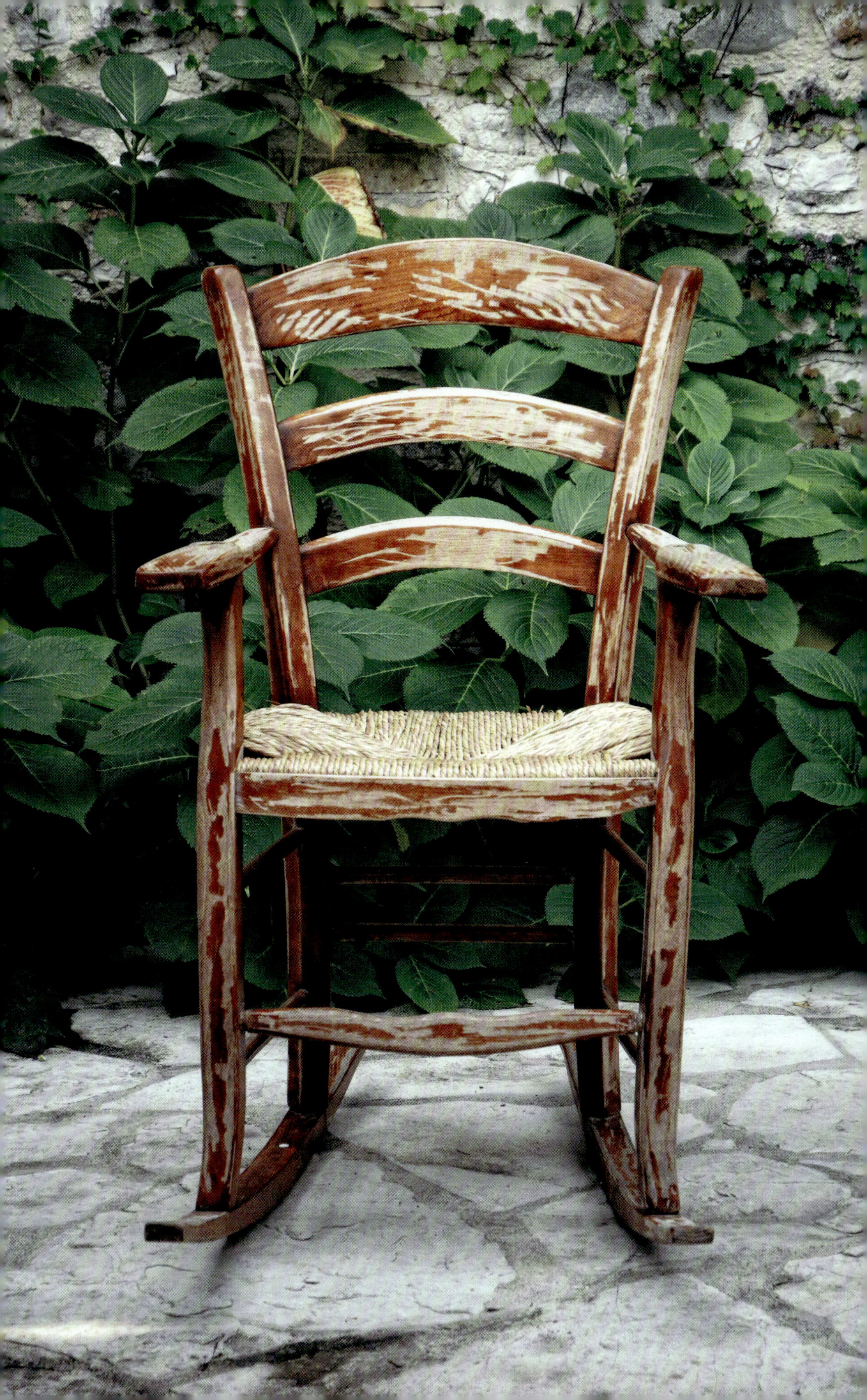

SUSTAINABILITY PROTOCOL, A MANUAL OF GOOD MANNERS

"Following the protocol": in Italy the expression conveys the idea of behaving properly, of having good manners. The viticultural protocol (or vademecum) is a technical and regulatory guide that show winemakers the correct ways to defend the vines from pests and diseases, while respecting the environment and inhabitants as far as possible. It is a voluntary, not compulsory guide, hence the instructions it contains are advice, not regulations to be applied strictly. A manual of best practice to minimize the impact of plant protection products on people and the environment by heightening the awareness of wine growers. Technically, the viticultural protocol provides guidance on agronomic methods and strategies to be used to protect crops and control weeds while reducing the impact on people and the environment and ensuring the product is economically viable. Conegliano Valdobbiadene Prosecco Superiore DOCG first adopted the viticulture protocol in 2011, while in the Prosecco DOC plains the first viticultural guide was issued in 2013. More frequently in recent years, many wineries have begun to use greener systems for protecting vines, although the combination of organic and traditional viticulture makes it difficult to completely banish all traces of chemicals from the vineyards due to their volatility. In addition to organic products for defending the vines, in the Prosecco zone there are some winegrowers who have had a dash more courage and tried to restore a natural dimension to viticulture. The Oenological School in Conegliano has surrounded its organic vineyard with hedges, the ideal habitat for good insects that feed on parasites. Others, for the same reason, have planted roses. There are also those who release insect allies directly into the vineyards, while many now weed the rows mechanically instead of using chemical sprays.

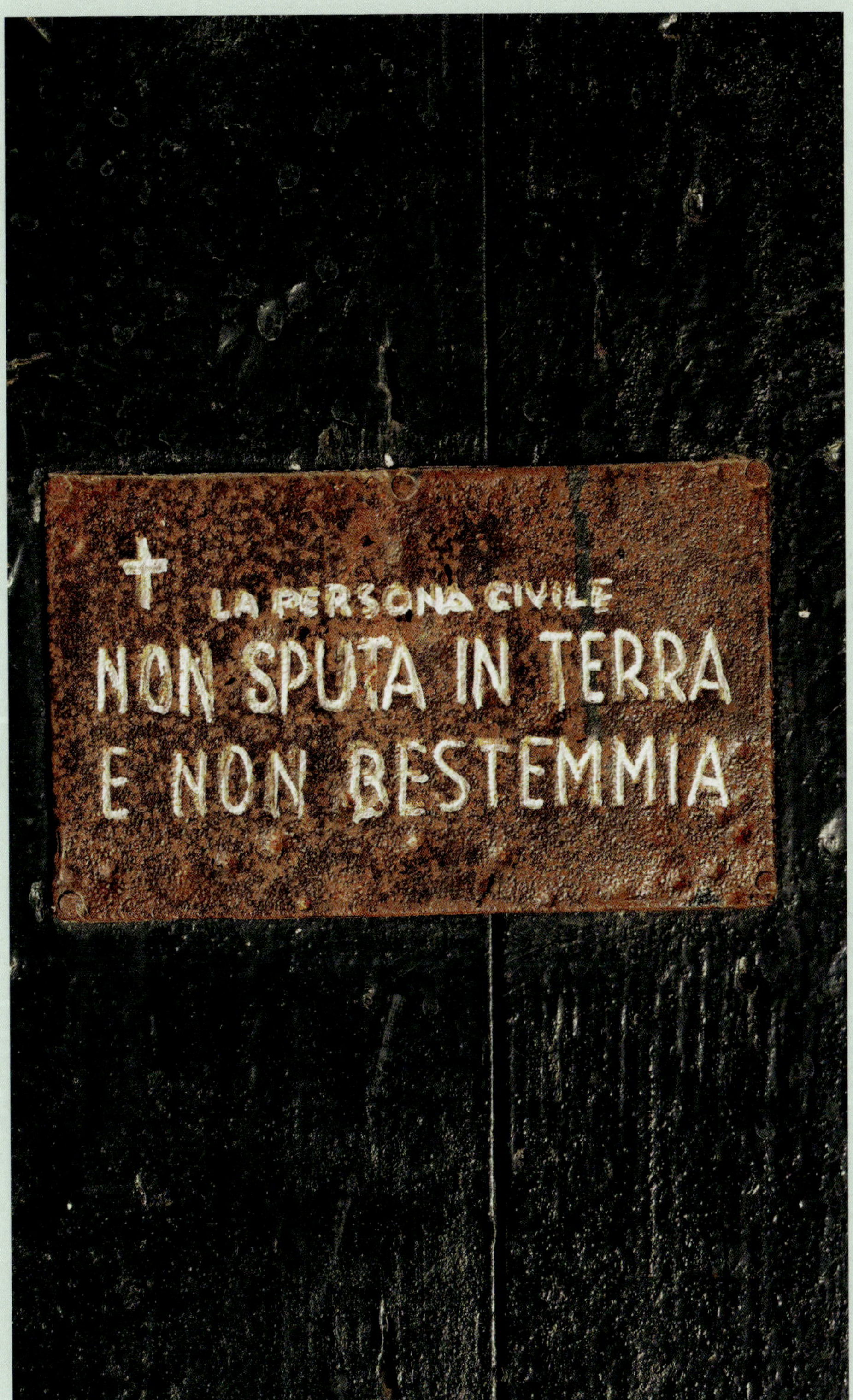

Salgareda, Campo di Pietra locality

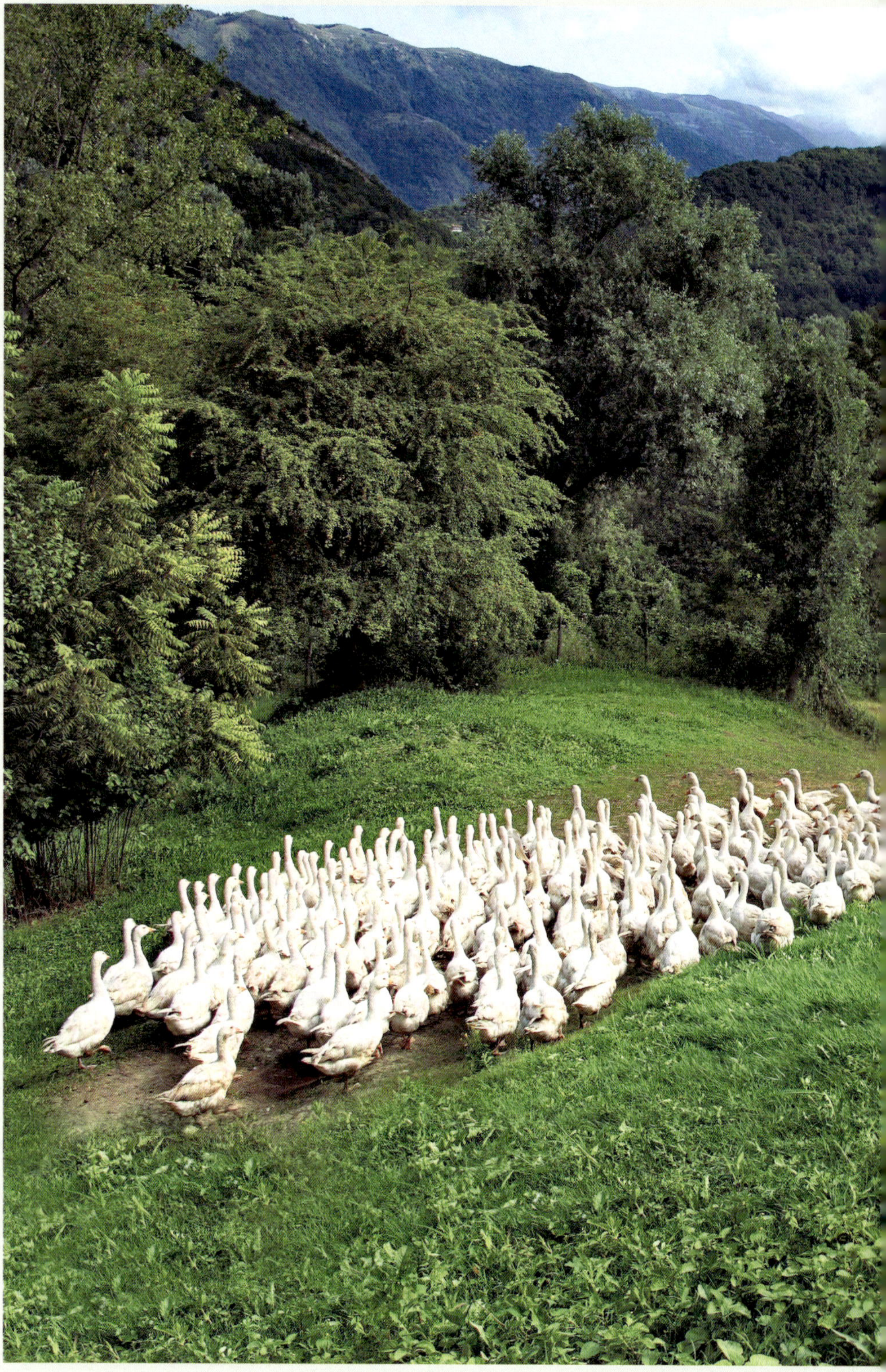

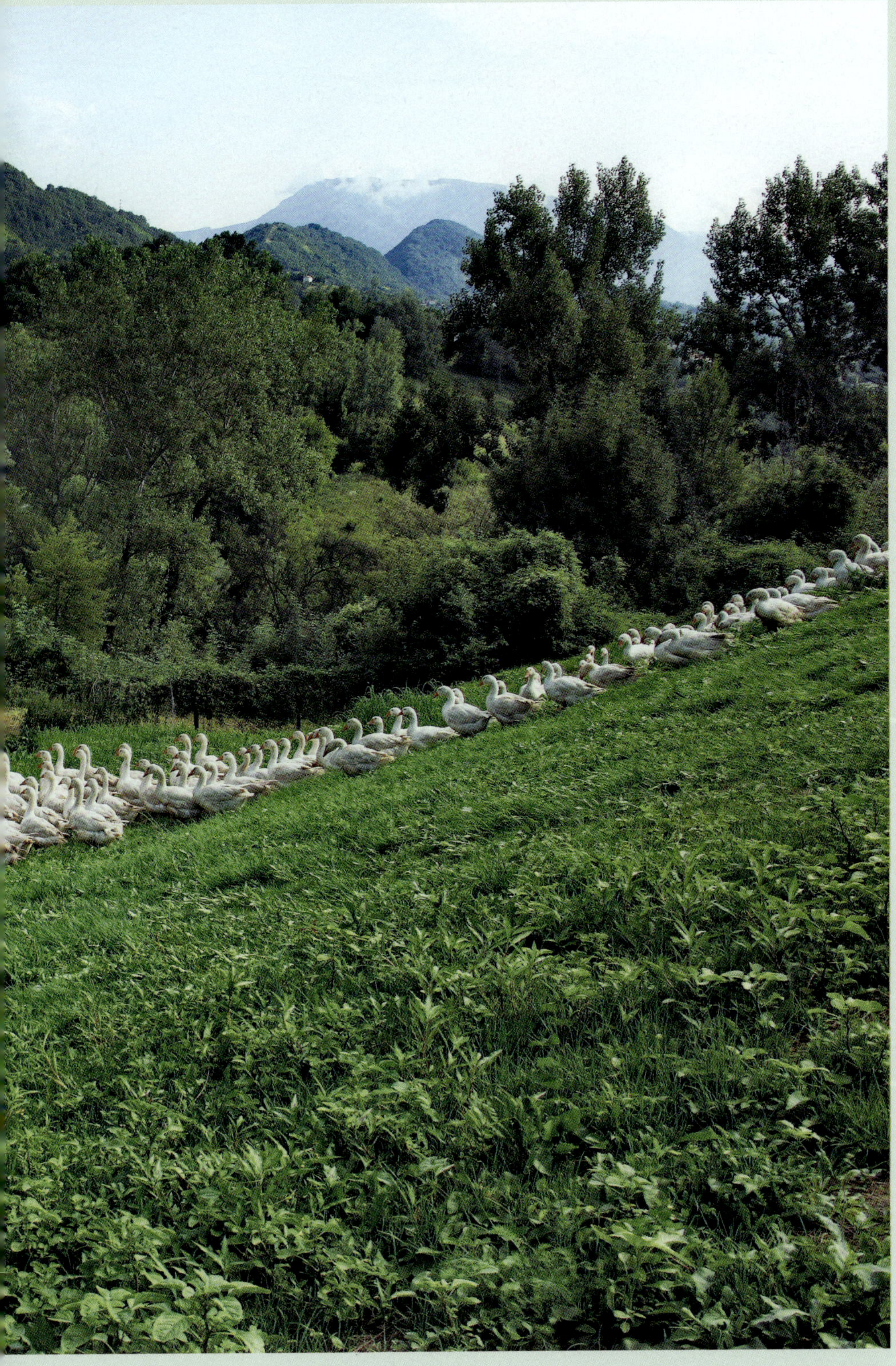

Arfanta

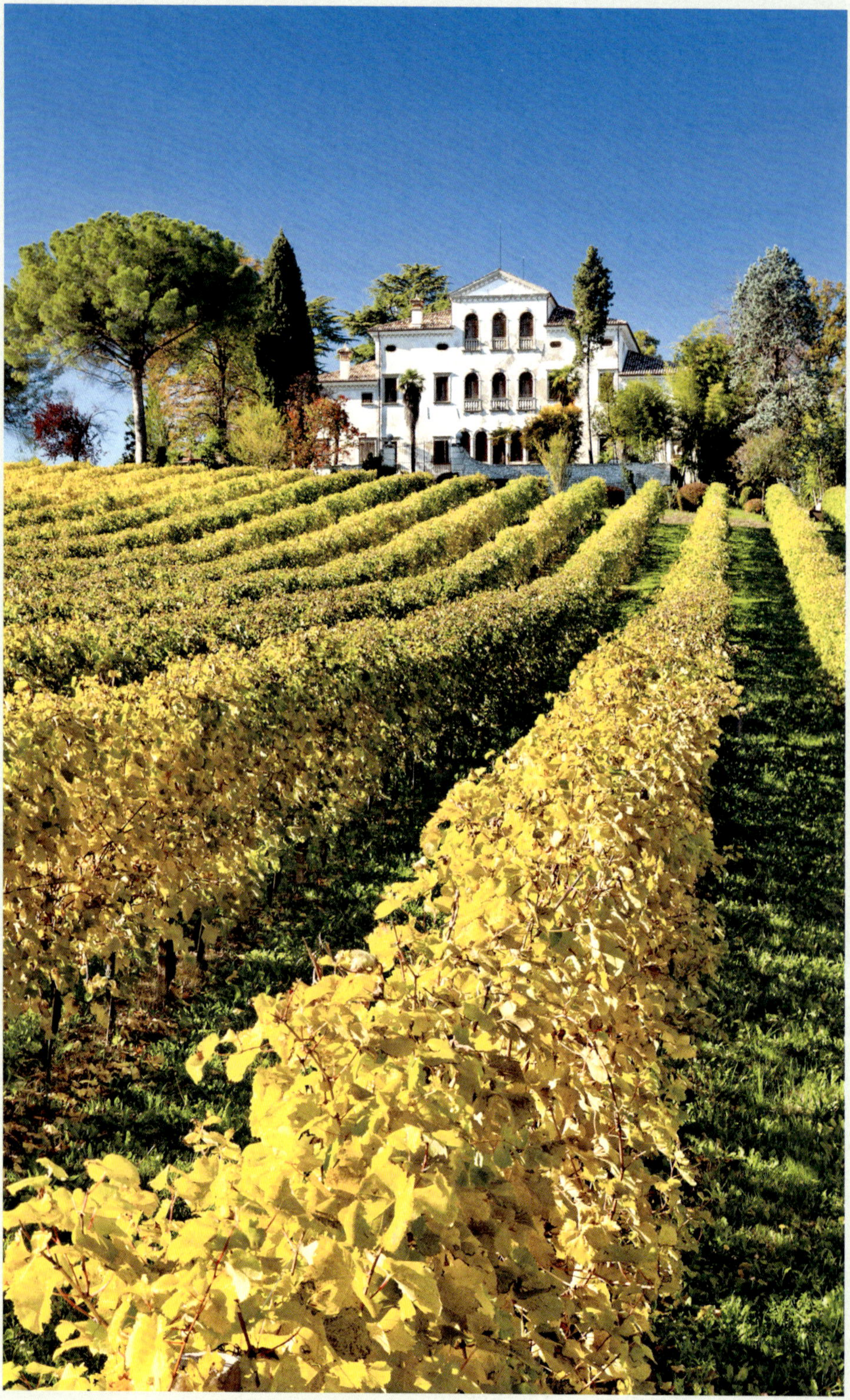

Ogliano, Villa Gera Amadio Maresio

UNESCO AND THE HILLS OF CONEGLIANO VALDOBBIADENE

Rugged hillsides chain-stitched with rows of vines. Little villages with church steeples soaring above them. Hills and dells dotted with ancient stone houses. If you listen carefully, you can still hear the vats bubbling, the polenta pot grumbling on the fire, the little chicks peeping behind the mother hen, while the heat of the sun nurtures the grapes clustering on the vines. On the hills of Conegliano and Valdobbiadene, nature and people have worked together for centuries in an enduring partnership. The key to this harmony is respect. It is not a natural but a cultural landscape, so defined by Article 1 of the UNESCO Convention, which protects the world cultural heritage. The hills of Conegliano Valdobbiadene are candidates for UNESCO World Heritage listing. It is a cultural landscape because it is shaped by the interaction between man and nature. "In particular, the hills of Prosecco Superiore belong to the second category of landscapes (II – organically evolved landscape), namely those generated by a continuous process that has evolved in history, but still vital, through which the local community and its artistic, technical and productive culture have been organized in response to the characteristics of the fragile and distinctive physical environment" (from the dossier of the UNESCO candidature). Nature, architecture, art, tradition and innovations in viticulture and winemaking are the elements that together distinguish the hilly landscape of Conegliano and Valdobbiadene. Candidacy for recognition as a UNESCO World Heritage Site has been advanced for the fifteen municipalities of the DOCG Prosecco: Conegliano, San Vendemiano, Colle Umberto, Vittorio Veneto, Tarzo, Revine, Cison di Valmarino, San Pietro di Feletto, Refrontolo, Susegana, Pieve di Soligo, Farra di Soligo, Follina, Miane, Vidor and Valdobbiadene – and 6 villages that skirt the hills and possess the same distinctive qualities: Fregona, Moriago della Battaglia, Sernaglia della Battaglia, San Fior, Colle Umberto and Santa Lucia di Piave. The bureaucratic process, begun in 2010, is long and the commitment to maintaining harmony between nature and humanity requires irreproachable conduct. However, the ambitious goal stimulates consciences and goes straight in the direction of protecting the environment.

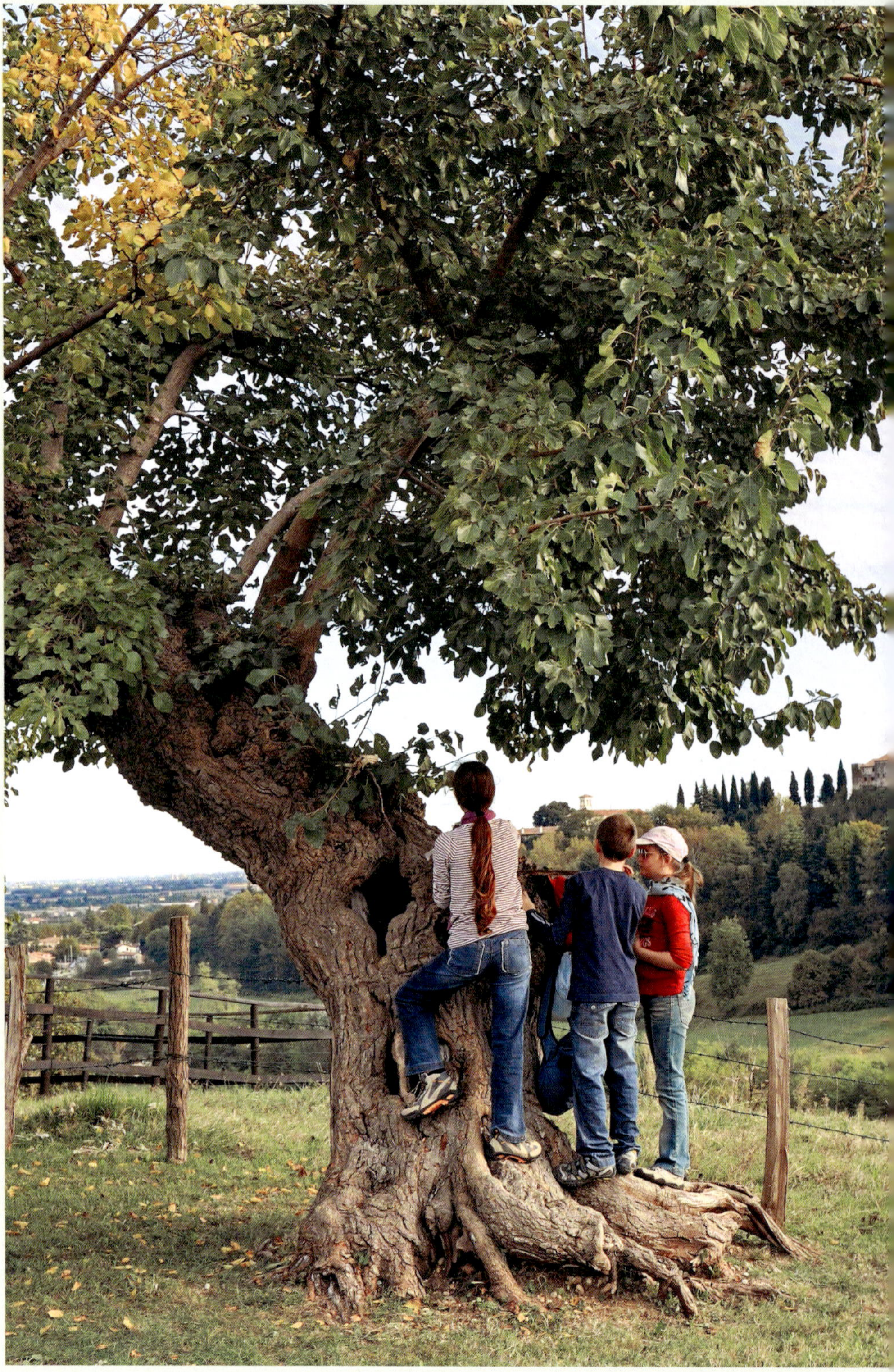

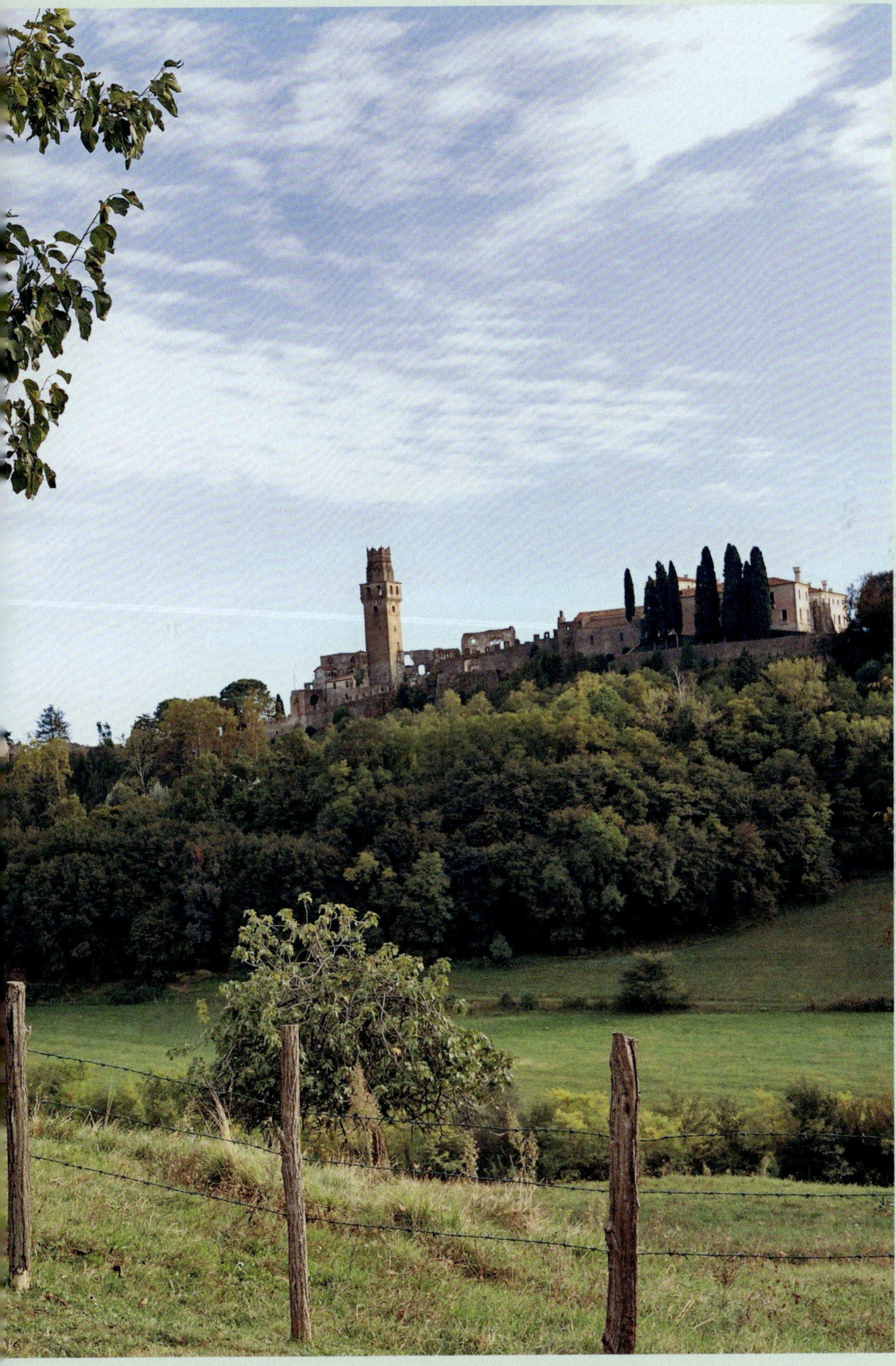

Susegana, San Salvatore castle view from Casa Forcolera

TERRITORY

Villa di Maser

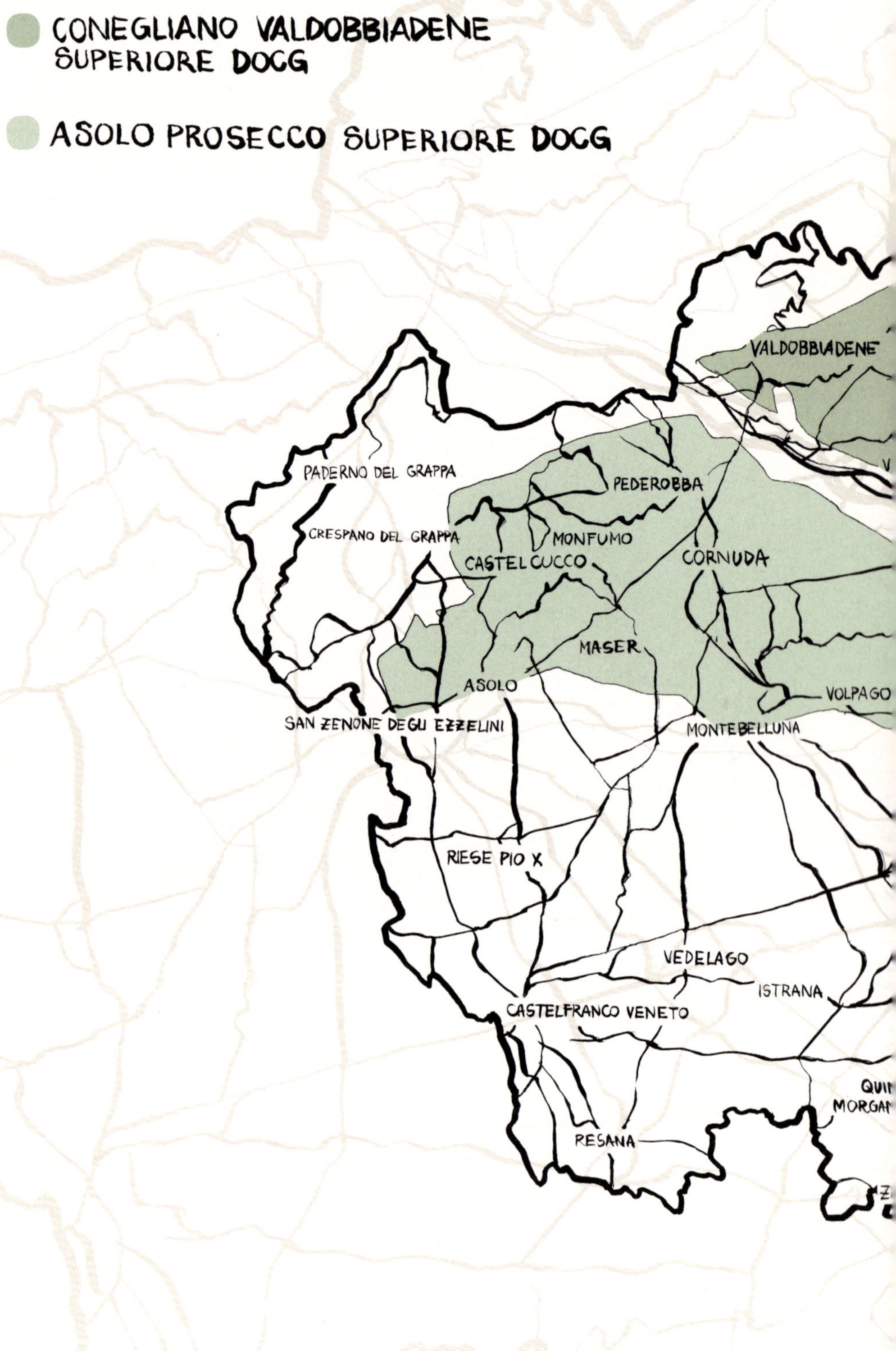
CONEGLIANO VALDOBBIADENE SUPERIORE DOCG
ASOLO PROSECCO SUPERIORE DOCG
VALDOBBIADENE
PADERNO DEL GRAPPA
PEDEROBBA
CRESPANO DEL GRAPPA
MONFUMO
CASTELCUCCO
CORNUDA
MASER
ASOLO
VOLPAGO
SAN ZENONE DEGLI EZZELINI
MONTEBELLUNA
RIESE PIO X
VEDELAGO
ISTRANA
CASTELFRANCO VENETO
RESANA

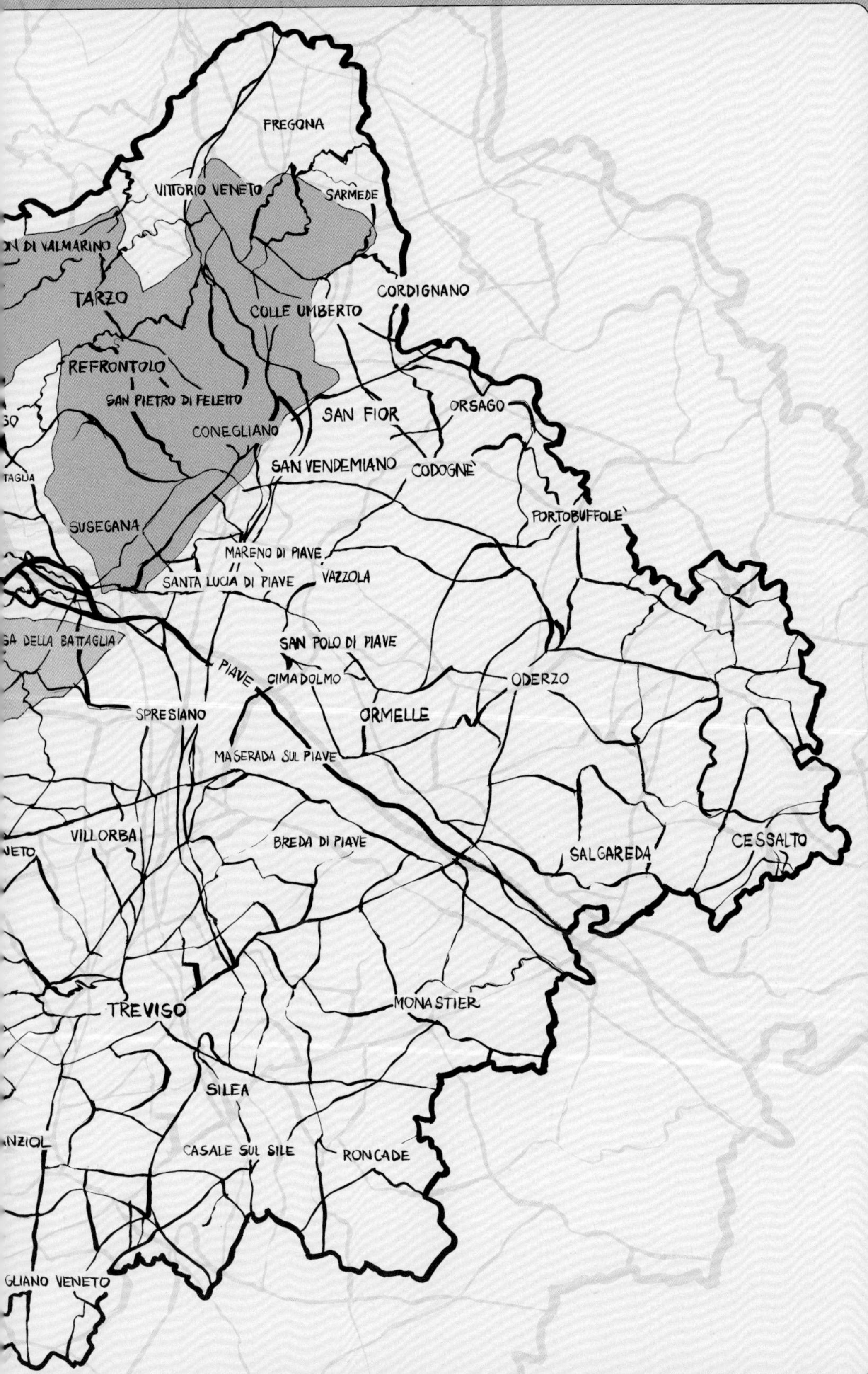
FREGONA
VITTORIO VENETO
SARMEDE
ON DI VALMARINO
TARZO
CORDIGNANO
COLLE UMBERTO
REFRONTOLO
SAN PIETRO DI FELETTO
SAN FIOR
ORSAGO
CONEGLIANO
SAN VENDEMIANO
CODOGNÈ
PORTOBUFFOLÈ
SUSEGANA
MARENO DI PIAVE
SANTA LUCIA DI PIAVE
VAZZOLA
SAN POLO DI PIAVE
PIAVE
CIMADOLMO
ODERZO
SPRESIANO
ORMELLE
MASERADA SUL PIAVE
VILLORBA
BREDA DI PIAVE
SALGAREDA
CESSALTO
MONASTIER
TREVISO
SILEA
CASALE SUL SILE
RONCADE
GLIANO VENETO

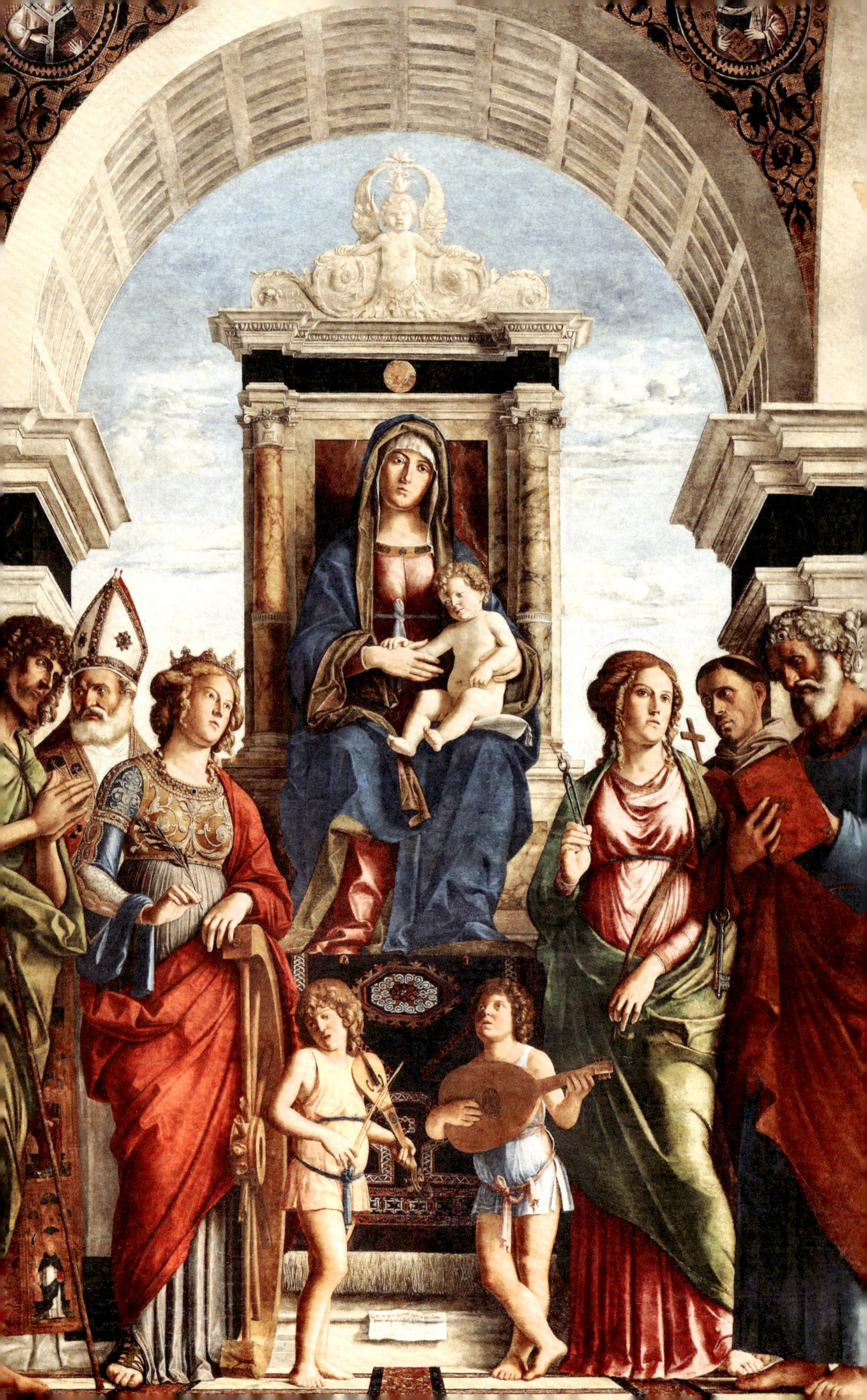

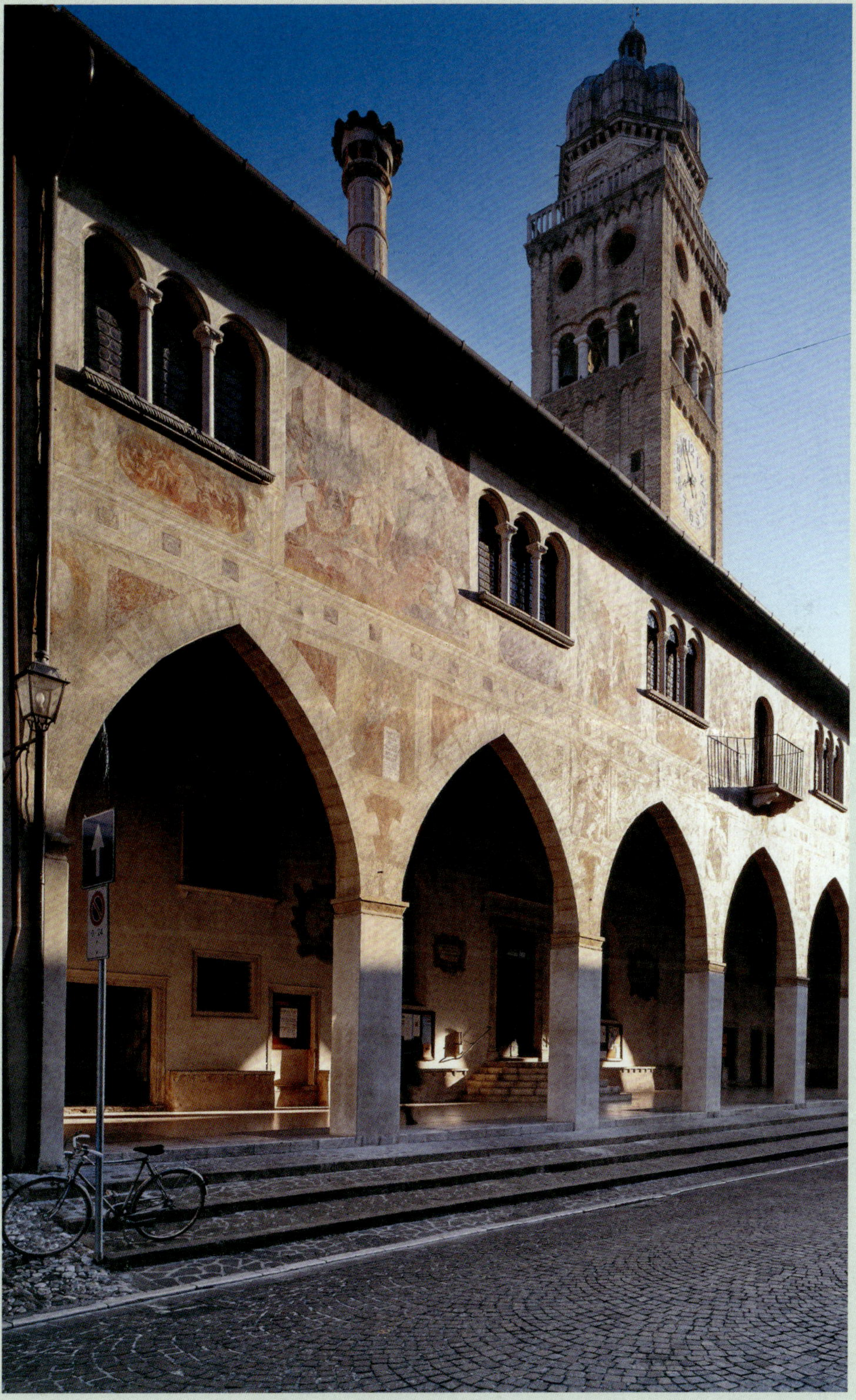

Conegliano, the altarpiece by Cima and the Duomo in via XX Settembre

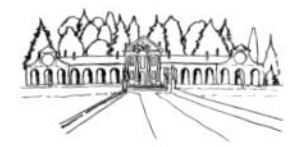

CONEGLIANO

Though it recently celebrated its thousandth birthday, Conegliano carries its years lightly. In 1016 the first official document attests to the city's existence as a fortress of the bishop of Belluno, but the origins of the village that would eventually be called Conegliano lie in the late Neolithic period, some 6,000 years ago. It is famous as the birthplace of the renowned 15th-century artist Giambattista Cima (aka Cima da Conegliano). Visitors to Conegliano for the first time will immediately notice the Torre del Castello looming up on Colle di Giano. All that remains of the medieval structure is the tower named the Torre della Campana, which today houses the Civic Museum. Inside there is a fine art gallery with works by Palma il Giovane and Pordenone, some remarkable sculptures and an archaeological section with prehistoric and Roman relics. At the top of the tower is a terrace which gives you wonderful panoramic views stretching from the mountains to the sea. On a clear day, your can see all the way to Venice and its lagoon. Running through the historic center of Conegliano is ancient Via XX Settembre (Contrada Granda). Together with Piazza Cima, it is the heart of the city. In ancient times, the town was surrounded by walls and entered through three gates: Porta Rujo to the west, Porta Monticano to the east and Porta San Polo to the south. Ranged along the street, through a succession of architraves and archivolts, and walls embellished with frescoes, are its most important buildings: the cathedral, the Teatro Accademia and the Town Hall, as well as magnificent palaces dating from the 15th century. The cathedral was built in the 14th century. Its facade is decorated with a huge fresco, held to be the largest in the Veneto, painted in the sixteenth century by Pozzoserrato. Entering the cathedral, you can admire the only work by Cima to be preserved in his hometown: the Conegliano altarpiece, dated 1492 and placed behind the high altar. Directly adjoining the cathedral is the Sala dei Battuti, dating from the 14th century, when it was built as the meeting place for the religious confraternity of the same name. The room is adorned with refined frescoes by Francesco da Milano, Jacopo Pozzoserrato and Girolamo da Treviso. A short walk from the cathedral is Cima's house. When it was restored, fragments were found dating from the Bronze Age

(1400–1300 BC). Currently the house contains reproductions of paintings by Cima and a small archaeological museum. Outside the town, on the hill of Cabalan, lies the Jewish cemetery, the burial place of Conegliano's Jewish community from 1545 until the late 19th century. The Museo degli Alpini (devoted to Alpine troops) and the Museo del Caffè (coffee museum) are also worth visiting.

Conegliano is famous not only for wine. From art to sports, from science to industry, the area has given birth to people who have distinguished themselves by their talent. Apart from Giambattista Cima, another famous artist is Francesco Beccaruzzi; in medicine and research, Ugo Cerletti, a neurologist and psychiatrist, the son of the engineer Giovanni Battista Cerletti, an illustrious oenologist and the first director of Conegliano's School of Oenology; the medical researcher Paolo De Coppi and astrophysicist Piero Benvenuti; in sports the soccer player Alessandro Del Piero, the soccer coach Gianni De Biasi, the referee Gabriele Gava; Gianfranco Zoppas, a leading industrialist.

This is a region rich in historical and artistic interest. Susegana is dominated by two castles, San Salvatore and Collalto. Well worth a visit is the Museo dell'Uomo (ethnological museum). Memories of the Great War take us to Nervesa della Battaglia, where the tremendous Battle of the Solstice was fought (June 15–23, 1918). On the hilltop is a shrine of silence and remembrance, the Ossuary Monument which holds the remains of Italian and Austro-Hungarian soldiers from World War I. Not far away is the monument to Francesco Baracca, a daring air ace of the Great War. Also noteworthy is the Abbey of Sant'Eustachio, built in the early 11th century. Here Monsignor Giacomo della Casa wrote the "Galateo," a Renaissance courtesy book.

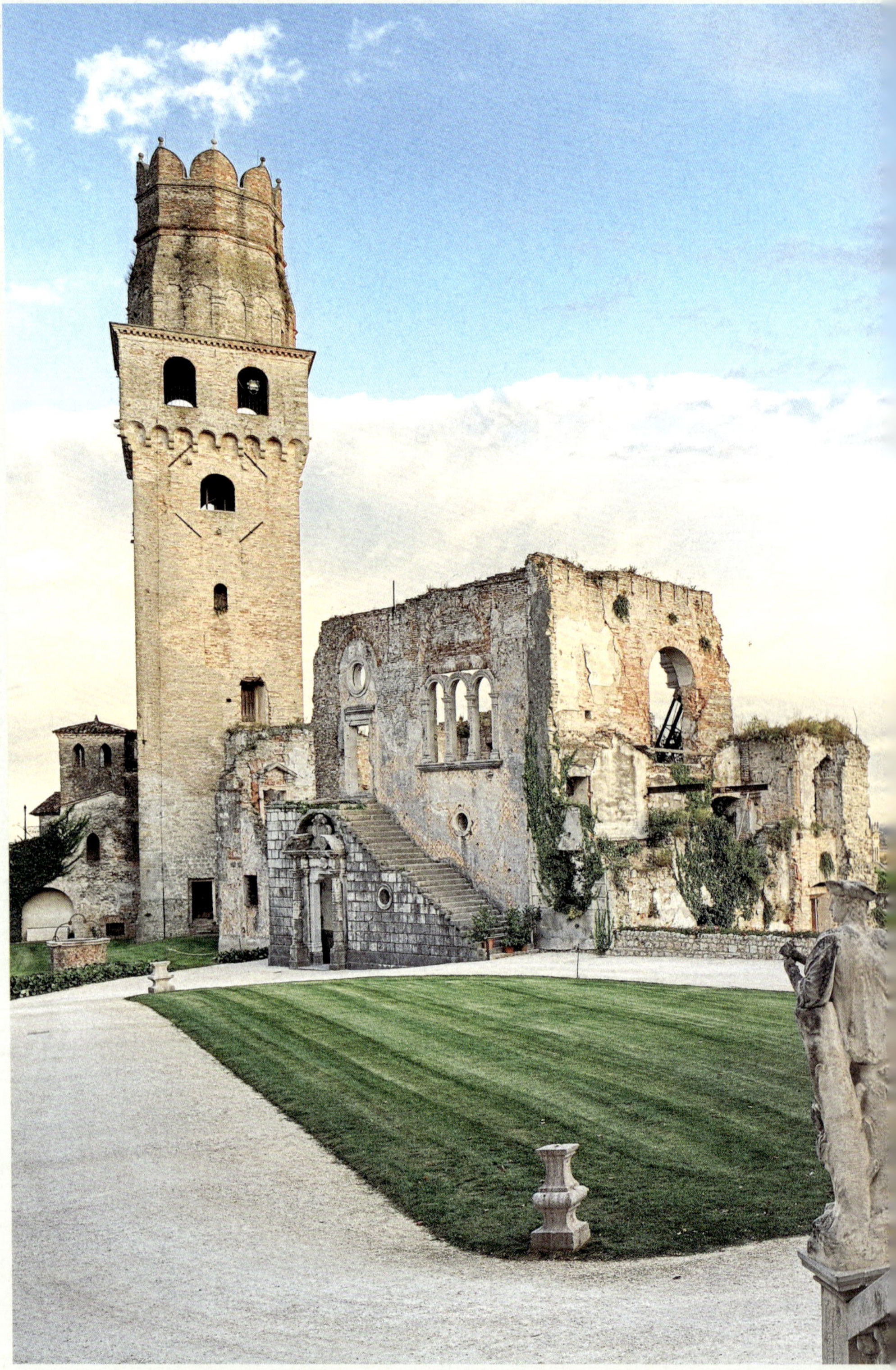

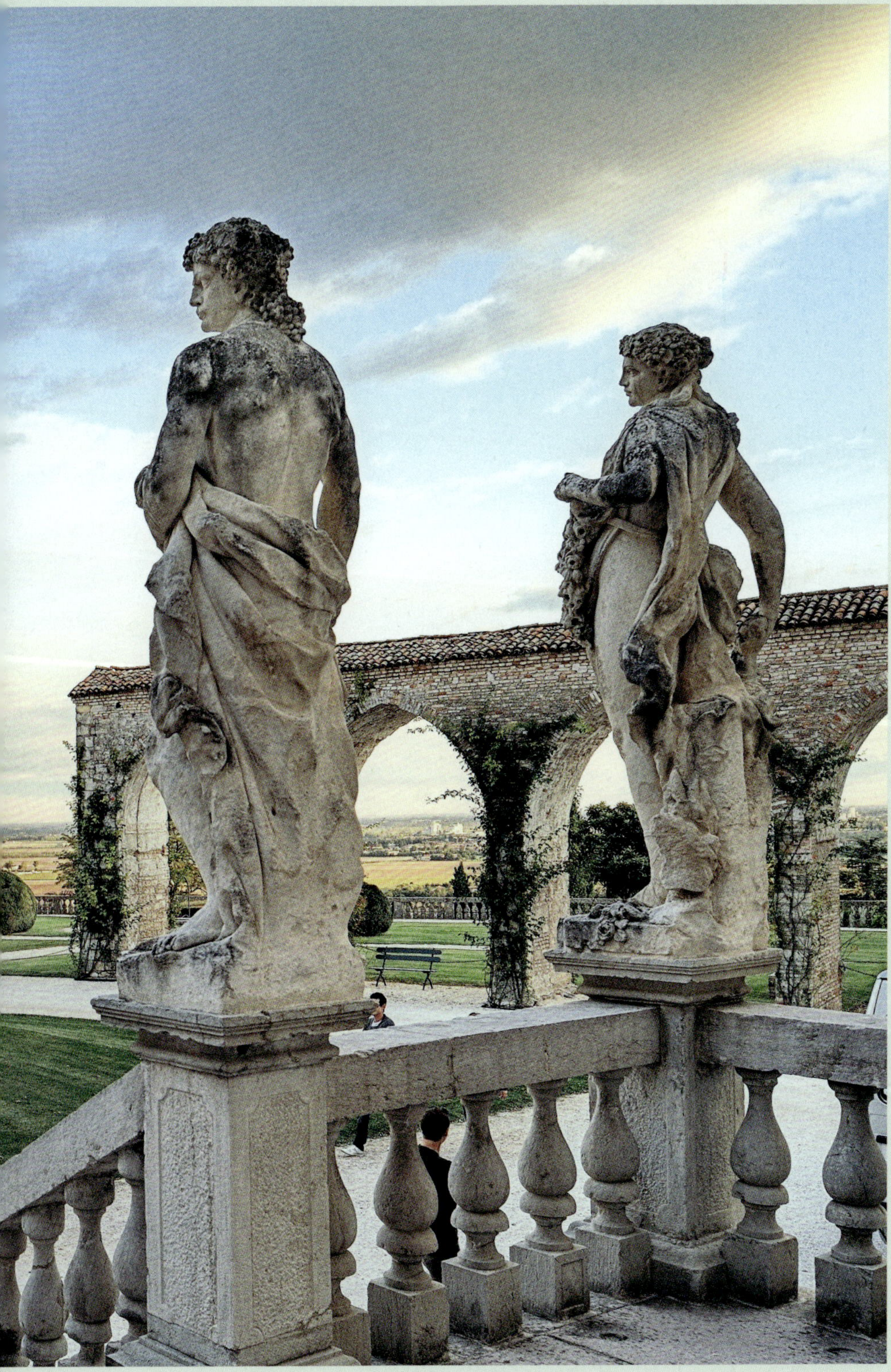

Susegana, San Salvatore castle

VALDOBBIADENE

"On all sides you can admire hills covered with vineyards and a gentle breeze shakes the vine leaves." As early as the 6th century AD, Saint Venantius Fortunatus, considered the last great Latin poet, described Valdobbiadene, his native land, notable for its vineyards. Still today, the gaze is lost amid rows and rows of Glera vines rippling across the hillsides. Clearly the cultivation of the vine dictates the rhythms of life for those who live here. The earliest human settlements in Valdobbiadene date from some 40,000 years ago, but it was not until 1116 AD that the earliest documents record the existence of the village. In the early Middle Ages the local rulers were the Ezzelini family. Then Duplavilis, the name given to Valdobbiadene in the past because the River Piave forks here, passed under the rule of the Venetian Republic. After the passing of Napoleon and the Austrian domination, the bourgeoisie of merchants, notaries and landowners grew steadily until World War I. The scourge of war was followed by reconstruction, which depended partly on winegrowing. And today the area is on the crest of success.

The historic fame of the city is linked to the figure of Saint Venantius Fortunatus, bishop of Poitiers. Tradition has it that the hamlet of San Vito di Valdobbiadene, was the birthplace in 1303 of Nicolò Bocassino, who became Pope Benedict XI.

In the central square stands the cathedral of Santa Maria Assunta, with the altarpiece of the Assumption by Francesco Beccaruzzi and another altarpiece by Paris Bordon of the Virgin and Saints Sebastian and Roch. The bell tower dates from the mid-18th century. The addition of the spire made it a local landmark.

From hill to hill and village to village, from Bigolino to San Vito, passing through Guia, San Giovanni, San Pietro di Barbozza and Santo Stefano, from hamlet to hamlet, from Saccol to Santa Lucia passing through Ron, Funer, Follo, Villanova, Ponteggio, Colderove and Guietta, you are immersed in nature, dotted with ancient stone-built farmhouses and wayside shrines. It is a land of hills and vineyards, as well as forests, mountains, valleys and rivers. You can climb up to the alpine pastures of

Monte Cesen and Pianezze. Wander through the meadows or seek the peace of the woods. Follow the course of the River Piave, sacred to the homeland. A little further north, as part of the municipality of Segusino, there is the small hamlet of Stramare. Founded in the 17th century as a place of refuge for the people of Istria, in the hamlet time seems to have stopped in the early twentieth century. At its center there is a fountain and the church dedicated to Saint Valentine, the saint of lovers. Legend has it that whoever drinks of the water of that fountain will be lucky in love. Many romantics come here on pilgrimage in the hope it will slake their thirst for love. Moving east to Conegliano, Refrontolo is well worth visiting. Offering wonderful views, it is set in the heart of the Prosecco hills of Conegliano Valdobbiadene. The area is famous for the production of Marzemino wine, here called Refrontolo Passito DOC. Along the course of the River Lierza, there is a watermill, the Molinetto della Croda, one of the most striking nooks of the Marca Trevigiana.
The ancient mill, a characteristic example of rural architecture dating from the 17th century, ground its last bag of flour in 1953. In its nearly four centuries of history it has inspired artists and enchanted thousands of visitors. Not far from Refrontolo, there is another panoramic terrace on the Prosecco hills at San Pietro di Feletto. From the ancient churchyard the eye can gaze as far as the Alpine foothills of Belluno. The 11th century church is one of the oldest and most prestigious in the Marca Trevigiana. Entering it is like traveling back in time to the Middle Ages, when Christianity still mingled with pagan cults. From the porch to the apse, from the bell tower to the baptistry, the frescoes instructed the faithful, a kind of bible of the poor, devised for those unable to read.

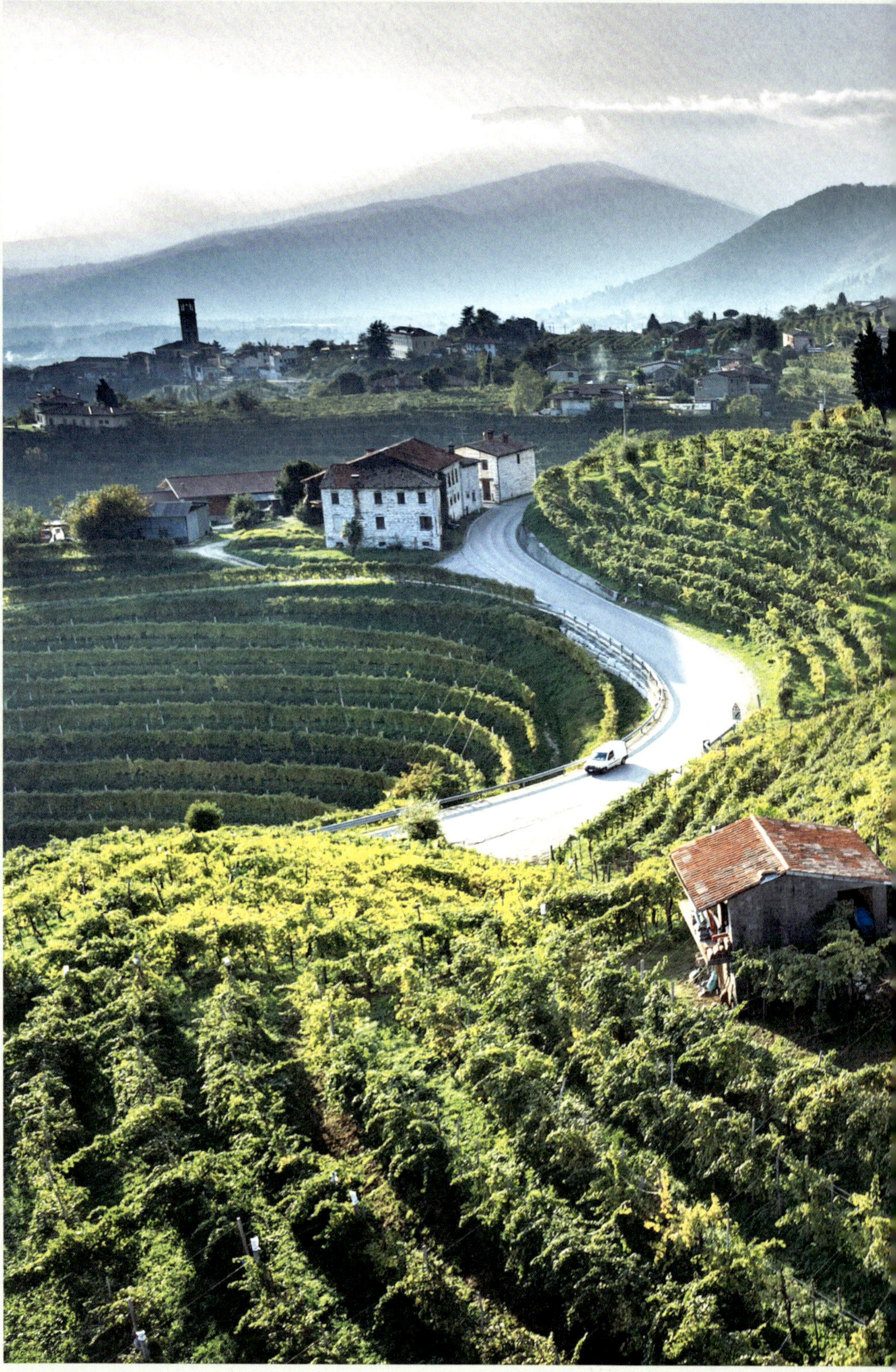

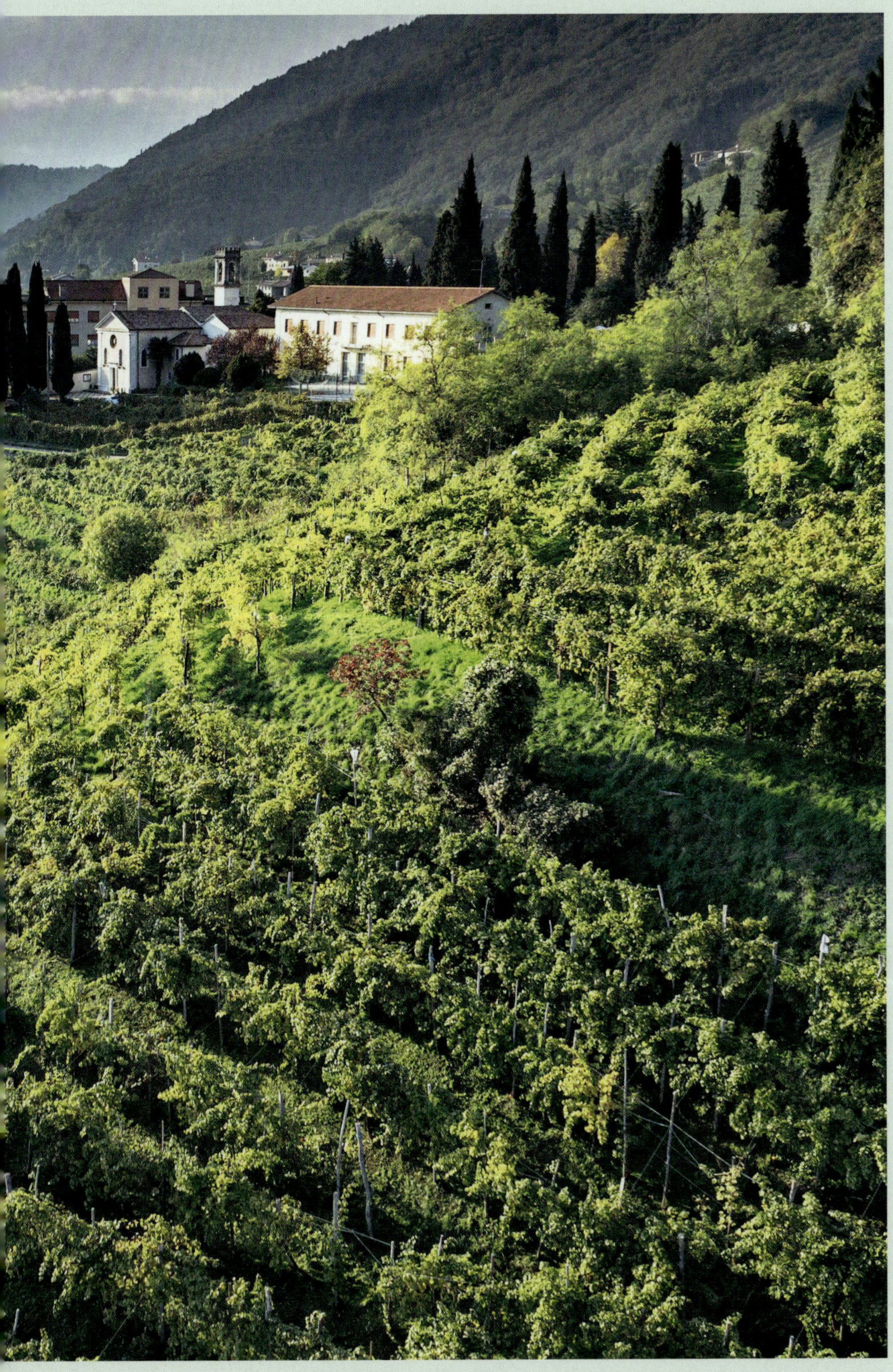

Valdobbiadene, the Prosecco route

FROM CISON DI VALMARINO TO FOLLINA

Cison di Valmarino is one of Italy's most beautiful villages. Perched on a height in the gentle hills of the Pedemontana Trevigiana, Cison seems immune to the hectic pace of modern life. Immersed in its natural setting, it offers glimpses of sheer wonder. Amid the ancient stone-built houses, that paths wandering up to the Alpine foothills and streams that draw smiles on the green of the fields, the Glera vines are luxuriant. The traces of human presence at Cison date from prehistoric times, but it was under the Roman Empire that the first permanent settlements were established. The village lies in the valley, rich in history and legends. The engineering genius of the Romans under the Empire appears in the ancient road, the Via Claudia Augusta Altinate. In the Middle Ages the power of the important feudal families emerged. For three hundred years the feud was held by the Brandolini da Bagnacavallo, an ancient family of condottieri in the service of the Serene Republic of Venice until its downfall in 1797. For centuries Cison di Valmarino was the little capital of the Counts Brandolini. The castle of the same name is a survival from that time, together with a large number of stately buildings that distinguish Cison from the other towns in the valley. The castle, known by the name of Castelbrando, stands on a rocky spur of the Col de Moi in a strategic and highly scenic position overlooking the valley. The castle can be visited, with an interesting historical tour, and also houses a luxury hotel. In the village you can also visit a museum of early radios, a pearl of history and culture. But nature is undoubtedly the main attraction. A fascinating feature is the wood called the Bosco delle Penne Mozze, a memorial containing the gravestones of Alpine soldiers who fell in war or in the course of duty. It is a place of pilgrimage for Alpine soldiers from all over Italy. In the valley of Valmareno you can make wonderful excursions of great historical, artistic and natural interest. For example, the Via dell'Acqua ("Way of Water") winds through the woods past an important complex of former water mills and other examples of industrial archaeology. Amid the rolling hills covered with beautifully groomed vineyards, dotted here and there with lush fruit trees and old farmhouses perfectly restored, south of Cison lies the village of Rolle, a rural hamlet and a landmark of the

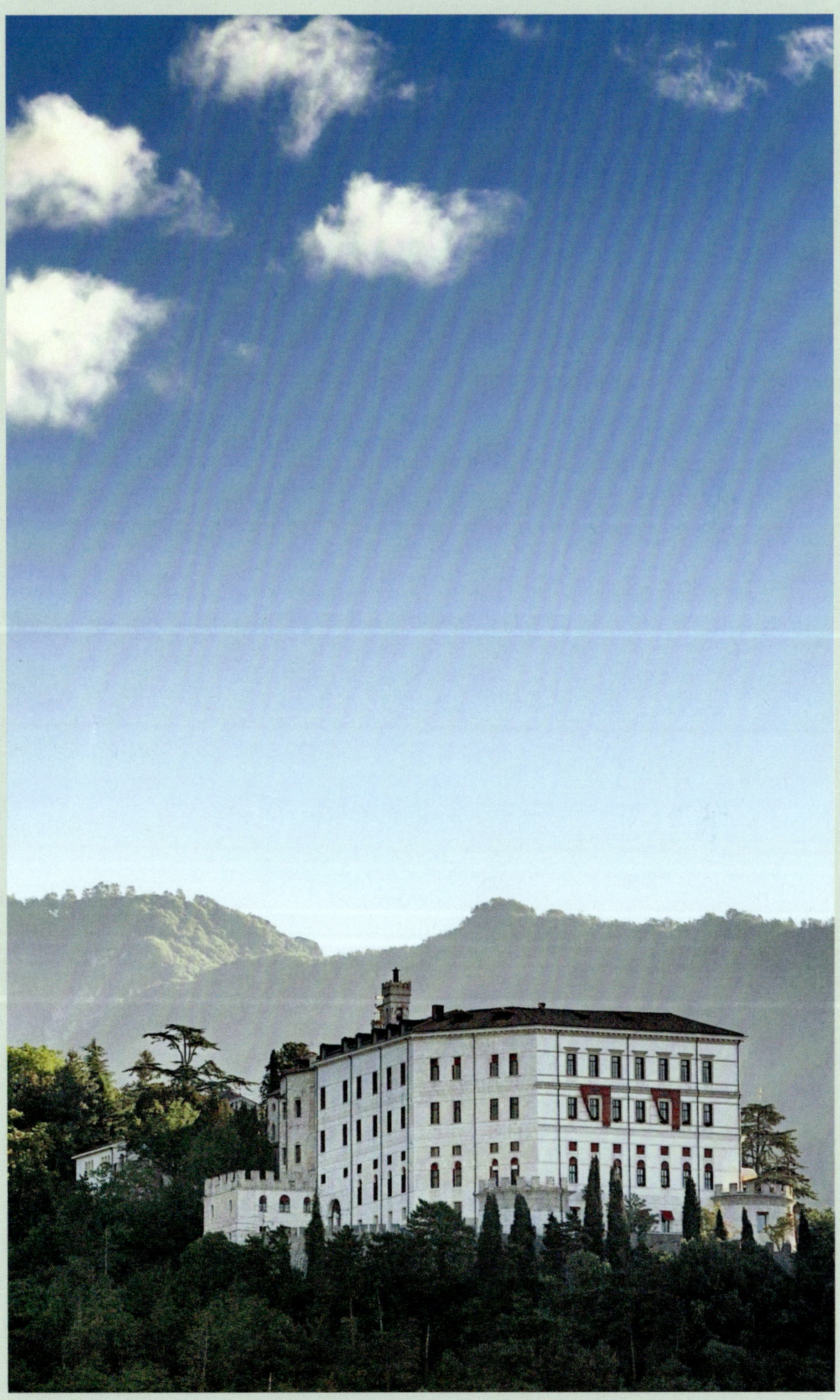

Cison di Valmarino, Brandolini Castle (Castelbrando)

FAI, the Italian Heritage Foundation. From the little piazza, you have a view over the vineyards at noon, pampered by the sun. A breathtaking view. A "postcard of the gods" as the poet Andrea Zanzotto wrote.

The hamlet is dominated by the "Sleeping Beauty," a mountain whose profile resembles a girl reclining.

Not far from Cison is Follina, another village that is a gem. Its history is closely bound up with the Abbey of Santa Maria, an early medieval Benedictine foundation. But it probably contains traces of much earlier prehistoric settlements (dating from about 120,000 BC), as well as Roman remains. Around the middle of the twelfth century, Cistercian monks took over from the Benedictines and transformed the abbey into the beautifully preserved architectural treasure it is today. The history of Follina is embodied in its abbey, a place of profound spirituality and centuries of culture. It was the Cistercian monks who first produced woolen cloth at Follina and turned the Valmareno into a dynamic center of the textile sector in the medieval and modern periods. As you stroll in the streets of Follina, you can admire the fine buildings of the old town, built out of the profits of the wool and silk-making industries.

Continuing towards Revine and Tarzo we come to the two glacial lakes of Santa Maria and Lago, known together as the Laghi di Revine. Separated today by a slender strip of land, they once formed a large body of water left after the great Piave glacier withdrew. Swimming is allowed in both and annually for many years past they have been awarded a Blue Flag for the quality of the water. These are two green oases to refresh body and mind. And you can also make a journey back into the past. Some flints in a peat bog at Colmaggiore, a hamlet of Tarzo, has proved that there used to be an ancient village built on stilts in the lake, visible today in the reconstruction in the archaeological park (Parco Archeologico Didattico) at Livelet.

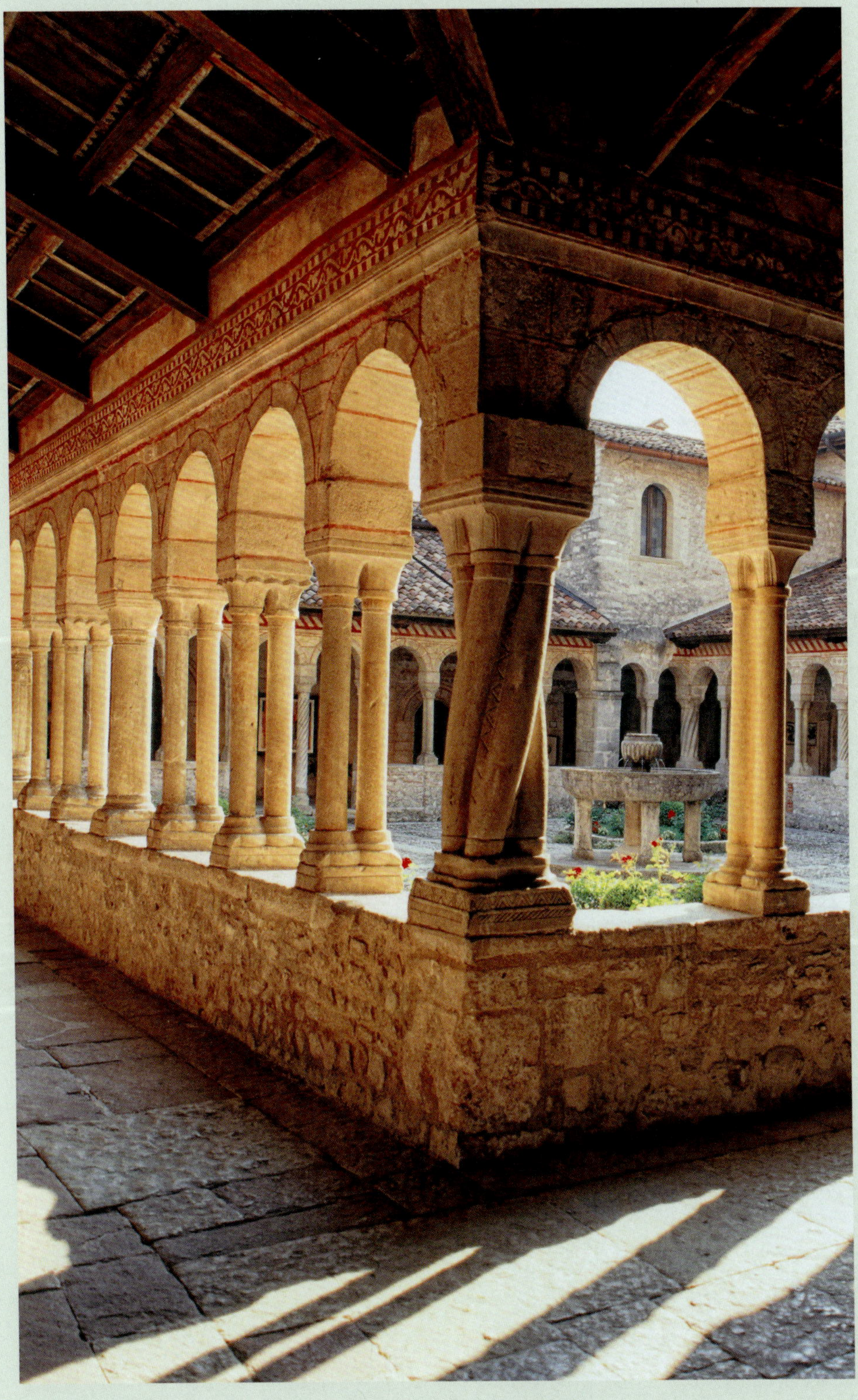

Abbey of Follina, the cloister

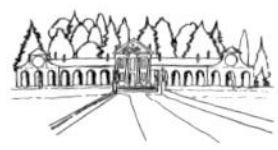

VITTORIO VENETO

Vittorio Veneto, or the city of the victory. Its name is in the history books, because it was here that the final battle of the Great War (1915-18) was fought. The city was also awarded a gold medal for valor for its role in the Resistance during World War II. Vittorio Veneto stands midway between Venice and Cortina. The River Meschio flows through the town, offering enchanting views. The city is the gateway to the Prealps of Belluno and to the Dolomites. Formerly there existed two neighboring and independent towns, Ceneda and Serravalle, Romanesque in origin. In 1866 they were merged to form the present municipality. The built-up area of Ceneda, further south, of Roman or even Celtic origin, attained its greatest prestige in the 7th century when it became an important duchy under the Lombards. Made a bishopric in the 8th century, Ceneda is still the seat of one today. From this period date the early defenses of the Castle of San Martino, set on a hillside at the center of a fortified wall. For centuries it was the bishop's residence. The Loggia of the community of Ceneda now houses the Museum of the Battle, with a rich collection of documents and memorabilia from World War I. Serravalle, in the northern part of the city, also of Roman origin, was fortified by barbarian kings and princes. It became the feud of the Camino family in 1174. At the Renaissance, it was frequented by important Italian artists, including Jacopo Sansovino and Titian. In 1749 it was the birthplace of Lorenzo Da Ponte, a writer and the librettist of some of Mozart's most important operas. In the picturesque setting of Piazza Flaminio, in the noble old town of Serravalle, stands the cathedral, originally built in the 14th century. The current structure dates from 1779. The ceiling has a fresco by Canaletto and the interior contains a masterpiece by Titian. The bell tower has one of Italy's oldest clock dials. From the square the road leads to the Castrum of Serravalle, a fortress perched on a rocky spur. Vittorio Veneto is dominated by the mountains. To admire the city and valley from above, both Ceneda and Serravalle have two exceptional panoramic viewing points, which can be reached on foot. From Ceneda it is worth climbing up to Monte Altare, where traces of pagan worship go back to the Celts. From Serravalle you can reach the shrine of Saint Augusta, where her remains are kept.

From the city of victory to the land of Fairytales. Not far from Vittorio Veneto is Sarmede. This was the home of Stepan Zavrel, an illustrator and exile from the Prague Spring, who founded the International Exhibition of Illustration for Children. In the summer, these hills are thronged with young people who come from all over the world to attend courses held by great illustrators. And spring sees the same masters engaged in peopling the walls of houses facing the streets with pictures of fanciful tales.

The little villages clinging to the slopes of the Prealps host some great events. An example is the hamlet of Montaner, where a lively Orthodox community arose in the late sixties. There is a church and a convent, where nuns of different nationalities devote themselves to various activities, including painting the sacred icons and making rosaries.

We are on the edge of the Cansiglio plateau, but before you reach it and discover one of the best preserved forests in Italy, there are more vineyards, producing the finest Torchiato di Fregona. This rare raisin wine is made from three varieties of white grapes: Glera, Verdiso and Boschera. It is named after Fregona, one of the three municipalities where it is produced, the others being Sarmede and Cappella Maggiore. In the little village of Breda di Fregona, nature offers one of the most stunning spectacles in the whole province of Treviso. This is the Grotte del Caglieron, a series of caves formed over the centuries by the work of nature and man in a gorge carved out by the waters of the Caglieron River.

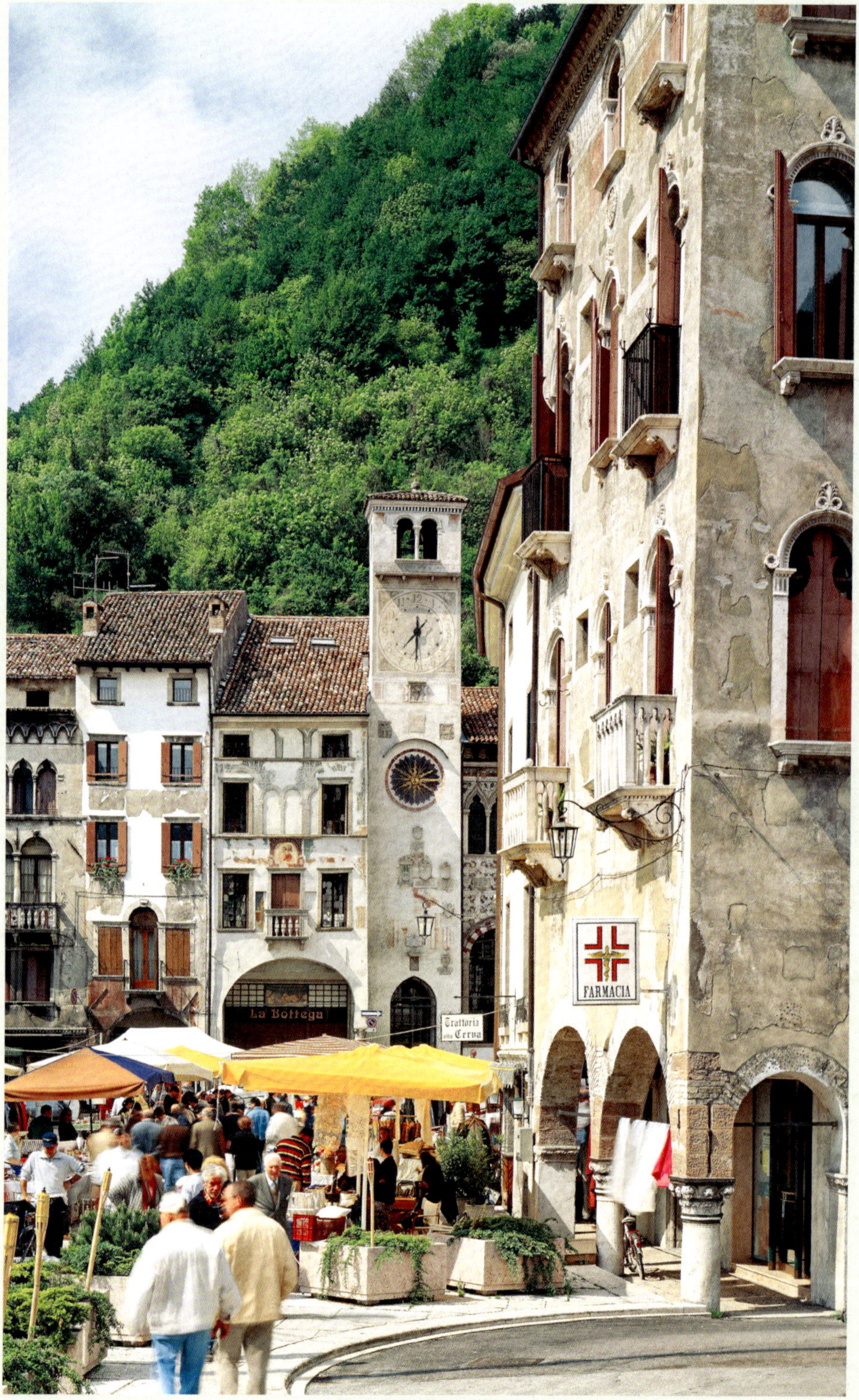

Serravalle in Vittorio Veneto, Piazza Flaminio

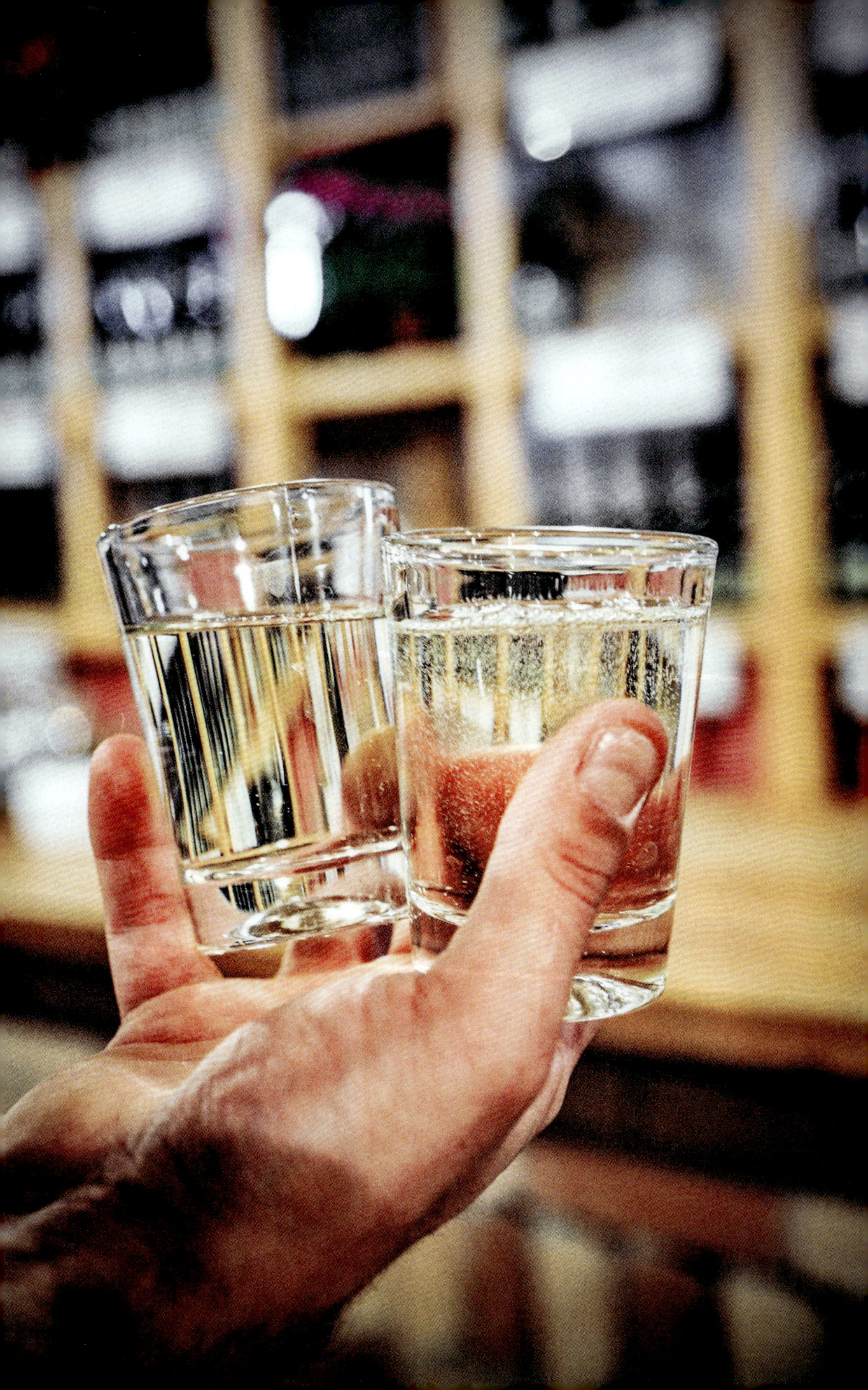

ASOLO

Set within its ancient walls and dominated by its medieval castle, Asolo can be visited in half a day. But once you have seen it, you will feel the urge to remain for the rest of your life, seduced by the same charm that has conquered poets and artists from around the world. From Pietro Bembo, who in the reign of Queen Cornaro wrote "Gli Asolani" here, to the English poet Robert Browning, who in the 19th century settled in the town and dedicated "Asolando" to it, Giosuè Carducci who called it "the town with a hundred horizons," and Freya Stark who chose it as a refuge between her journeys of exploration. From Lorenzo Lotto and Giorgione, whose works bring the grace of its landscape to life, to Palladio, Canova, and Eugene Benson; from Gustavo Modena to Eleonora Duse, who had a house in Asolo and was buried here; from Igor Stravinsky to Gian Francesco Malipiero.

The town's favorable position and climate meant Asolo was inhabited from prehistoric times and later an important Venetian settlement. Between the 11th and 14th centuries. it was dominated by various powerful families, but it was with the Republic of Venice that it reached the height of its splendor.

In 1489 Venice invested the lordship of Asolo in Caterina Cornaro, the former queen of Cyprus, who created a brilliant Renaissance court of artists, writers and poets. The severe rule of the Austro-Hungarian Empire did not tarnish its enchantment, which even survived the Great War.

The most important events in the town's history in the 19th century are recorded by the old pendulum clock concealed behind the counter of a wine bar in Via Browning.

The castle, rising on the summit of Monte Ricco, is the symbol of the town. Its historic center is reached through Porta Loreggia, the point of arrival of the ancient Roman Via Aurelia. To the left is a fountain known as the Fontanella Zen and to the right Villa Stark. In the garden of the villa are preserved the remains of the Forum and Roman Theater. As you stroll through the porticos lining Via Browning, you come to Piazza Garibaldi, the heart of the city. Facing the Fontana Maggiore rises the cathedral dedicated to Saint Mary of the Assumption. Also overlooking the piazza is the Loggia della Ragione, a Renaissance frescoed palace. This houses the Civic

Museum, which contains artworks, archaeological relics and documents recording events and figures that have made the town's history. Not far from Piazza Maggiore is the Castle of Queen Cornaro, which houses the theater dedicated to Eleonora Duse. Beneath the town there are still the well-preserved remains of the Roman aqueduct. From house to villa and from church to cathedral, Asolo continues to enchant with its hundred horizons, remote from the world and timeless.

A few kilometers away is Possagno, the home of Antonio Canova, the great neoclassical sculptor, born there in 1751. The Tempio Canoviano is impressive. The summit of its dome offers panoramic views over the Asolan hills, while at the bottom of the long flight of steps and the descent, there is Canova's birthplace with a gallery of plaster casts of his works.

The sculptor's body lies in the Tempio Canoviano.

The area contains traces of another great artist, Andrea Palladio, who lived two centuries before Canova. As an architect, Palladio is famous worldwide for his Venetian villas, many of which are UNESCO World Heritage Sites. Villa Barbaro at Maser is one of them. The villa was built by Palladio in around 1560 for Daniele Barbaro, patriarch of Aquileia, and his brother Marcantonio, ambassador of the Republic of Venice. Another example of Palladio's genius is Villa Emo at Fanzolo di Vedelago, the finest example of the villa-farm, perfectly integrating the noble residence into the countryside. Between Maser and Fanzolo, another important architect, the Venetian Carlo Scarpa, has also left his mark here. At the hamlet of San Vito, in Altivole, he built the Brion Tomb, one of the most interesting funerary monuments in modern architecture.

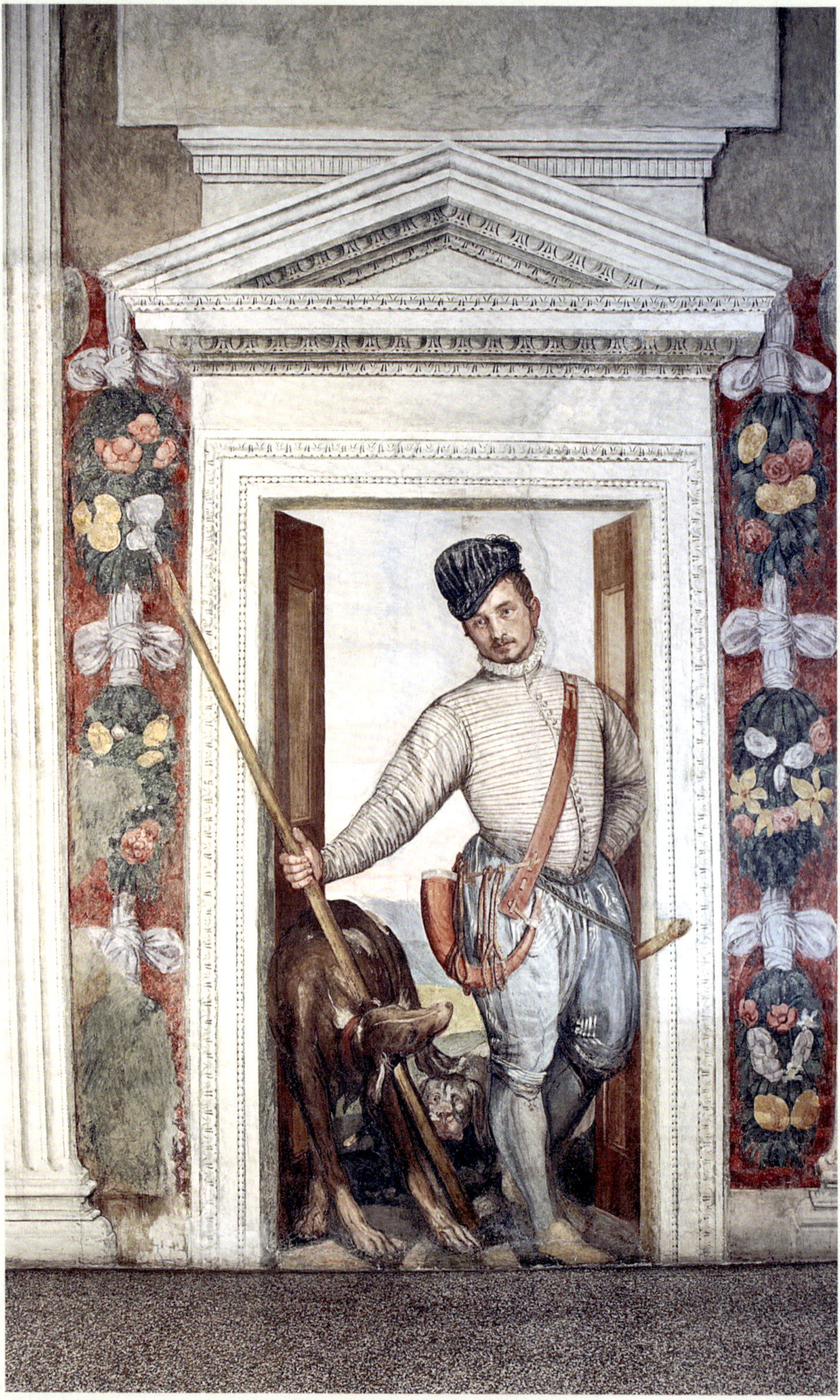

Villa di Maser (Villa Barbaro), Self-portrait of Paolo Veronese. Right: Asolo, Villa Contarini

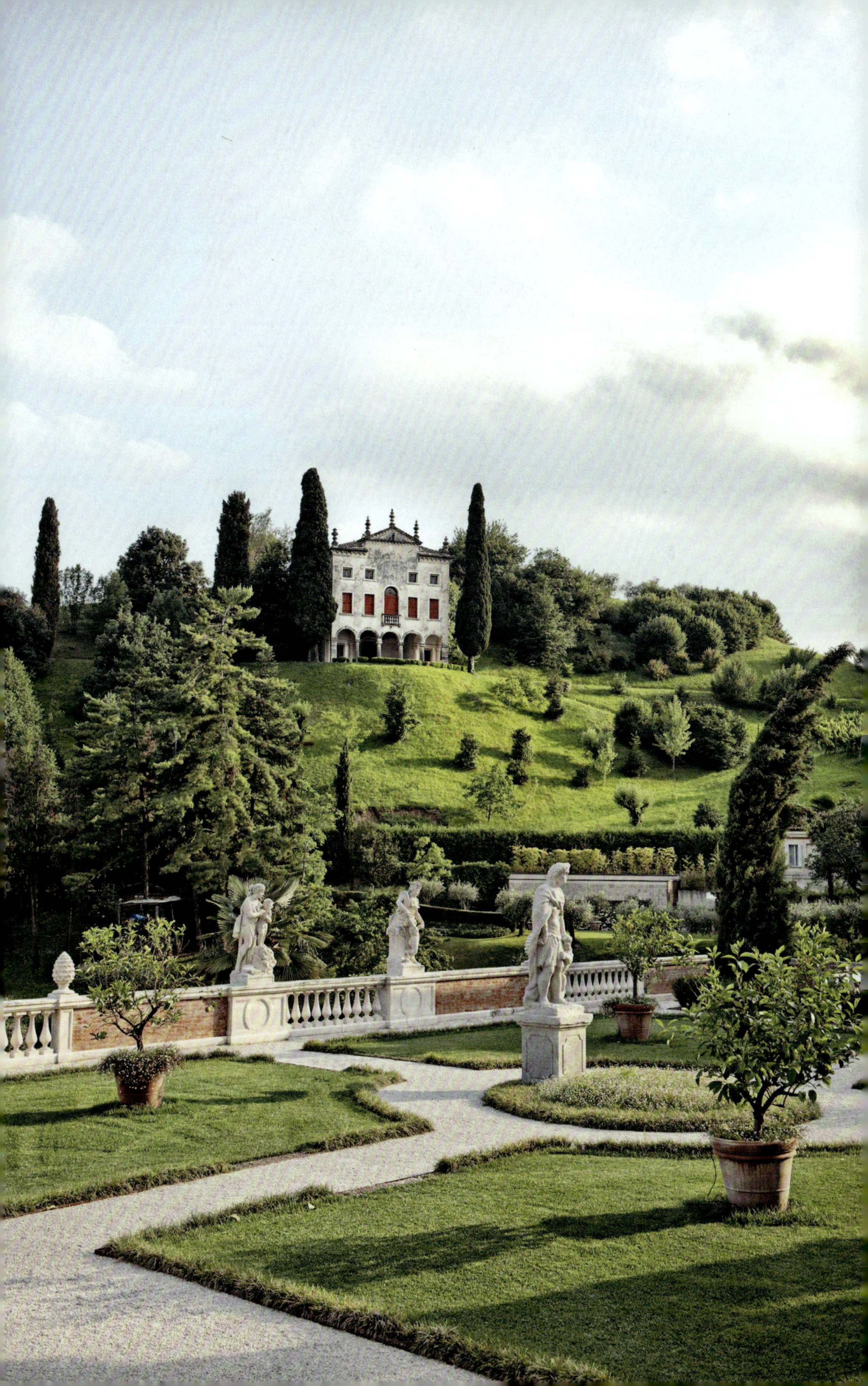

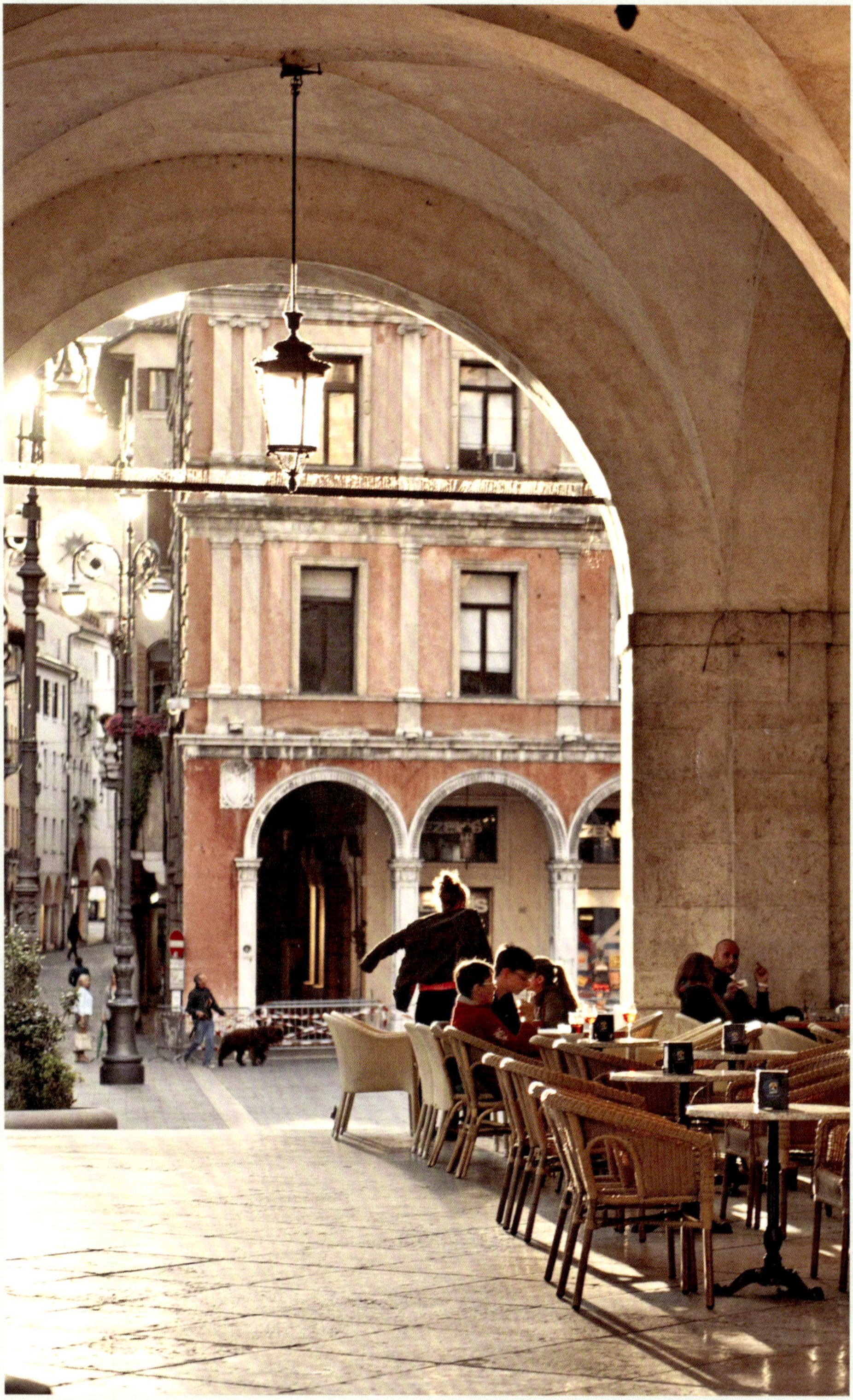

Treviso, Piazza dei Signori

TREVISO

If we had to give the city a gender, we would undoubtedly say that Treviso is feminine. The curves of the Sile River traverse the city sinuously. The Renaissance palazzi are strikingly ranged along her narrow streets, rising like models on size 12 heels. The churches scrutinize the city's life like matrons, at times severe, at others indulgent. A pleasurable chatter arises at the cocktail hour, with bosom friends exchanging secrets. Convivial, hospitable, hard-working, sometimes moody, the city is the capital of the "joyous and amorous March" of Treviso, as it was described by a chronicler in 1200. Like Venus, she was born from the waters, and Dante Alighieri put her in Paradise. At first blush it might sound like a compliment to describe her as a "little Venice" but if you think about it, these are words that could offend the singularity of a city that has no need resemble any other, because its sophisticated and sometimes provincial charm makes it unique.

The city's origins are uncertain, as is its name. It seems that for the Romans "Tarvisium" came from the Celtic torvos (bulls), or from the Gallic trev (wooden village), or from the statue of a girl with three faces, hence tre-visi. Most likely it derives from the Latin Tervisus which means "three hills," now identified with Piazza Duomo, Piazza dei Signori and Piazza Sant'Andrea, on which the first settlements were built. Archaeological finds show that as early as the 16th century BC, in the middle Bronze Age, some villages of the Paleoveneti existed in the area.

The decline of the Roman empire affected Tarvisium. Although spared by Attila, the city was fought over by Goths and Byzantines and later the Lombards and Franks. After these upheavals, in the Middle Ages the city experienced a period of economic and artistic development. Those were the years when it was dubbed urbs picta because of its many richly frescoed houses. The years of feud were prosperous, despite the conflicts between Guelphs and Ghibellines. In 1600 the city was known as a "little Athens" for the fervent intellectual activity of poets, artists and men of letters. It remained faithful to the Republic of Venice until, in 1866, it became part of Italy and then was ravaged in the two world wars. In particular on Good Friday, 1944, it was subjected to a terrible air raid which in a few minutes destroyed half the city. Fortunately, the bombs spared much of its artistic and architectural heritage. The architecture of the old town emanates a special charm: the city's plan is Roman, its development medieval, and the final impression is Venetian. Piazza dei Signori contains a succession of ancient palaces from the communal period, creating a solemn and harmonious whole. In the piazza and its immediate vicinity are the city's most important monuments: the Palazzo del Podestà or del Governo, with the Torre Civica, the Palazzo dei Trecento and the Loggia dei Cavalieri. An alley connects the piazza with the Monte di Pietà, with the magnificent Cappella dei Rettori, and the combined churches of Santa Lucia and San Vito, rich in frescoes, canvases and sculptures. From the center you come to the Cagnàn River near the island of Pescheria. A few paces more offer you another view. On the opposite bank of the river, you reach the Gothic church of San Francesco, which contains the tombs of Petrarch's daughter and Pietro Alighieri, Dante's son. Starting from the city center and taking Via Calmaggiore, you come to the cathedral, a crucible of styles, originally built between the eleventh and twelfth centuries on the foundations of an early Christian church. In the arcade that connects the Piazzetta della Torre with Via Calmaggiore, there is the singular fountain, the Fontana delle Tette: in the days of the Serenissima, it would flow with white and red wine on special festive occasions. In the former church of Santa Caterina you will find the Archaeological Collection and three public galleries: the Pinacoteca, the Collezione d'Arte Moderna and the Collezione Salce. The Sala del Capitolo in the church of San Nicolò, on the left bank of the Sile River, contains a fresco by Tommaso da Modena: it depicts the first pair of spectacles to be depicted in the history of art. Amid palaces, churches, museums, city walls, gates and bridges, you can read the history of Treviso.

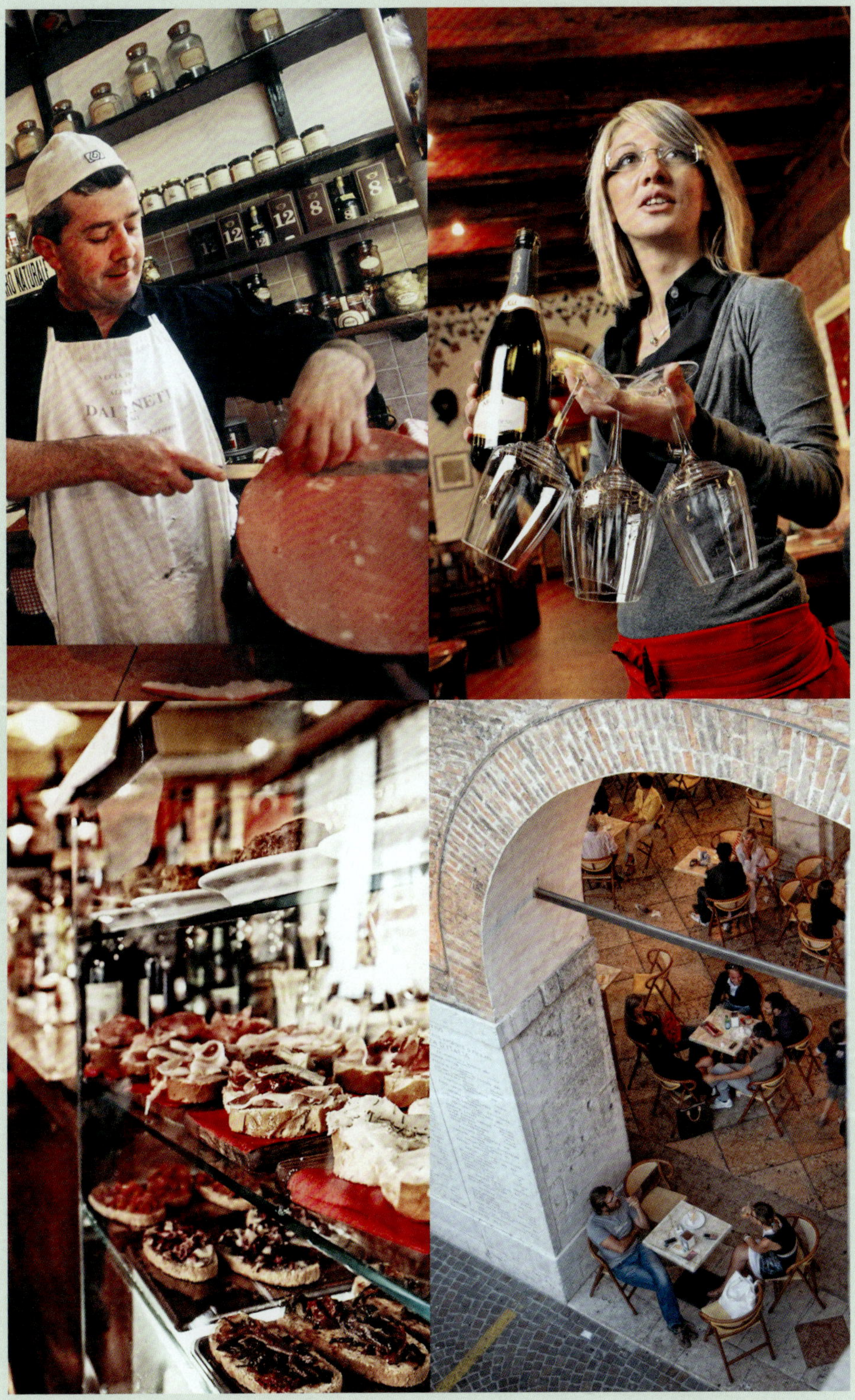

Treviso, typical osteria

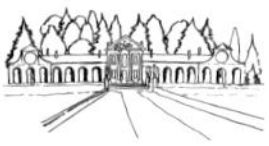

VENICE AND THE PLAIN OF DOC

Water is definitely the dominant natural element in the Po Valley, with this part of it known as the Venetian Plain, from the foot of the Dolomites to the Venetian Lagoon. The plain of Prosecco DOC, furrowed and contoured by the River Piave, Italy's sacred river ever since World War I. The Piave ("la Piave" as the locals call it) has left its mark on the landscape and the soil. The flowing river is a metaphor for life and the Piave has for centuries been not only a source of water but also an economic factor. Its waters have been used to cultivate fields and vineyards. It transported logs from the woodlands of the Prealps to the Arsenal where they were used to build Venice's ships. The river was a line of defense against the enemy in the Great War. Its stones have embellished the vacation homes of noble Venetians. It has inspired poets, writers and artists in all ages.

The Piave is undoubtedly the most important river, but it is not the only one. The Sile, Livenza, Brenta, Tagliamento and countless smaller watercourses flow more or less silently through the region and constitute the dense web of the vital lifelines of a land straddling two regions, which are also rich in springs. Finally there is the lagoon of Venice, which was formed between 6000 and 5000 years ago, at the end of the last glaciation.

A plain dotted with farmhouses, a testament to its richness and economic well-being, with castles and villas that are a heritage of the splendor of the Serene Republic of Venice and the rigor of the Habsburg Empire.

And cities rich in history, architectural and artistic works to be contemplated in rapture at their beauty.

In Vicenza Andrea Palladio's architectural genius has left a tangible sign. Since 1994 it has been a UNESCO World Heritage Site. Marostica, the chess capital, is not far from Bassano del Grappa with its famous Ponte Vecchio. Padua is the city of culture and science, with its university founded in 1222, one of the oldest in the world. Amid majestic ancient palaces and churches, you breathe the magnificence and spirituality of a past which lives on. Este, Arquà Petrarca, Abano Terme and Cittadella will sate your love of art and history and slake your thirst for nature. Traversing the province of Treviso , the Prosecco DOC area continues to Belluno, dominated

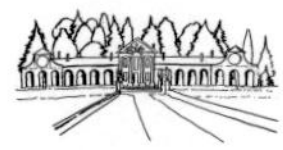

by the majestic Dolomites. The city was laid out by the ancient Romans around the decumano; its streets are lined with palaces and churches with northern forms and in Venetian Gothic style. Descending again and traveling eastward, the area crosses the Venetian border and enters Friuli Venezia Giulia. At Pordenone, dynamism and creativity are evident in the architecture and the city's artistic, musical and literary output. On the way to Udine the route rises again. The capital of Friuli contains piazzas rich in Venetian charm and the works of Giambattista Tiepolo, embraced by the protective gaze of the castle on the hill above the city. This is the land of the famous prosciutto crudo of San Daniele and the lavender of Venzone. But the Prosecco DOC district extends to the gates of the east. On the border with Slovenia there is Gorizia, where you will breathe the typical atmosphere of a frontier city. The Habsburg burghers loved this city and its mild climate, dubbing it the "Austrian Nice." In Gorizia medieval, baroque and twentieth-century architecture harmoniously coexist. All around, the landscape is dominated by the Karst. Further south and a little further east, overlooking the Adriatic Sea, we come to Trieste. Here Prosecco DOC has earned its own label. A Mitteleuropean city par excellence, from the Audace pier to the old Lantern, Trieste is a succession of sails, antique shops, splendid palaces in a crucible of styles ranging from Roman to Art Nouveau, from Neoclassical to Baroque and the unmistakable Habsburg tyle. Behind the Carso mountains, facing the gulf, Trieste has been a free port for imports of coffee ever since the 18th century. On the other side of the sea, a few miles farther south, lies Venice. Lying on the water, it casts its reflection in the lagoon and welcomes the world with the proverbial Venetian conviviality. It is here, among the canals and dockyards, that the wine trade began.

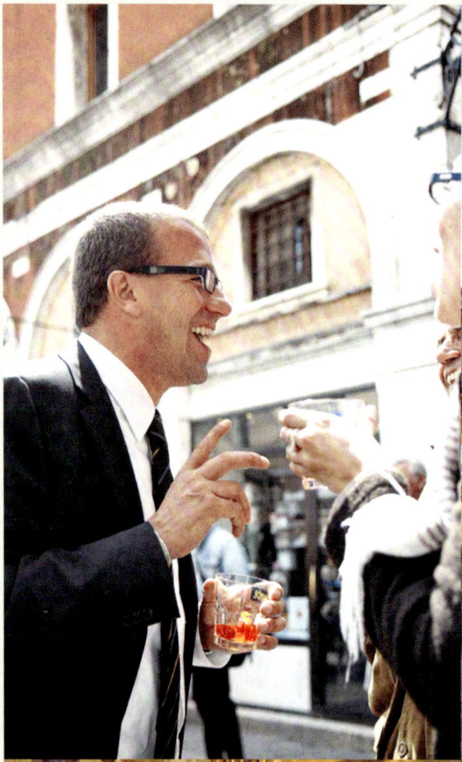

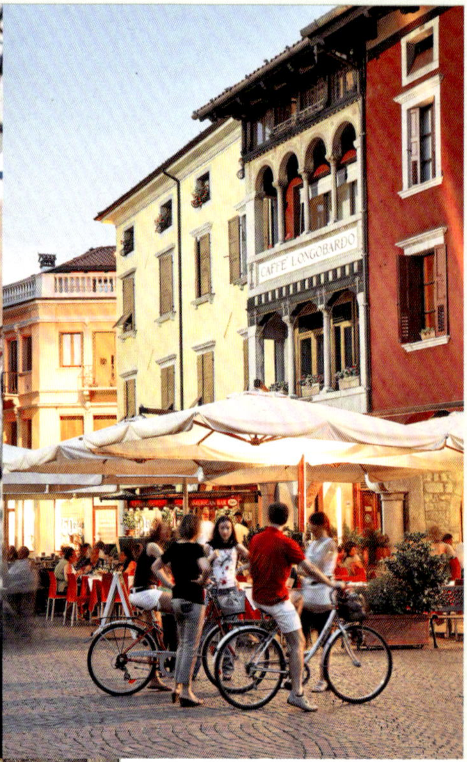

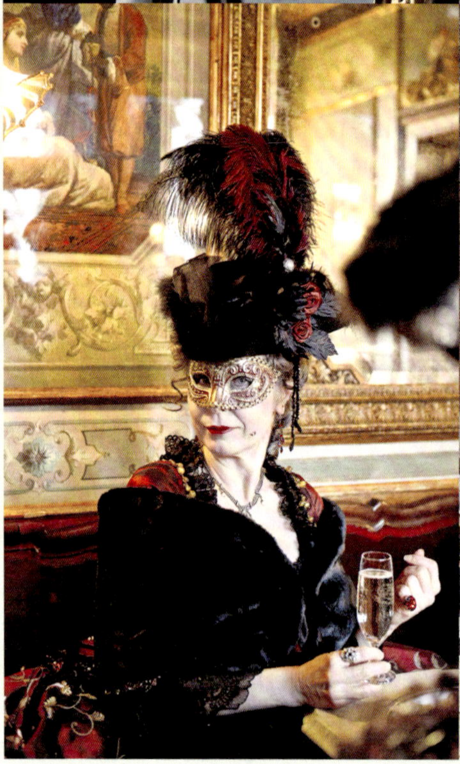

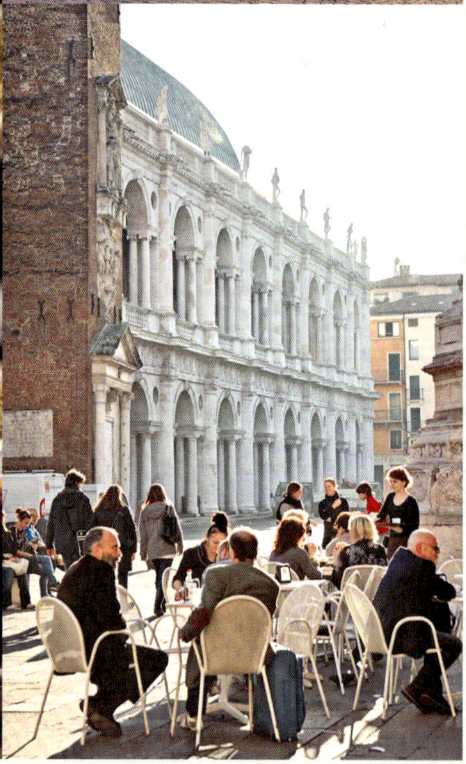

Venezia, Cividale del Friuli, Vicenza. Right: Trieste, Piazza Unità d'Italia

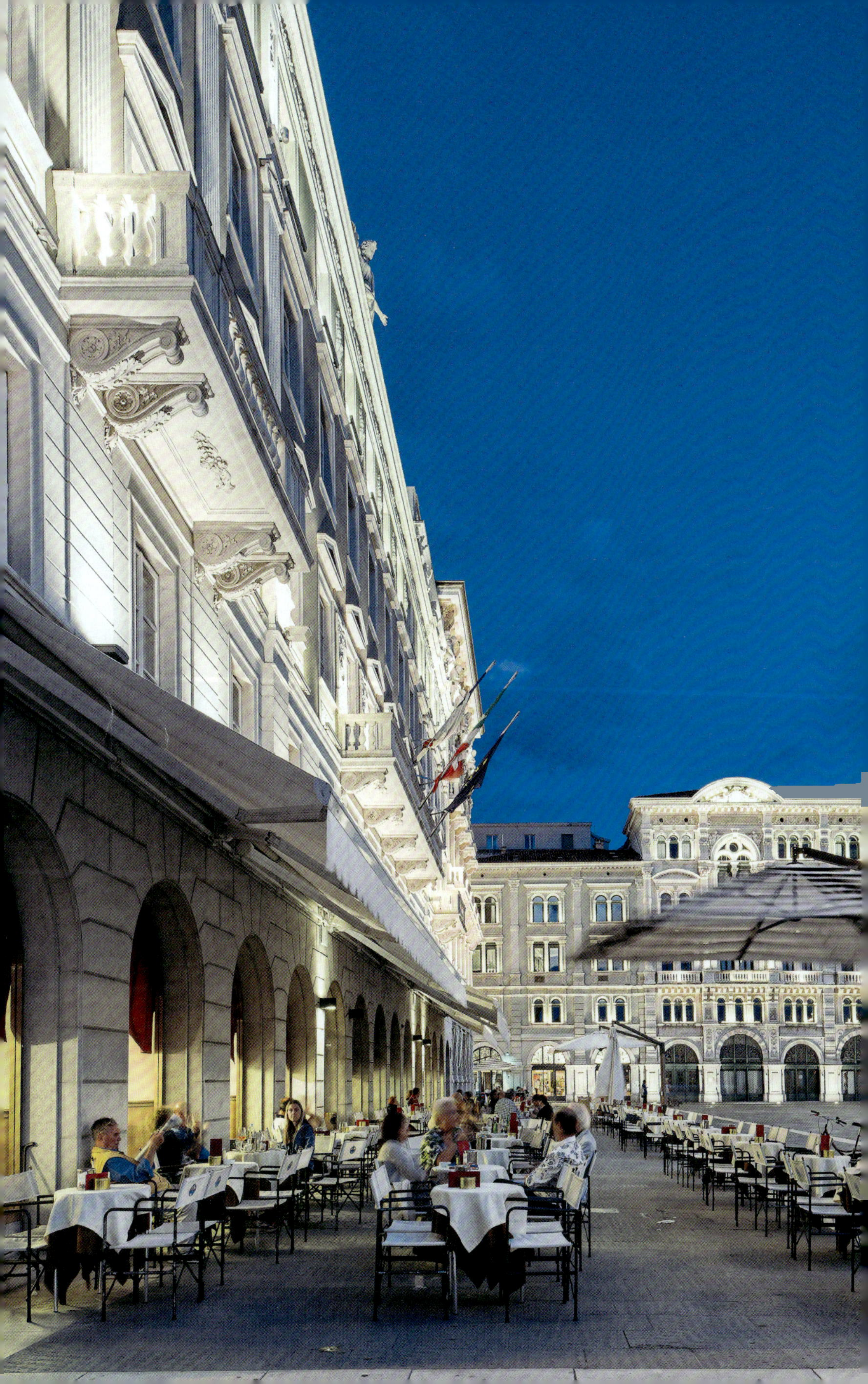

APERITIFS

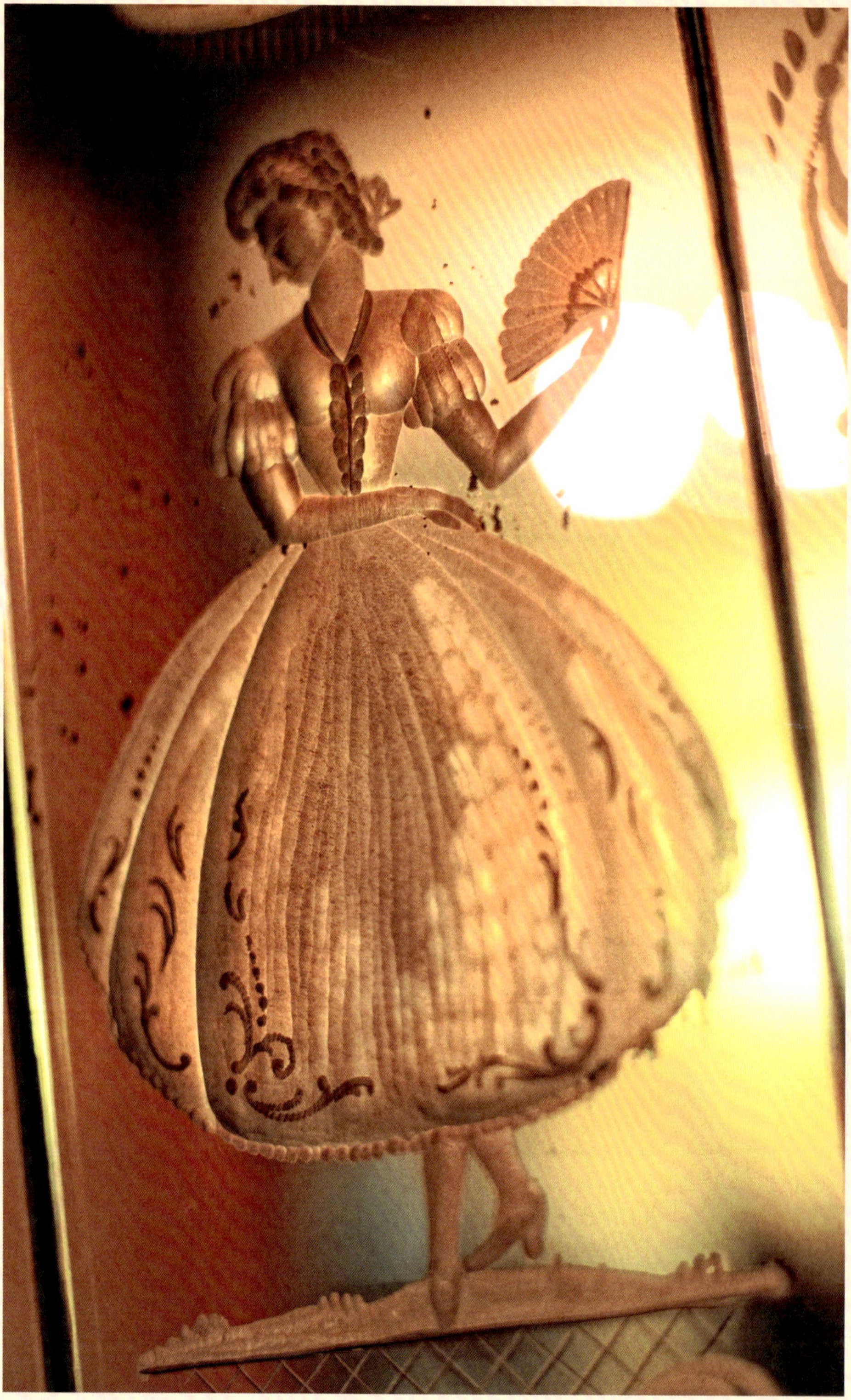

SPRITZ, APERITIFS AND OTHER DRINKS

Colored like a Kandinsky painting. Elegant as a Corinthian capital. Delightful as a jazz song. Cocktails are works of art enclosed in a glass. And the bartenders who prepare them all have a personal artistic flair. Cocktails call for imagination, professionalism, care for ingredients and attention to detail. And if there is passion into the bargain, as in our case, the magic works. Prosecco, strictly in the spumante version, is the key to Spritz and the cocktails devised by Leonardo Cisotto, bartender at the Grancaffè Quadri in Venice. In his recipes the ingredients are finely balanced, so that the Prosecco bouquet and flavor are always present, even combined with a liqueur. He often tells his staff to mix delicately, gently, so Prosecco does not shed its bubbles. Aperitifs, long drinks and after-dinner cocktails all feature fruit in season that he selects personally.

SPRITZ VENEZIANO

APERITIF

8 cl. (2¾ oz) Prosecco
3 cl. (1 oz) Soda water or seltzer
4 cl. (1¼ oz) Aperol
Garnish with a ½ slice of orange

PREPARATION

Fill a glass (old fashioned or goblet) and pour in this order:
Prosecco, soda water and Aperol.
Aperol can be replaced by liqueurs such as Bitter, Select or Cynar.

Curious fact

Spritz was invented in Venice under the Austro-Hungarian Empire. The soldiers, used to drinking beer, found the local wine too strong and added a squirt of soda, hence the name spritzer. But the drink was unpleasant to taste, so they added lemon zest. Over time the taste of this aperitif was enriched with the addition of various liqueurs. Broad public appreciation has led to Spritz being codified among international cocktails.

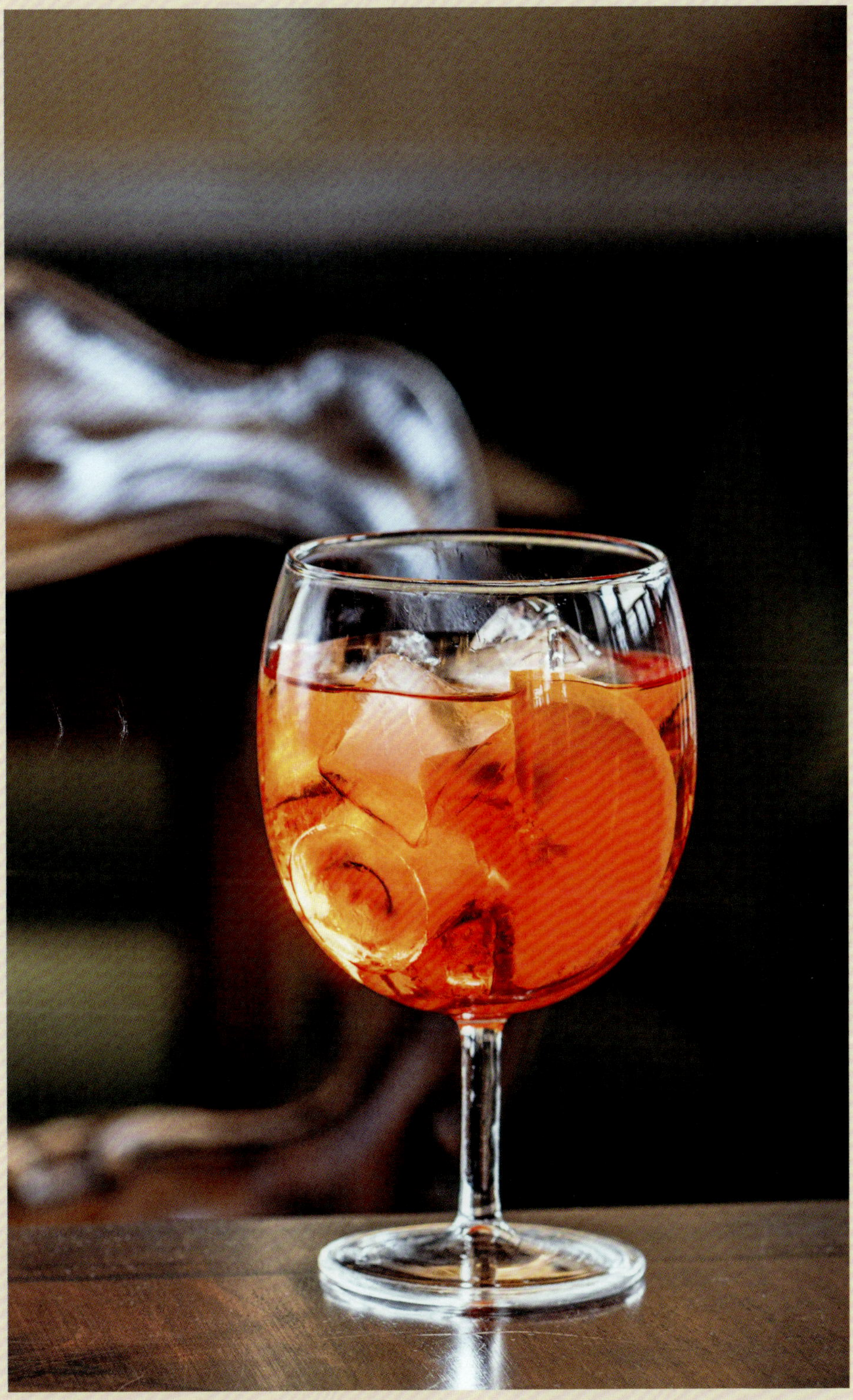

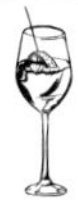

MIMOSA

APERITIF

10 cl. (3²⁄₄ oz) Prosecco
5 cl. (1¾ oz) fresh orange juice
Garnish with ½ a slice of orange

PREPARATION

Prepare straight in the glass,
pouring Prosecco and adding the orange juice.

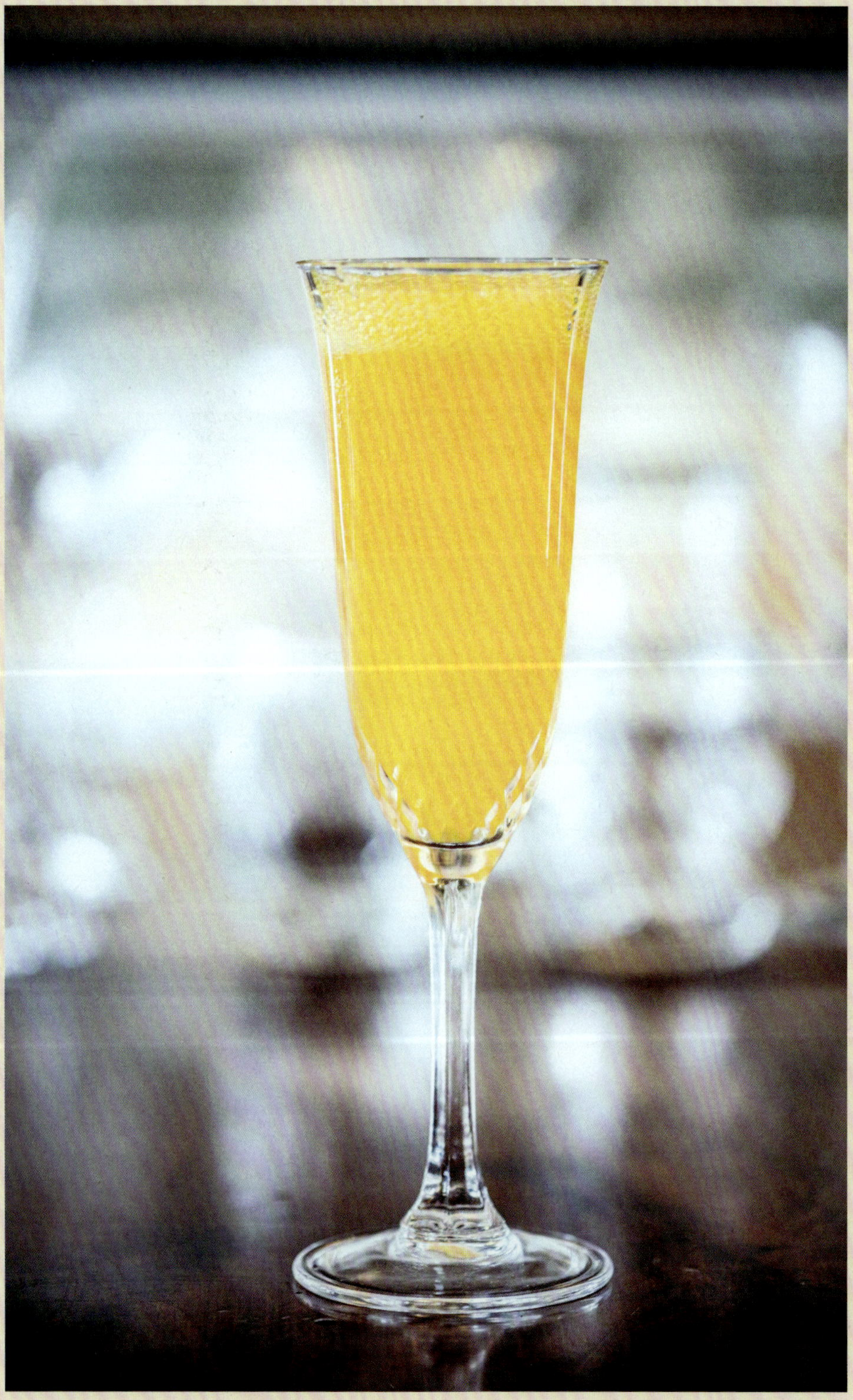

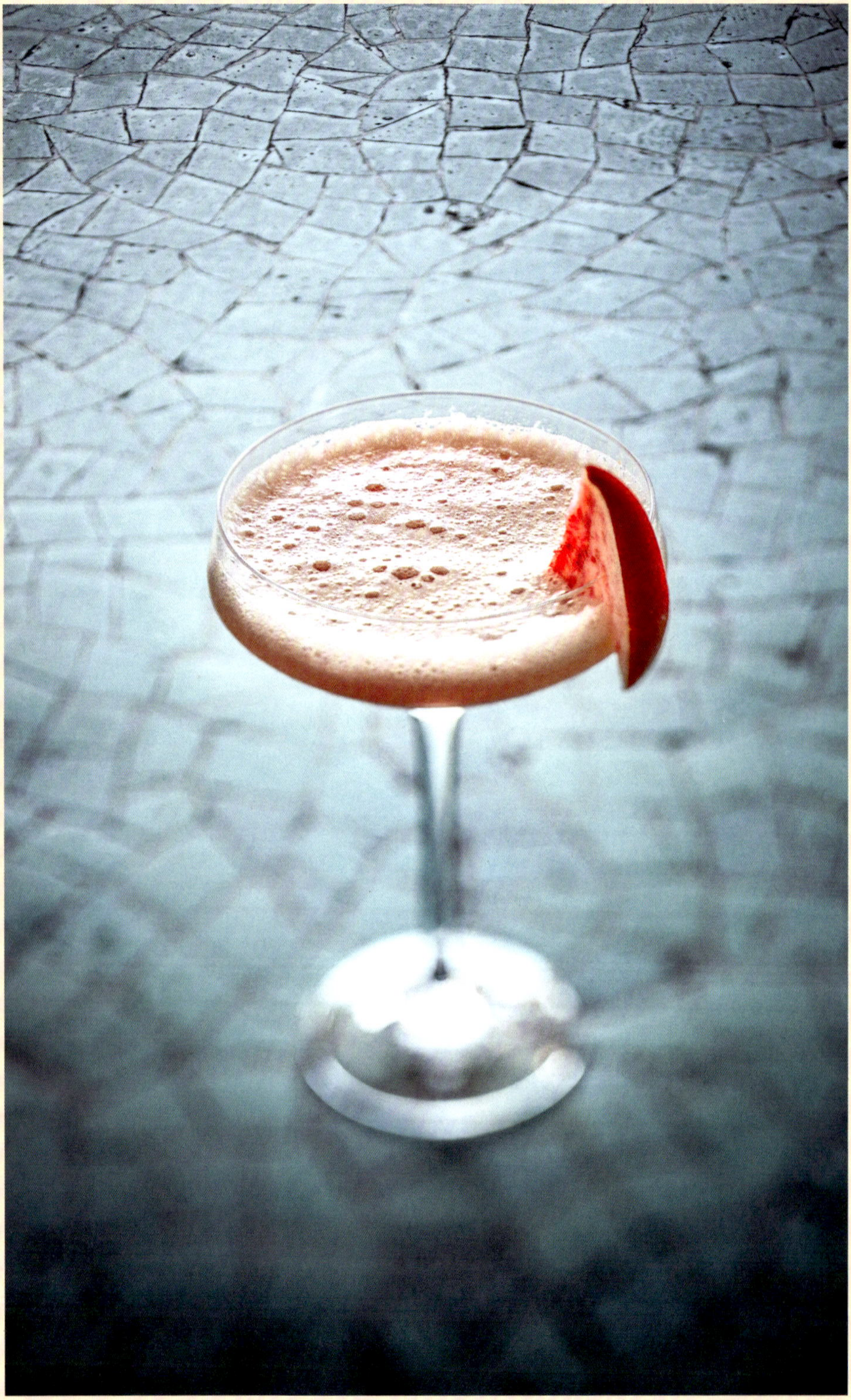

BELLINI

APERITIF

5 cl. (1¾ oz) white peach juice
10 cl. (3 2/4 oz) Prosecco
Garnish with a small slice of peach

PREPARATION

Take a ripe white peach, open it in half and remove the stone, strain the peach through the chinois, crushing it with your hands and remembering to add a few drops of lemon to prevent it from oxidizing. Sample the juice and correct it with a few drops of liquid sugar if desired. Pour the Prosecco, very cold, into a champagne flute or coupe. Add the peach juice.

Curious fact

The cocktail was invented by Giuseppe Cipriani at Harry's Bar in Venice, during a Bellini exhibition. Vittorio Gassman once complimented me on making the best Bellini he had ever tasted. So he said and wrote out on a dedication to me. Gassman was at Cortina for a book presentation and I was working in the bar of a famous hotel in Cortina. The difference to the cocktail, then, as now, is made by the peach, which should be crushed, not put in a blender.

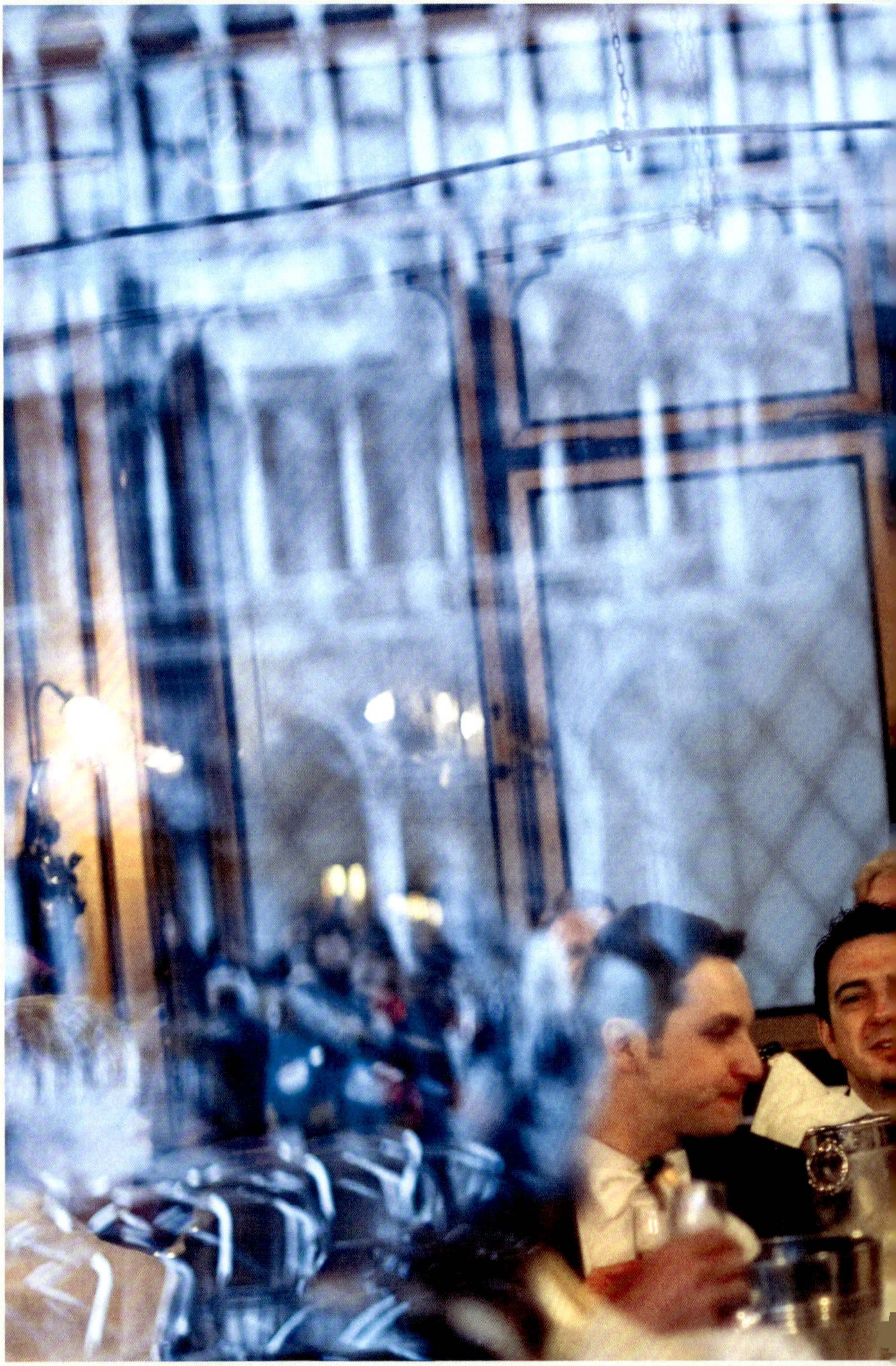

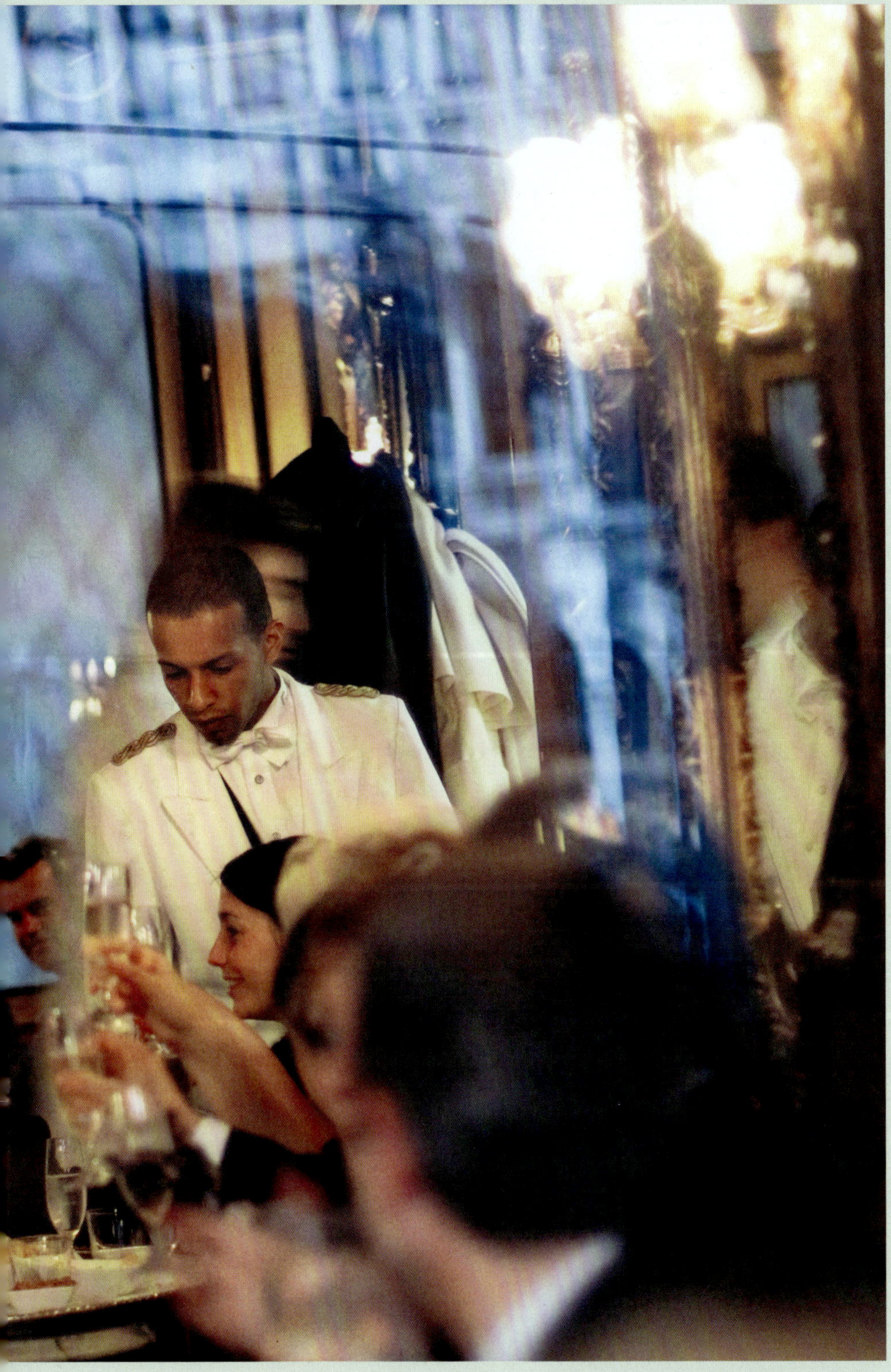

ROSSINI

APERITIF

5 cl. (1¾ oz) blended strawberries
10 cl. (3 2⁄4 oz) Prosecco
Garnish with a strawberry

PREPARATION

Blitz the strawberries in a blender with a few drops of lemon and sugar. Then pour into a chilled champagne flute or coupe of Prosecco and add the blended strawberries.

Curious fact

In my (long) experience as a barman, I've noticed that the Rossini is women's favorite cocktail.

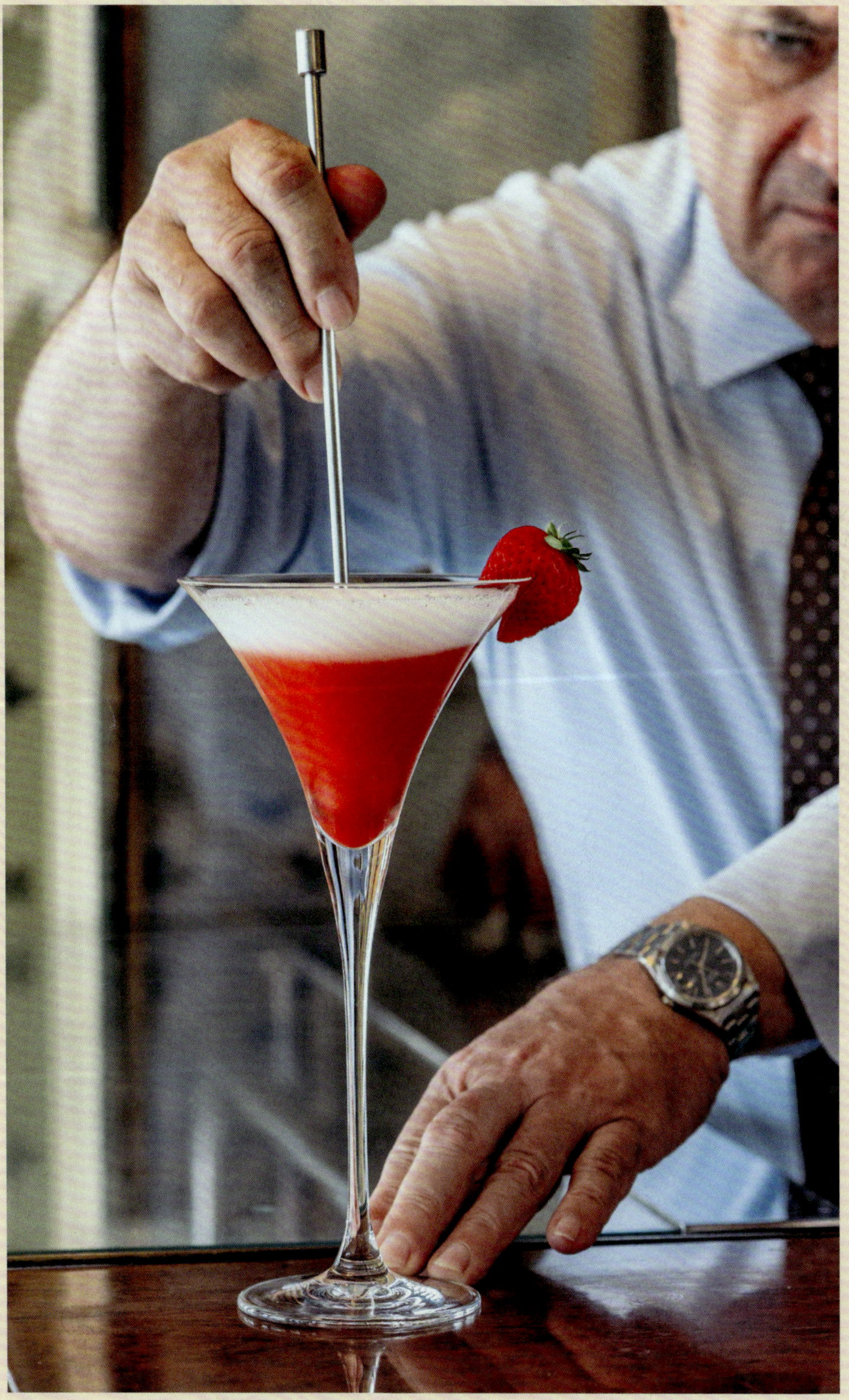

TIZIANO

APERITIF

5 cl. (1¾ oz) juice from fox grapes
10 cl. (3²⁄₄ oz) Prosecco
Garnish with some grapes

PREPARATION

Juice the grapes by passing them through a *chinois* and let the juice settle. Pour the chilled Prosecco into a champagne flute and add the juice.

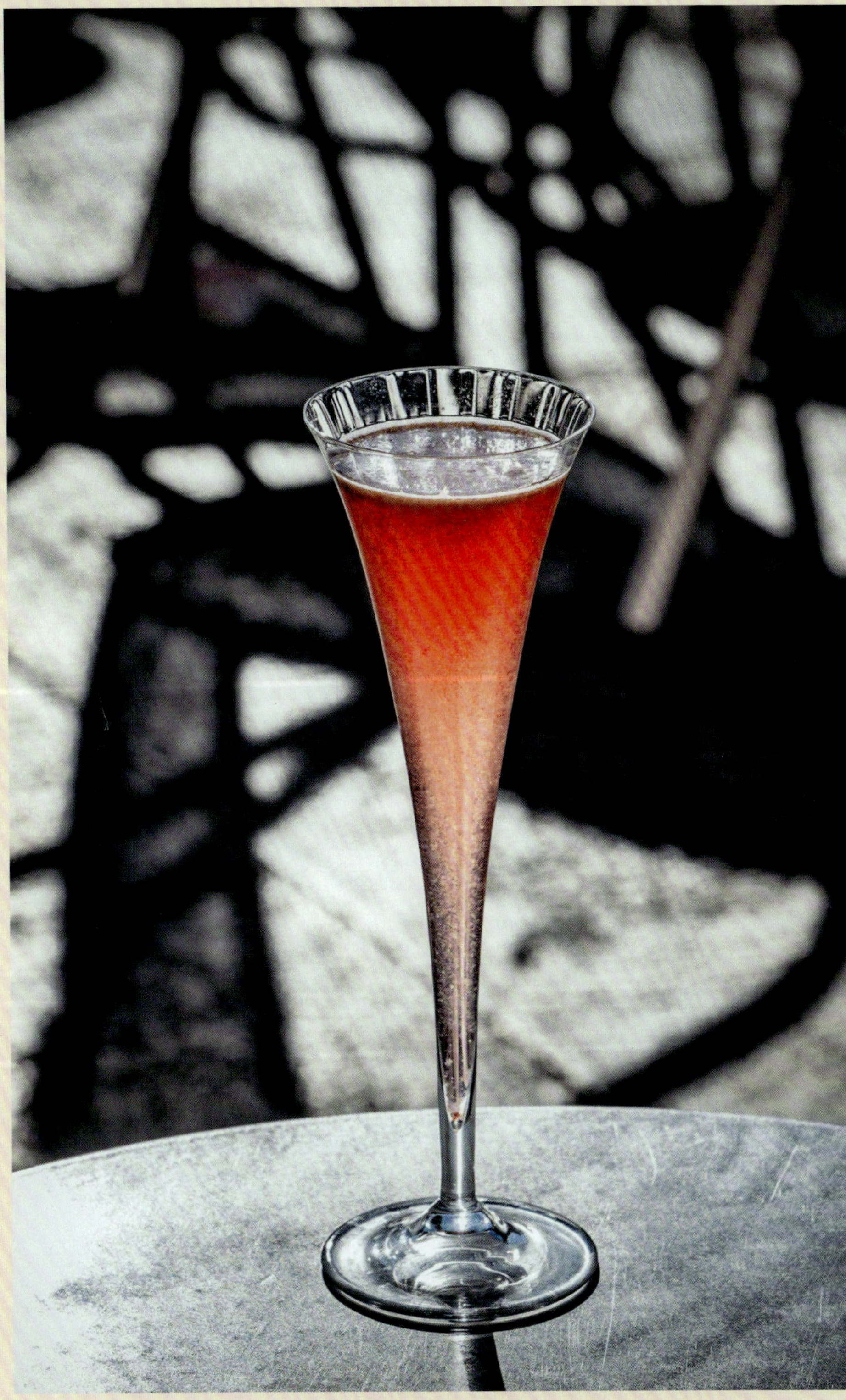

PUCCINI

APERITIF

10 cl. (3 2/4 oz) Prosecco
5 cl. (1¾ oz) mandarin juice

PREPARATION

Pour the Prosecco into a champagne flute and add the mandarin juice.

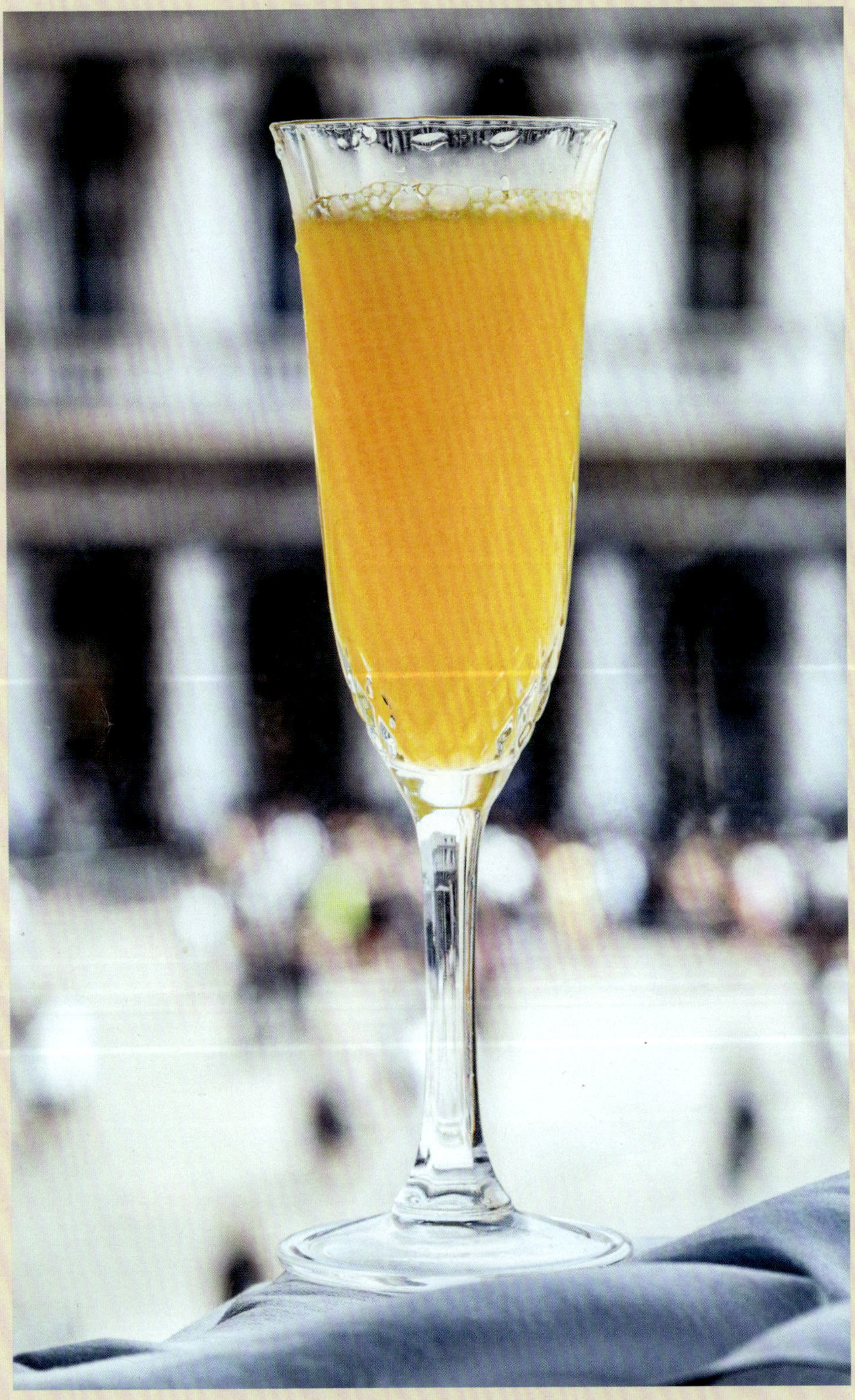

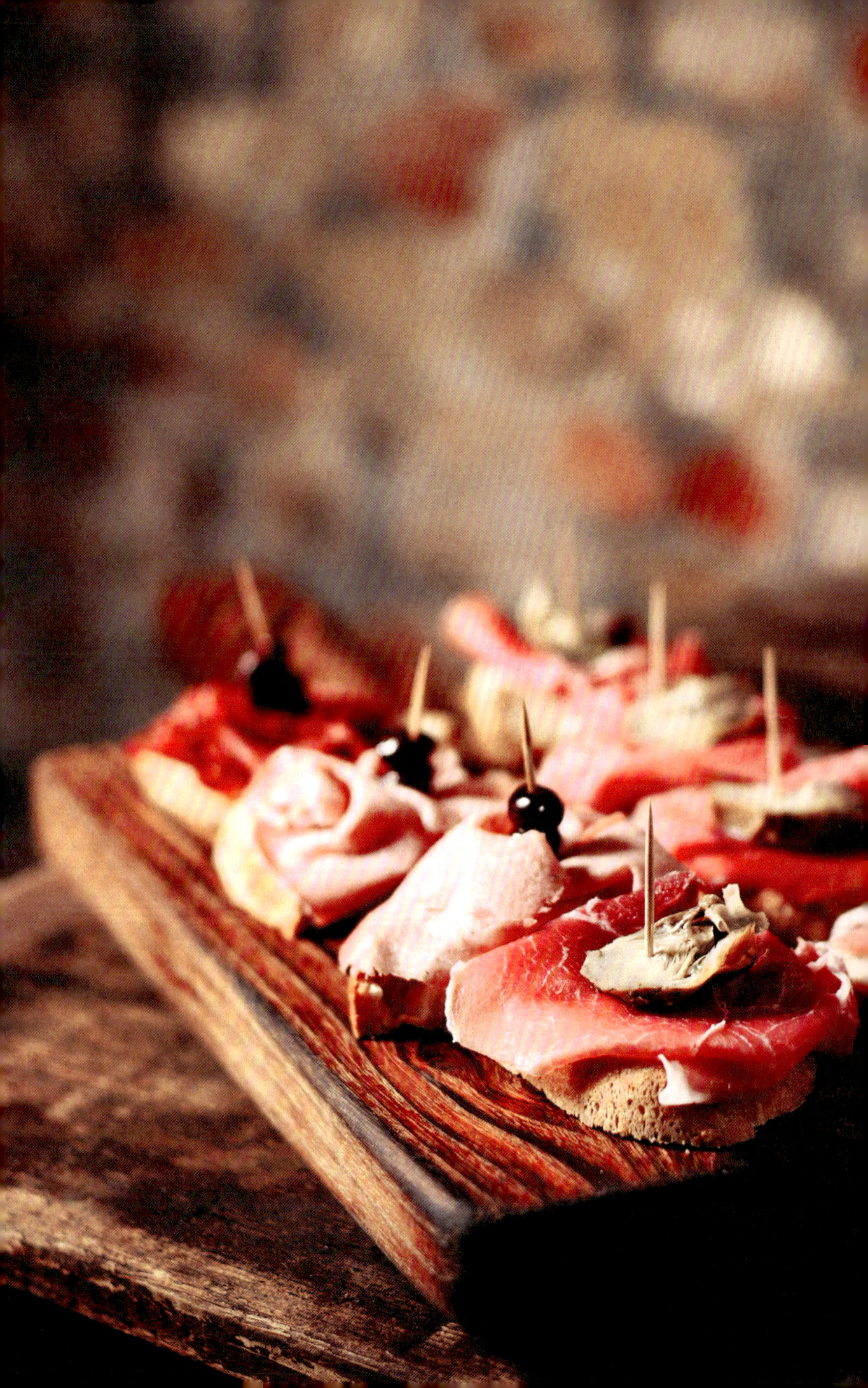

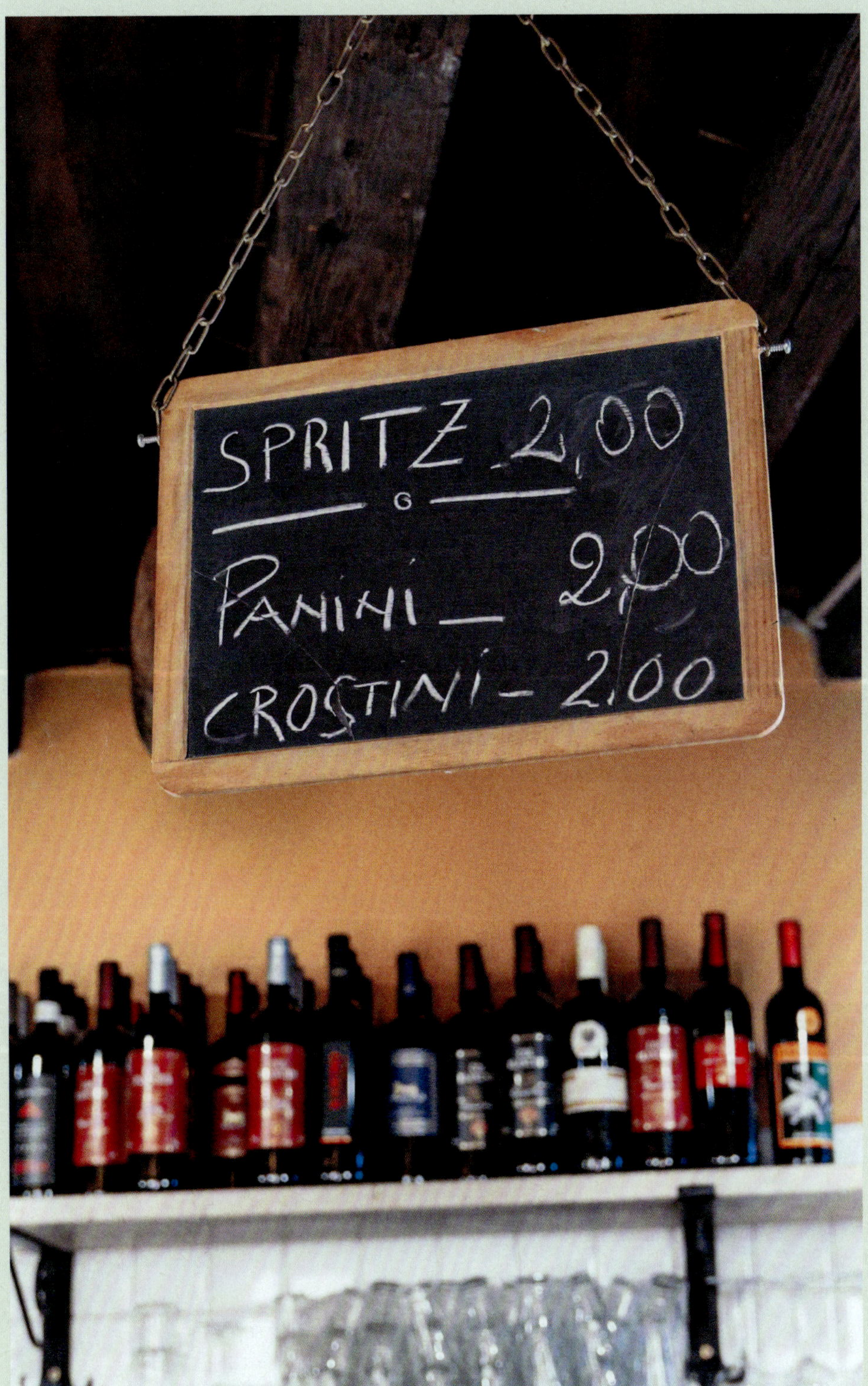
SPRITZ 2,00
PANINI 2,00
CROSTINI 2,00

CANALETTO

APERITIF

10 cl. (3 $\frac{2}{4}$ oz) Prosecco
5 cl. (1¾ oz) blended raspberries

PREPARATION

Pour the Prosecco straight into a flute or coupe and add the blended raspberries.

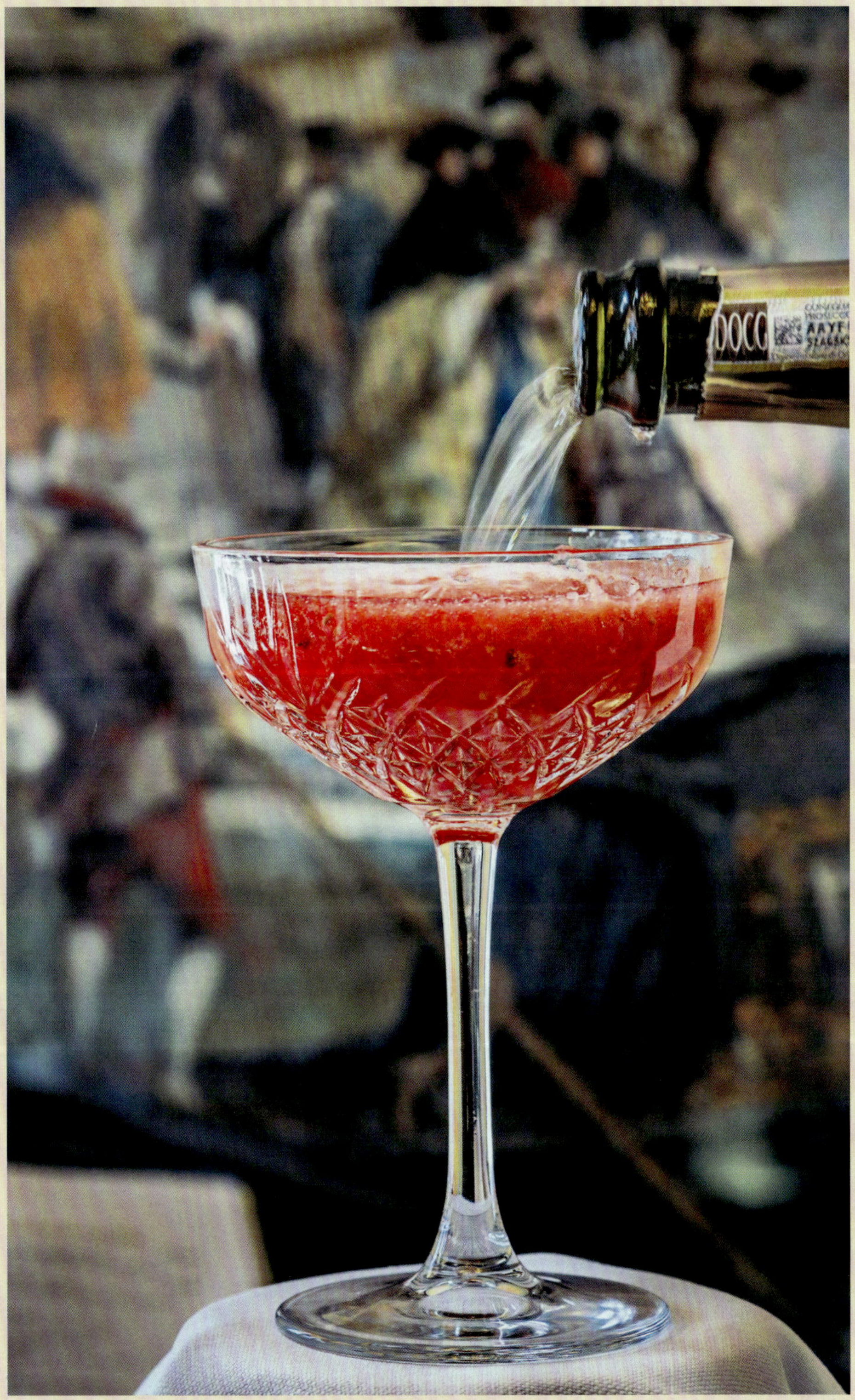

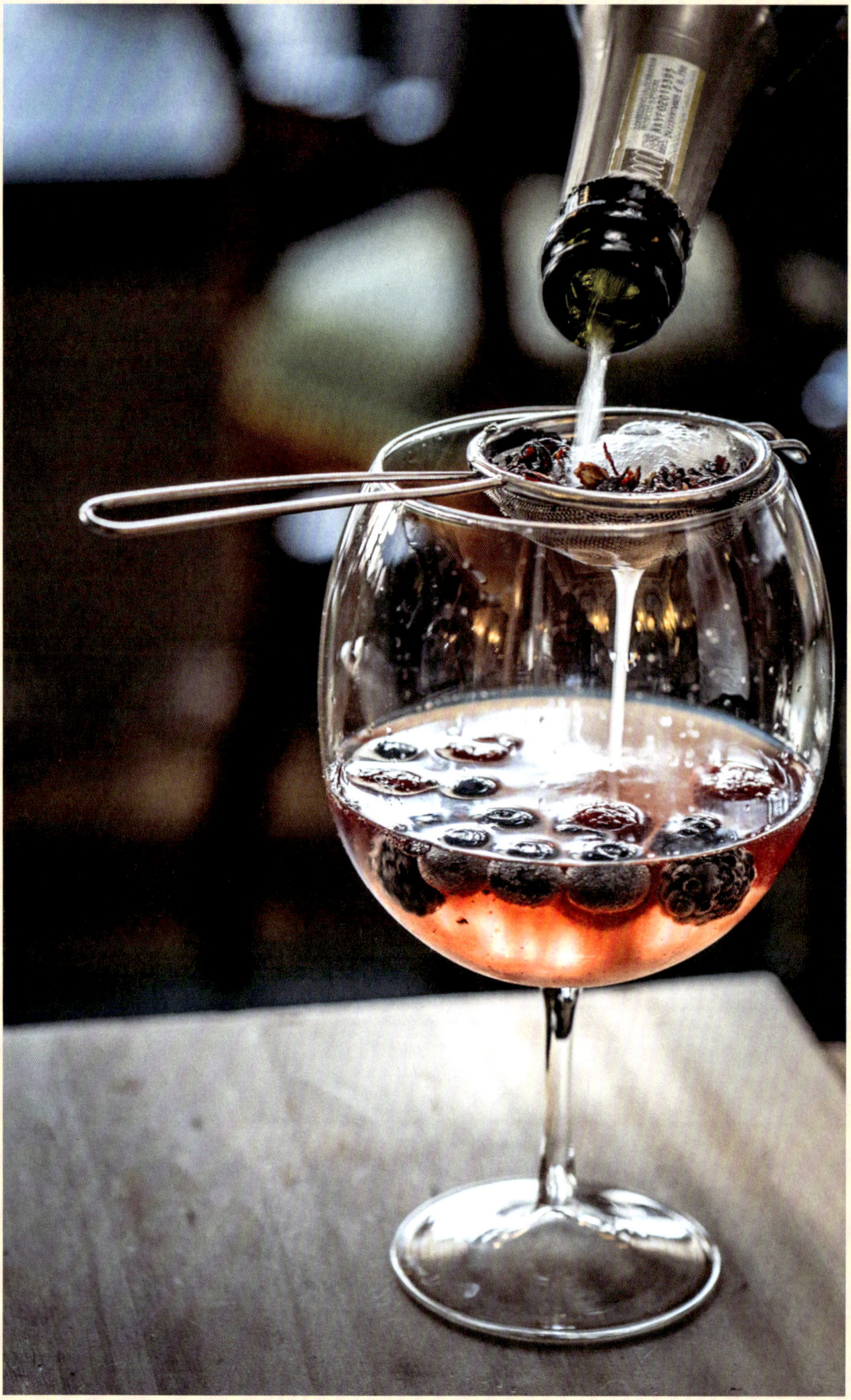

IN-FUSION SPRITZ

APERITIF

2 small slices ginger
2 spoonfuls dried red flowers and fruits
1.5 cl. (⅔ oz) liquid sugar
14 cl. (4¾ oz) Prosecco
Garnish with fresh red fruits

PREPARATION

In a large wine glass, bruise the 2 slices of ginger and then remove them. Put the dried flowers and fruits in a strainer over the glass and slowly pour the cold Prosecco over the flowers and fruits. Add the liquid sugar and stir gently.

Curious fact

This aperitif was invented a few years ago when herbs and infusions were starting to be the craze. I thought this was a good way to create an infusion using spumante instead of water and adding a healthy touch with the slices of ginger.

PROSECCO COCKTAIL

AFTER DINNER

1 sugar lump soaked in Aurum
14 cl. (4¾ oz) Prosecco
1 cl. (¼ oz) Brandy
Garnish with a ½ slice of orange and a cherry

PREPARATION

After soaking the sugar lump put it in the bottom of the glass, add the Prosecco and then the Brandy.
Stir gently.

Curious fact

This is a italian-veneto version of the Champagne Cocktail. Aurum is an orange-based liqueur, yellow gold in color, produced in Abruzzo. It's not very widely sold, but it's very good.

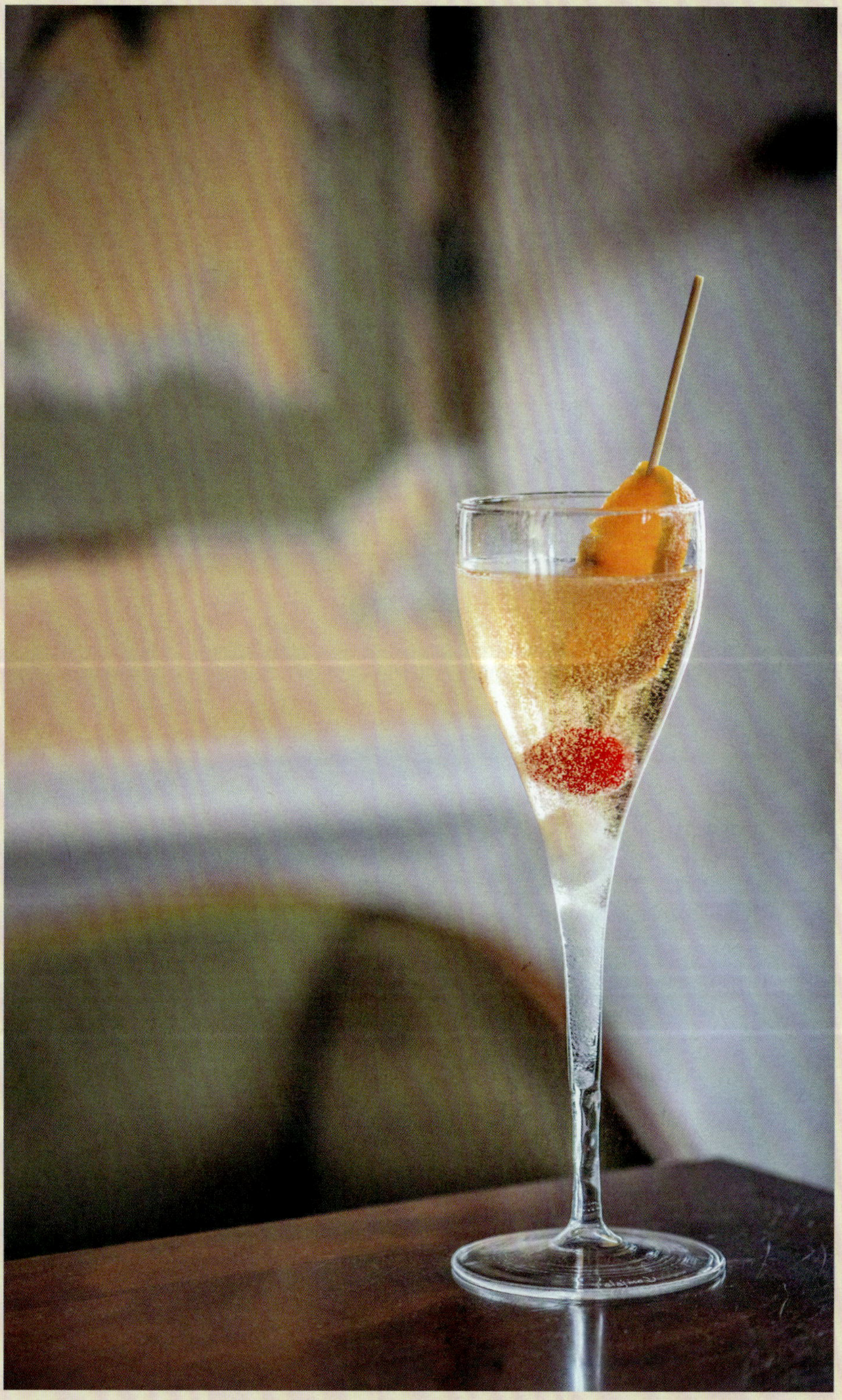

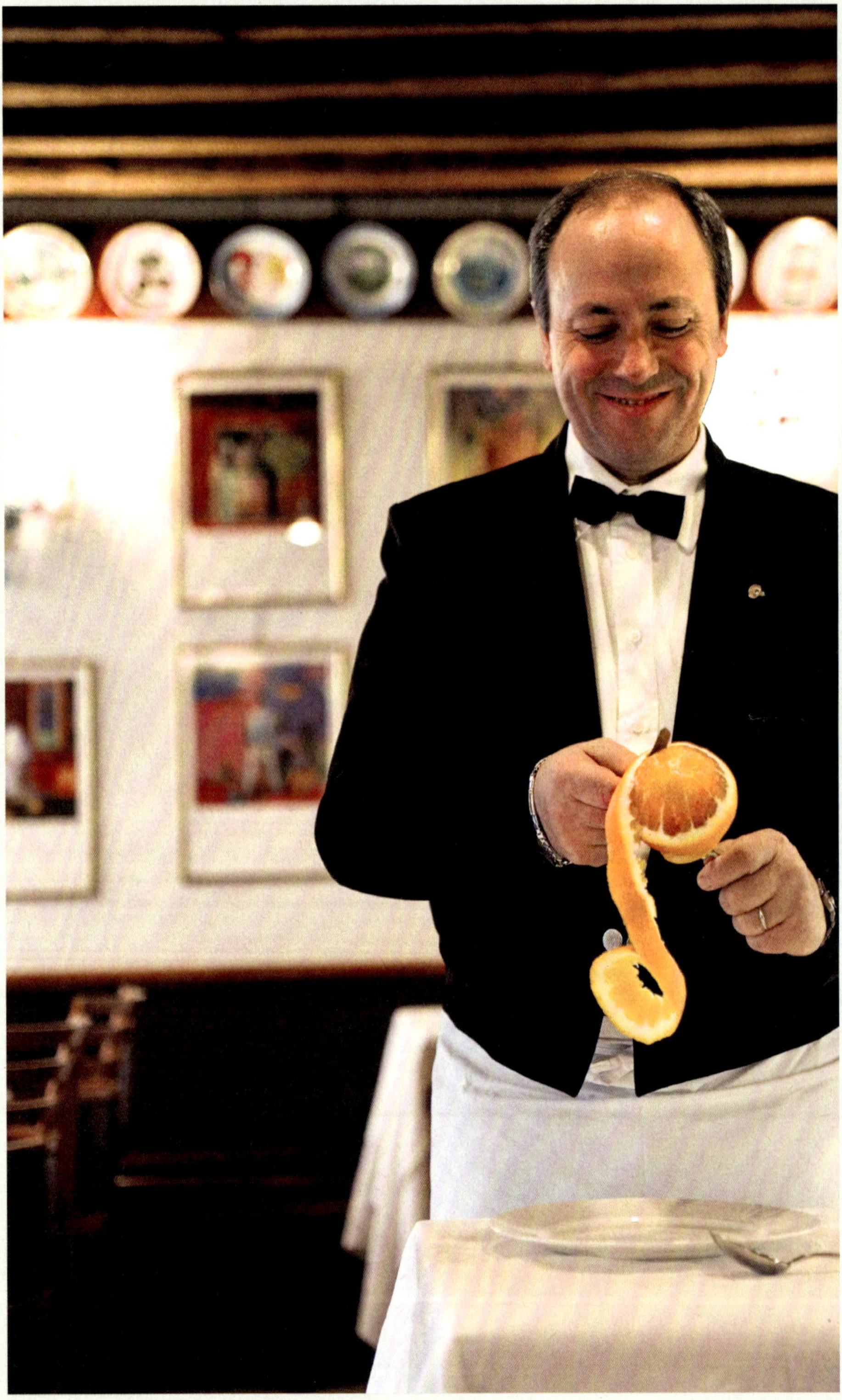

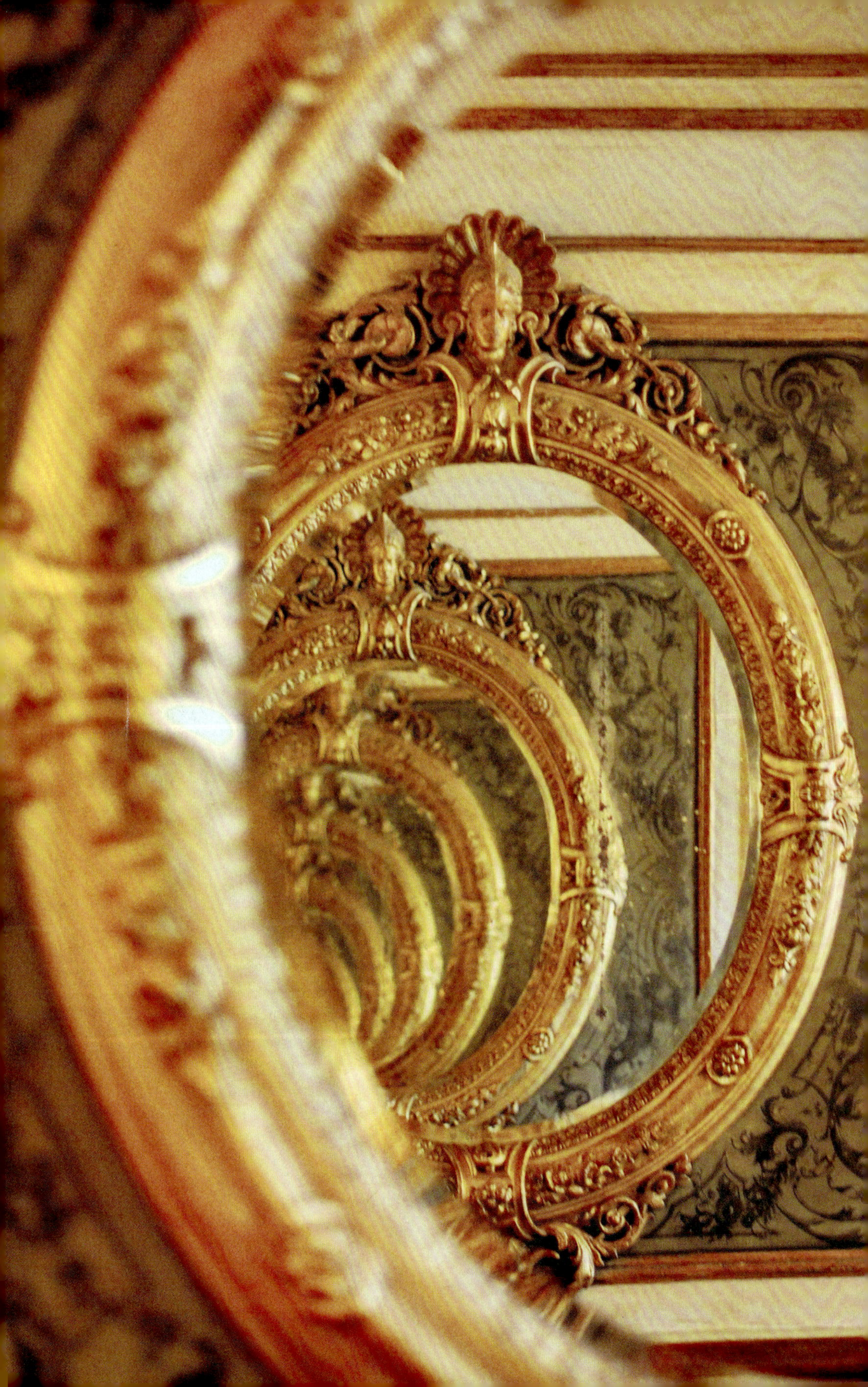

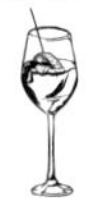

OLTRE IL GIARDINO

APERITIF

3.5 cl. (1¼ oz) apple juice
1.5 cl. (2⁄4 oz) grape distillate
10 cl. (3 2⁄4 oz) Prosecco
Garnish with a cherry

PREPARATION

Pour the ingredients straight into the glass and stir gently.

Curious fact

Grape distillate is made straight from grapes, so it is nobler and lighter than grappa. I called the cocktail "beyond the garden" because I imagined a cottage on a hill, with a big garden in front. Beyond it stretch away vineyards and orchards, their scents and flavors mingling in the glass.

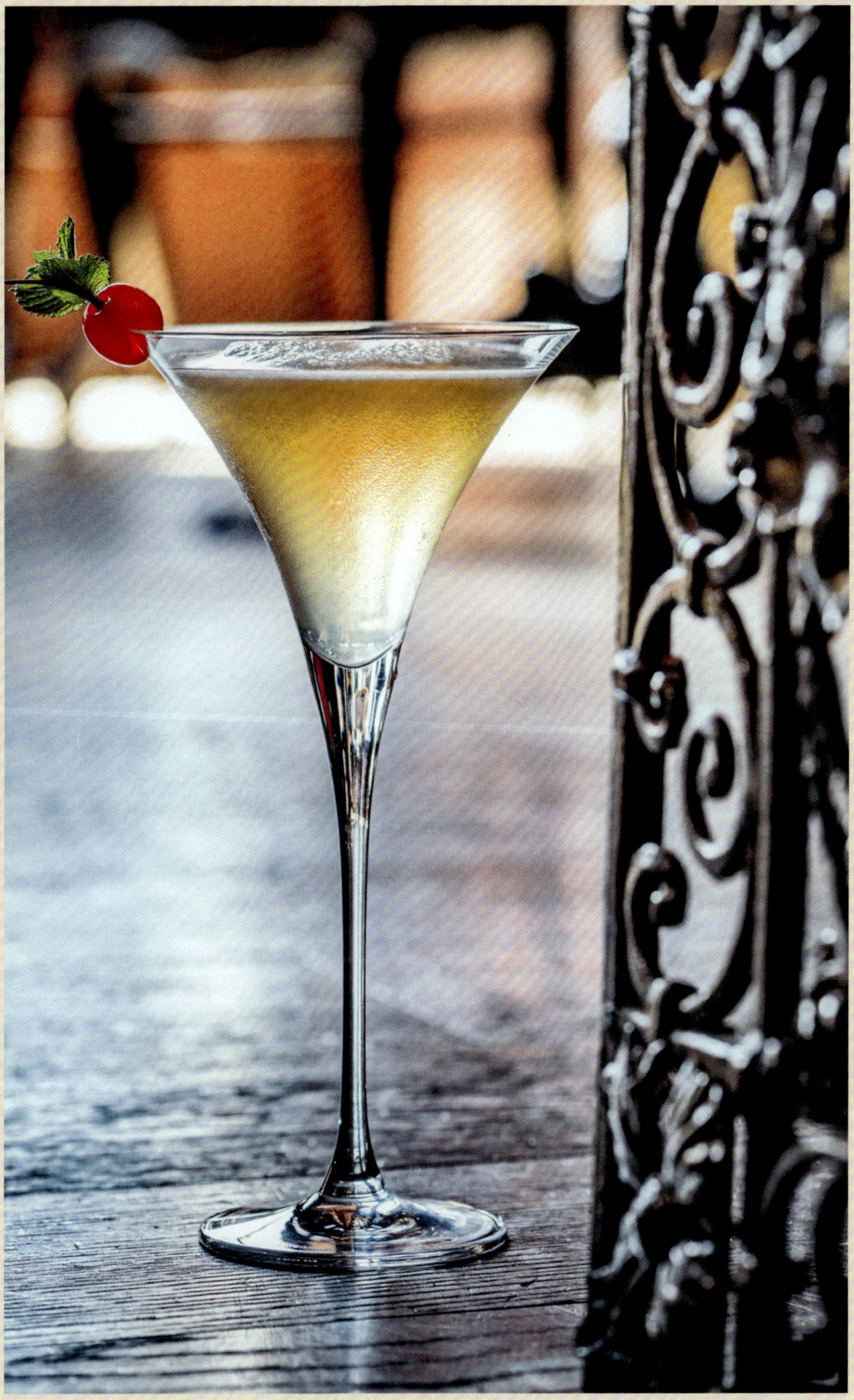

BEN-ESSERE

APERITIF

Diced fruit:
apple, pear, pineapple, kiwi, banana, peach, melon
2 cl. (¾ oz) Maraschino
13 cl. (4 2/4 oz) Prosecco

PREPARATION

Dice the fruit, mix it with the Maraschino and a few drops of lemon juice, put it in a goblet and add Prosecco.

Curious fact

The fruit is mixed with Maraschino to bring out its flavors.

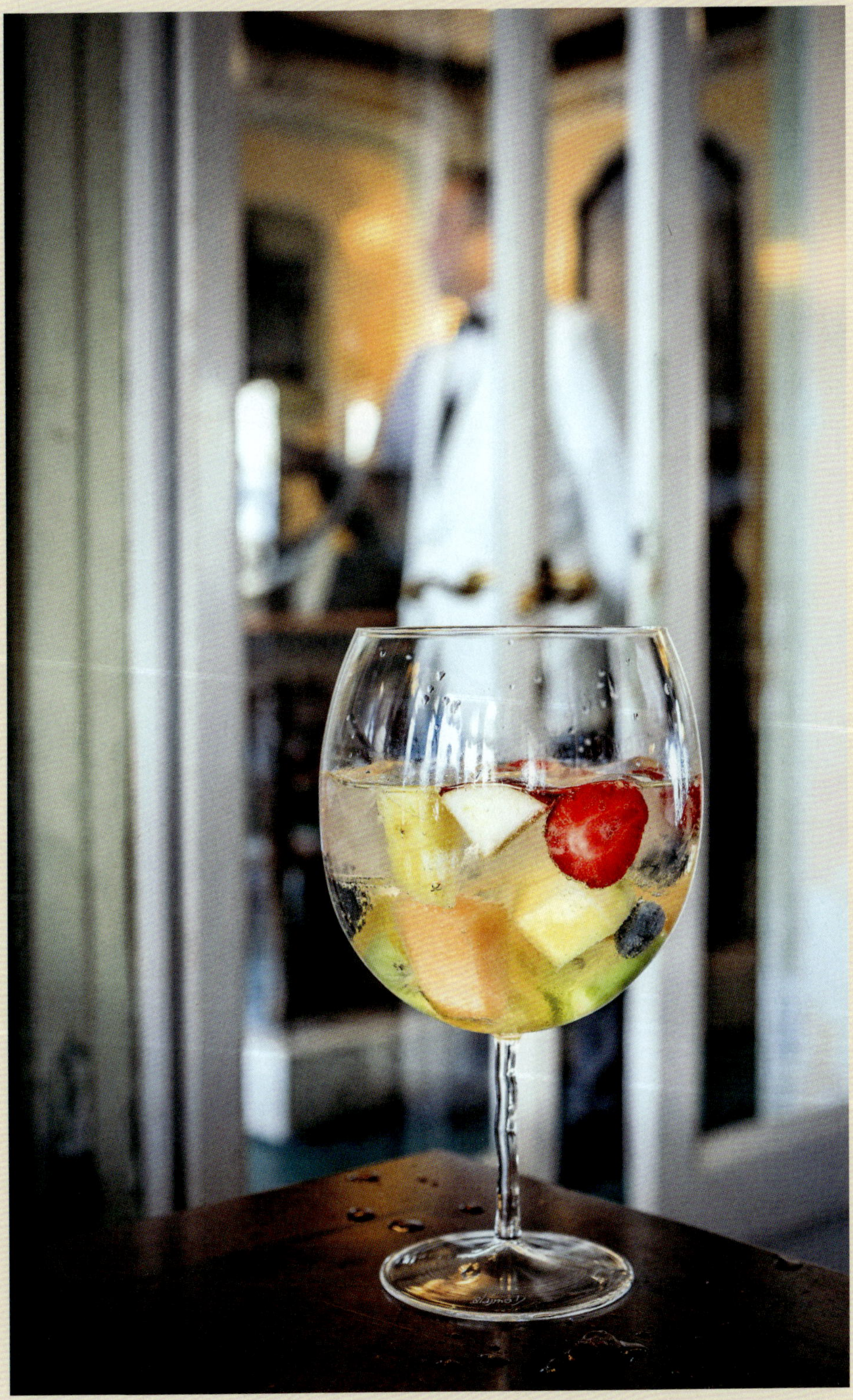

EL MOJO VENETO

LONG DRINK

3 cl. (1 oz) white rum
1.5 cl. (2⁄4 oz) lime juice
1.5 cl. (2⁄4 oz) sugar syrup
3 mint leaves
3 cl. (1 oz) soda water
9 cl. (3¼ oz) Prosecco
Garnish with a sprig of mint

PREPARATION

Put the first 4 ingredients into a tumbler, stir them for several seconds, add the soda water and Prosecco, stir and top up the glass with ice.

Curious fact

Mojo is a Voodoo term meaning a magic spell. I chose this name as a pun on mojo and mojito. This cocktail is a mojito with the addition of Prosecco. A handy hint: it is better not to crush the mint, so as to avoid extracting the oil, which is heavier to digest.

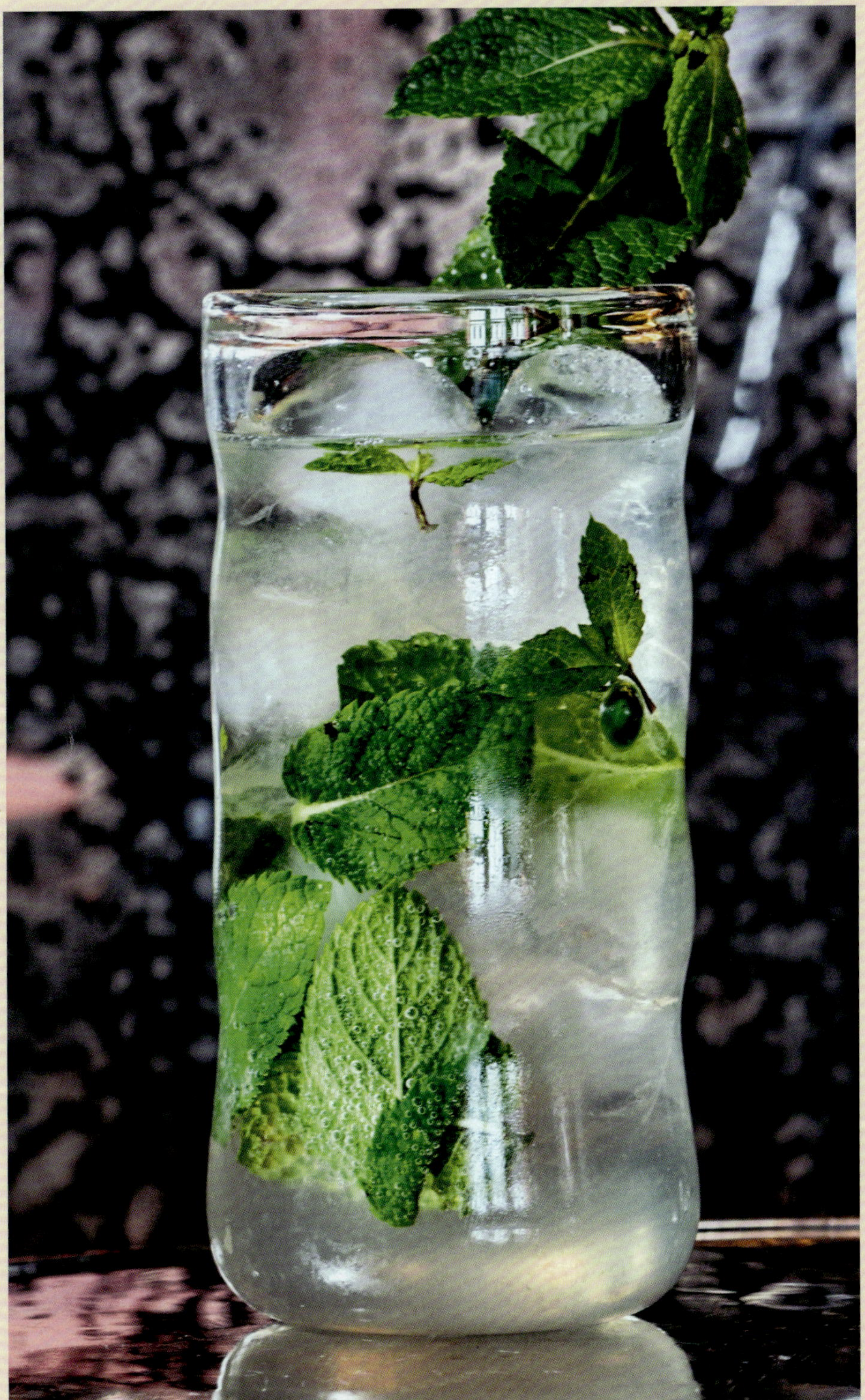

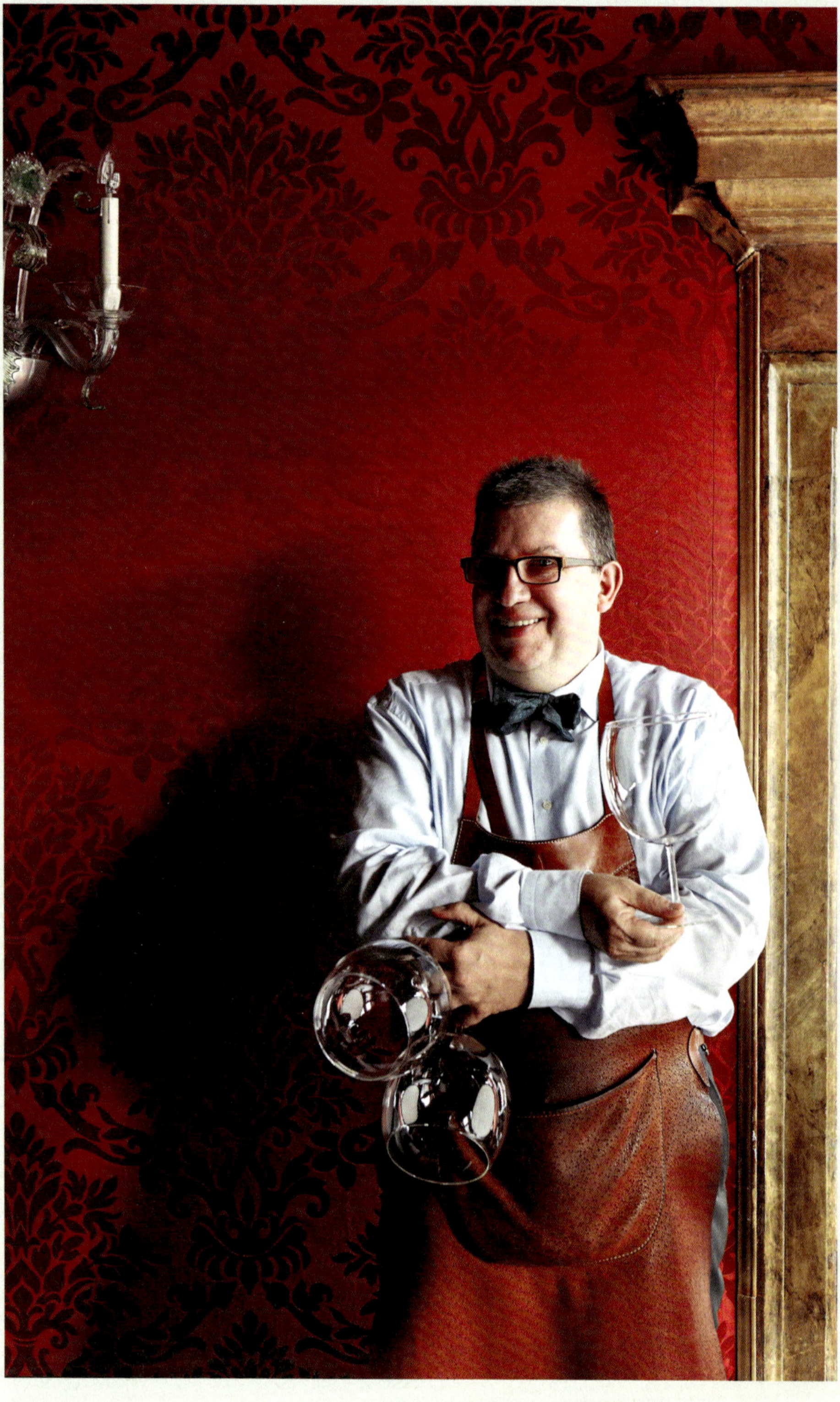

Possagno, Gallery of plaster casts by Antonio Canova >

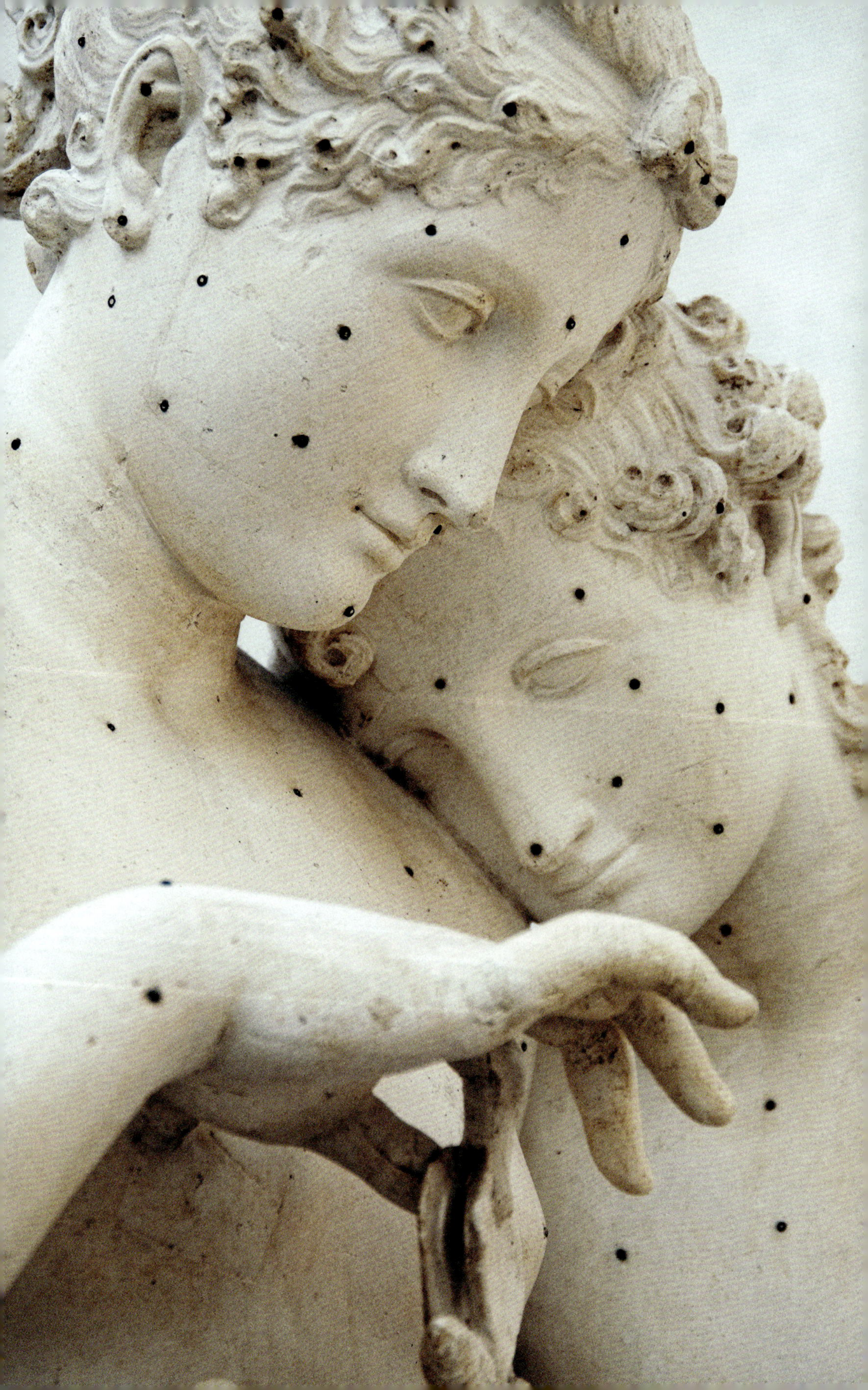

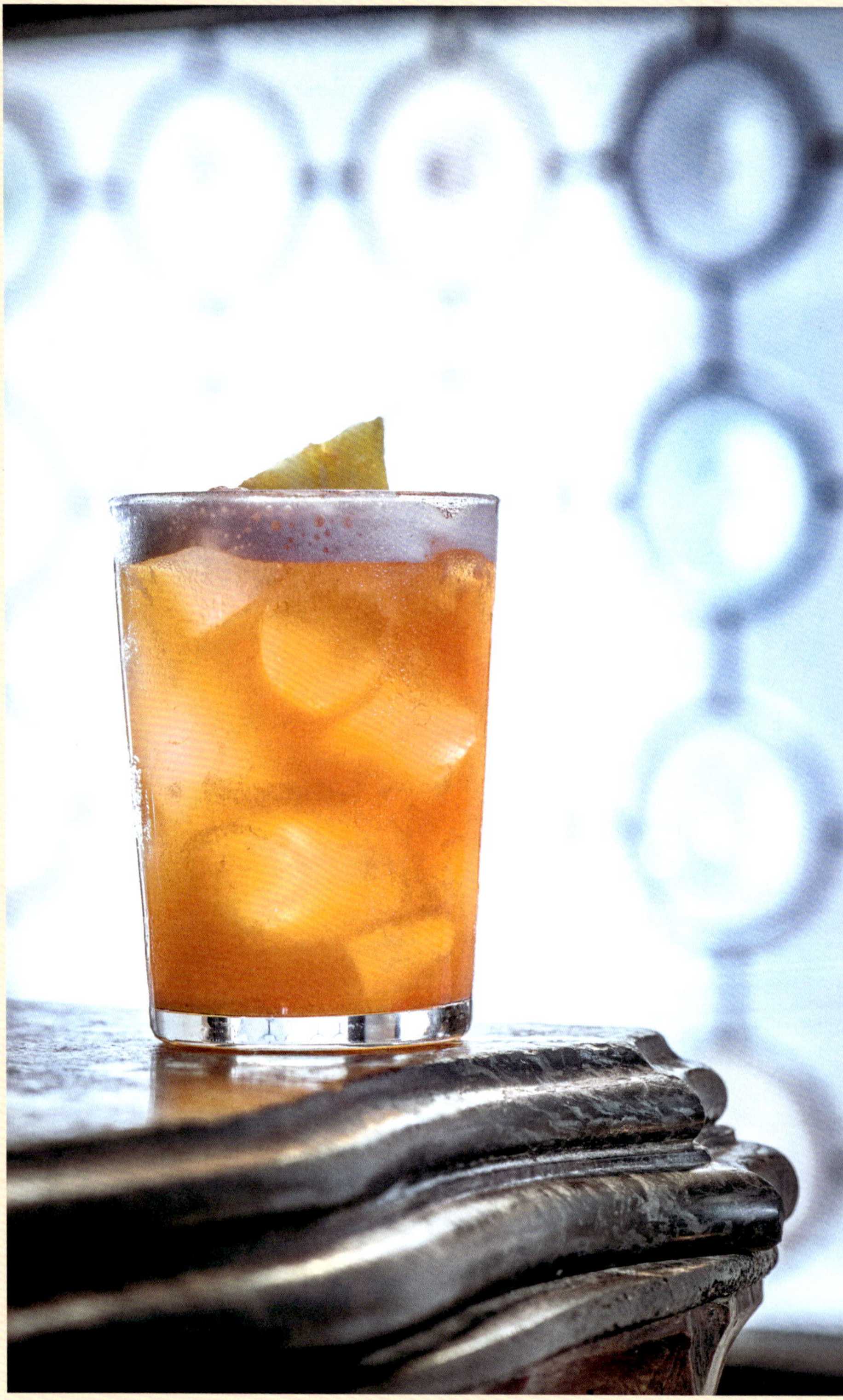

NEPENTHE

LONG DRINK

6 cl. (2 oz) pineapple juice
3 cl. (1 oz) Mandarinetto
2 cl. (¾ oz) White rum
9 cl. (3¼ oz) Prosecco
Garnish with pineapple slices

PREPARATION

Shake the first 3 ingredients.
Pour into a tumbler and add Prosecco.
Stir gently.

Curious fact

Nepenthe is the name of an old beverage the condottieri used to drink before a battle. It appears in Greek poetry and myths, but seems to date from the ancient Egyptians. I invented this cocktail as a young man.

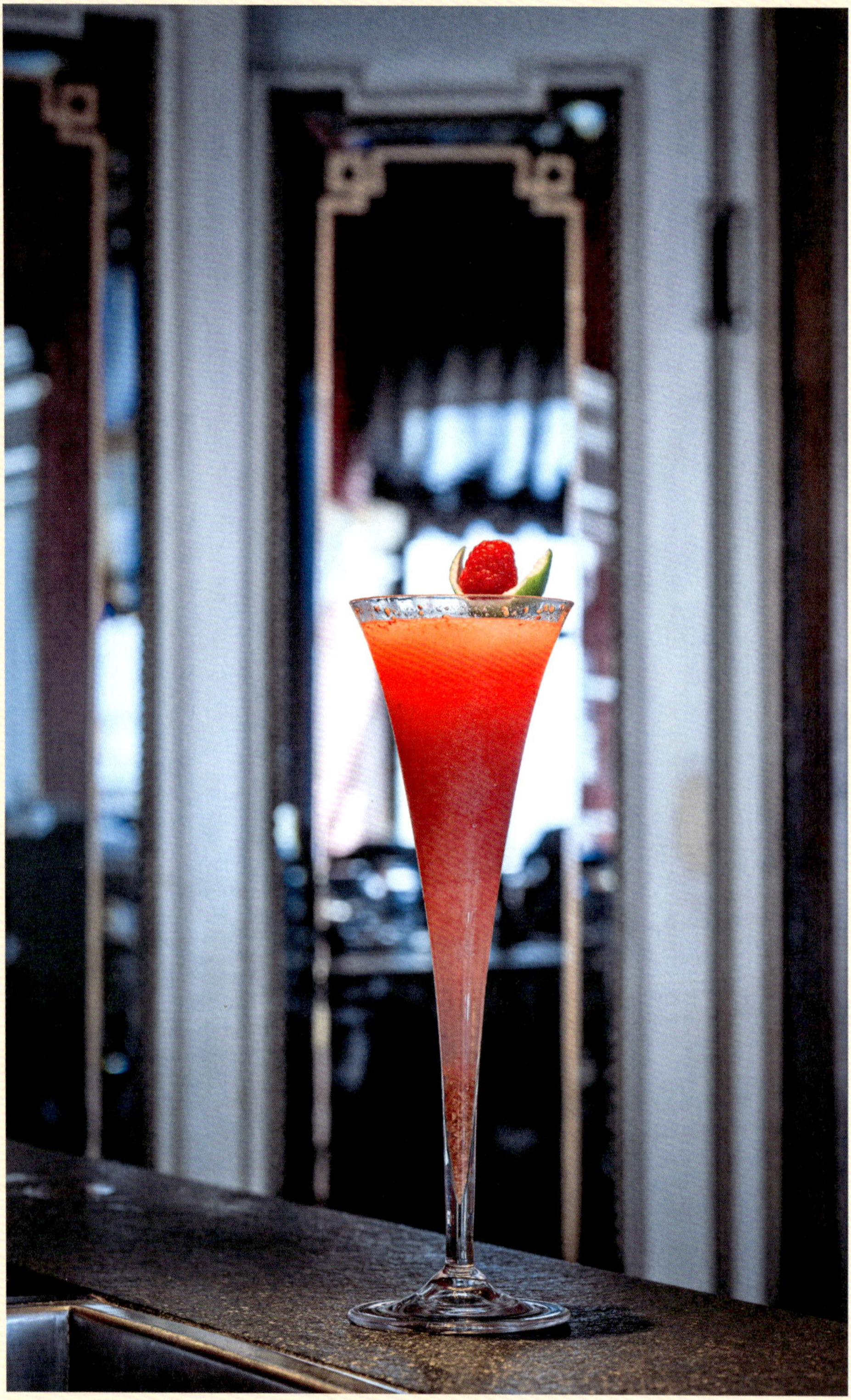

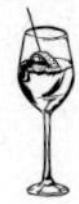

HEMINGWAY

APERITIF

7 cl. (2 2⁄4 oz) Prosecco
5 cl. (1¾ oz) blended raspberries
1 cl. (¼ oz) liquid sugar
2 cl. (¾ oz) vodka
Garnish with a raspberry

PREPARATION

Pour Prosecco into the glass.
Shake the first 3 ingredients and pour them into the Prosecco.
Stir gently.

TINTORETTO

APERITIF

11 cl. (3¾ oz) Prosecco
4 cl. (1¼ oz) pomegranate juice

PREPARATION

Pour the Prosecco straight into the flute,
add the pomegranate juice.
Stir gently.

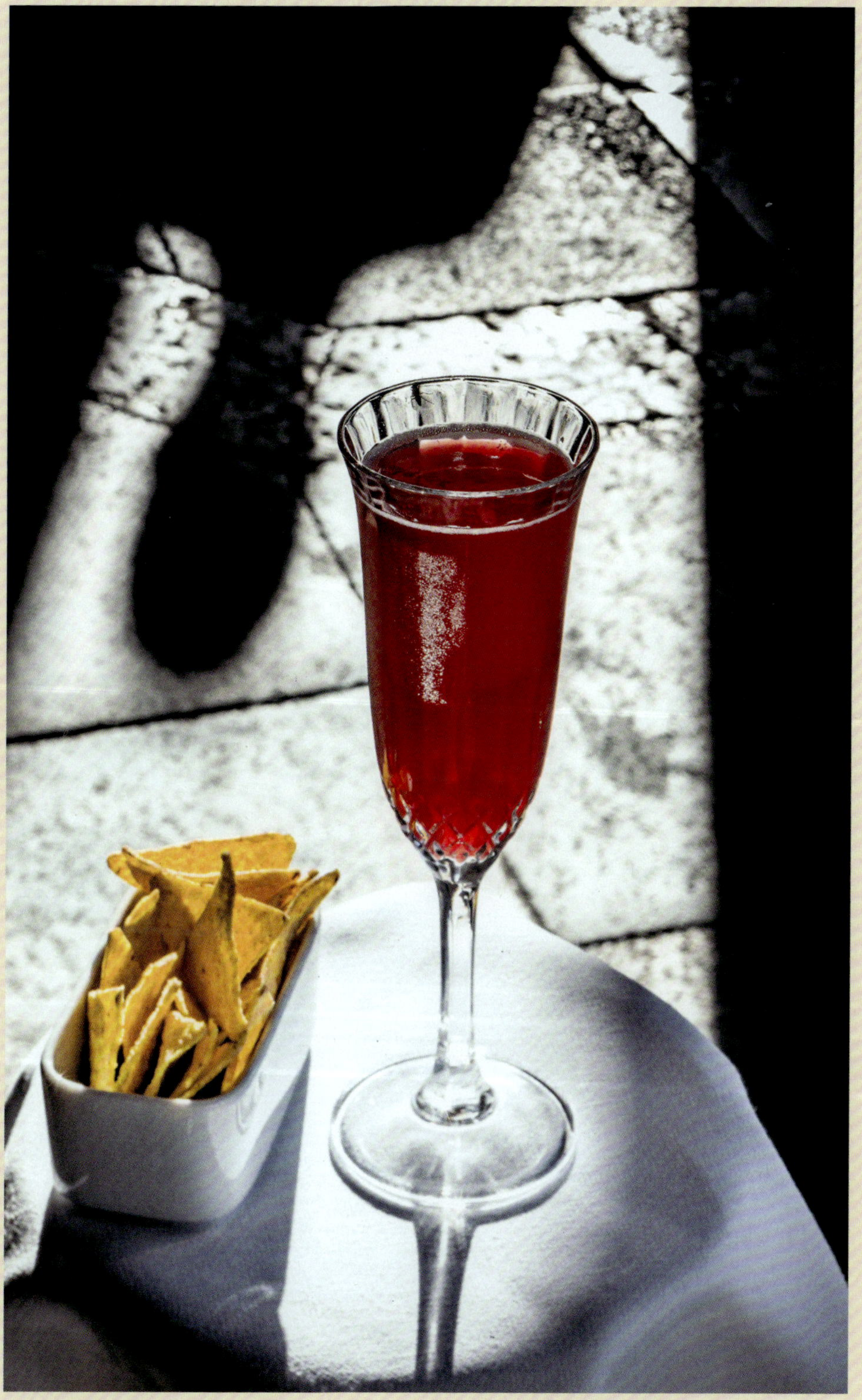

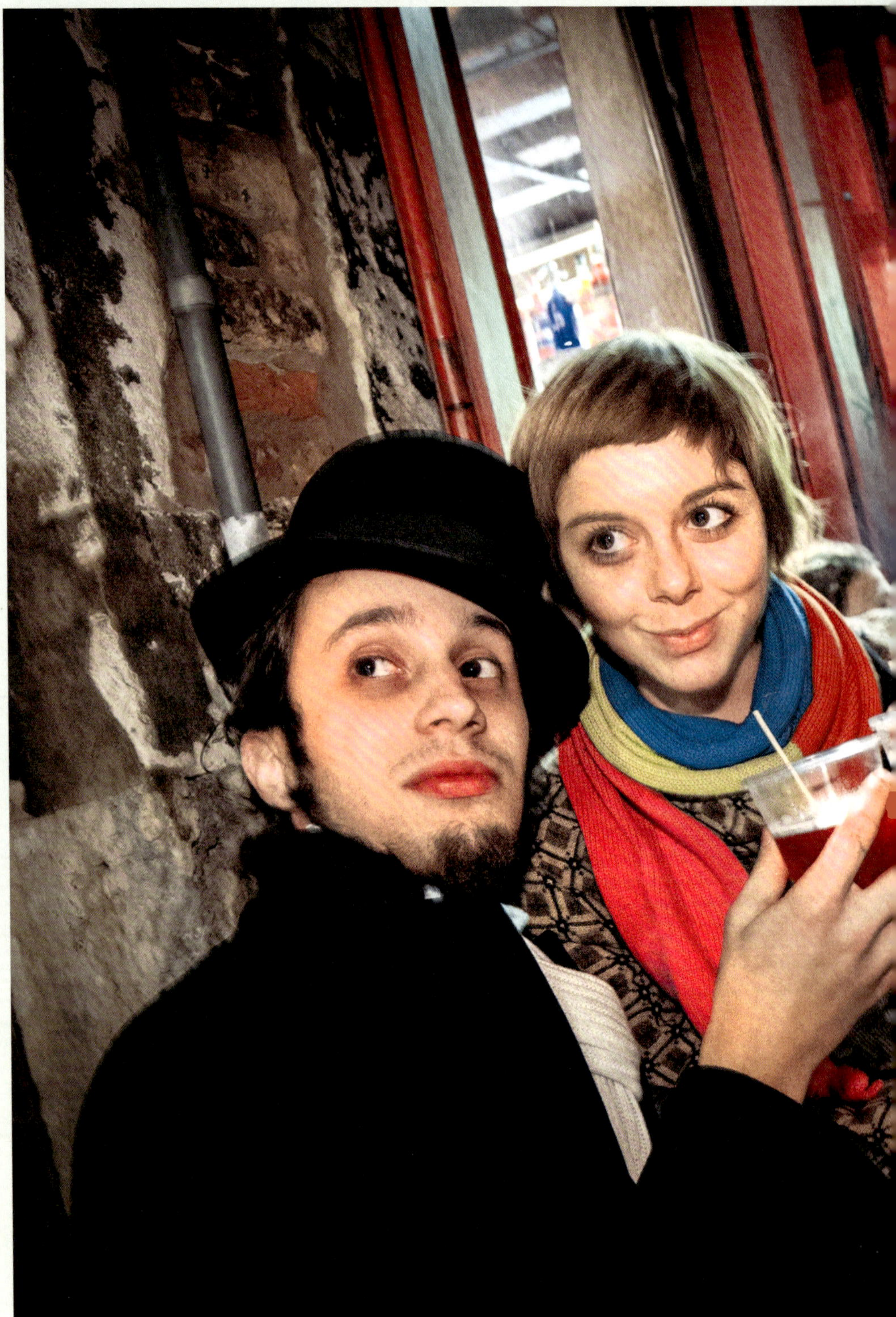

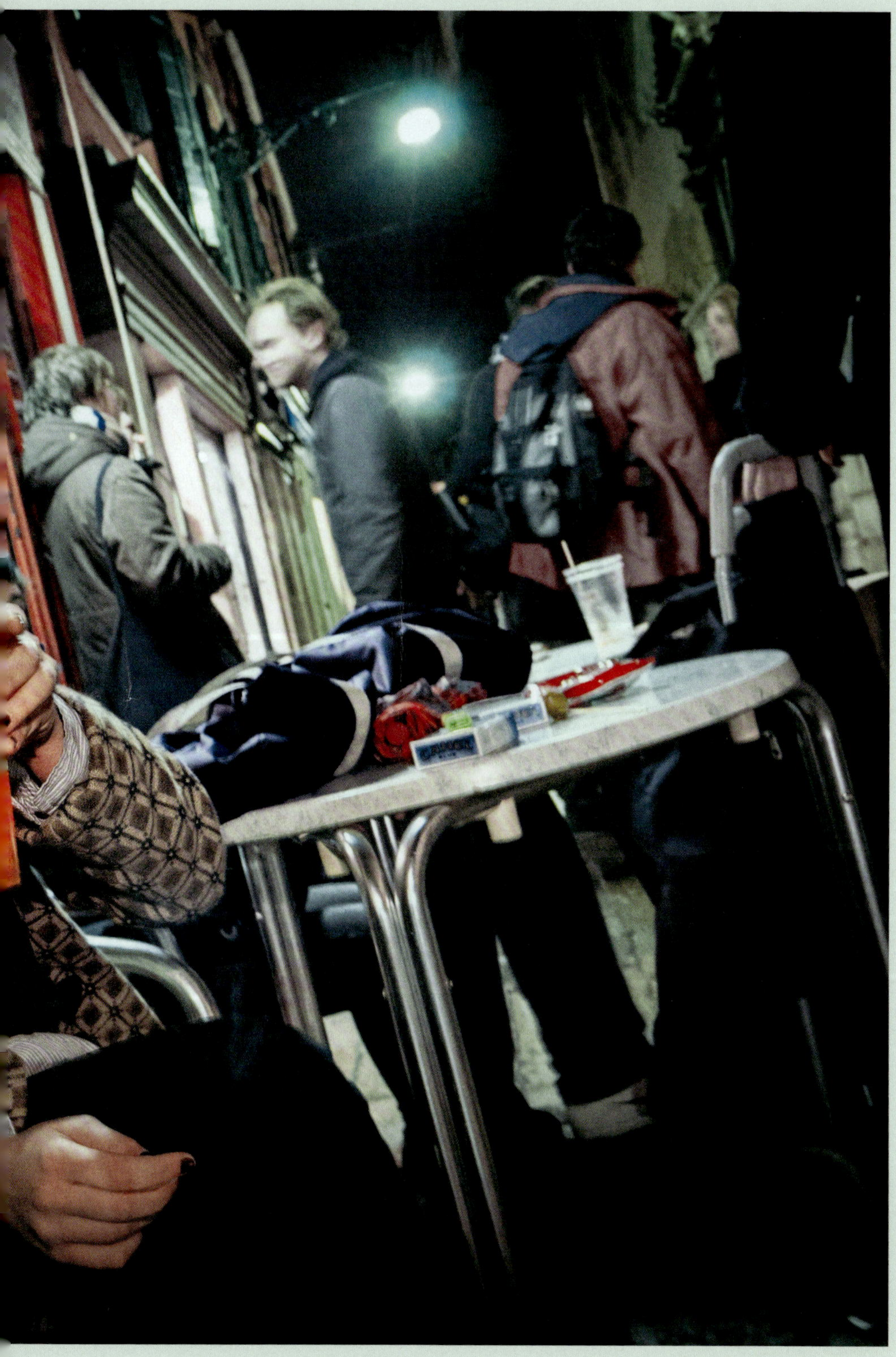

SCROPPINO

AFTER MEALS OR MID-MEAL

2 mini scoops of lemon ice cream
3 cl. (1 oz) Vodka
10 cl. (3 2/4 oz) Prosecco

PREPARATION

In an electric mixer or by hand, mix the ice cream with the vodka and 5 cl. (1¾ oz)of Prosecco, pour into a champagne flute and add the last 5 cl. (1¾ oz) of Prosecco.
Stir gently.

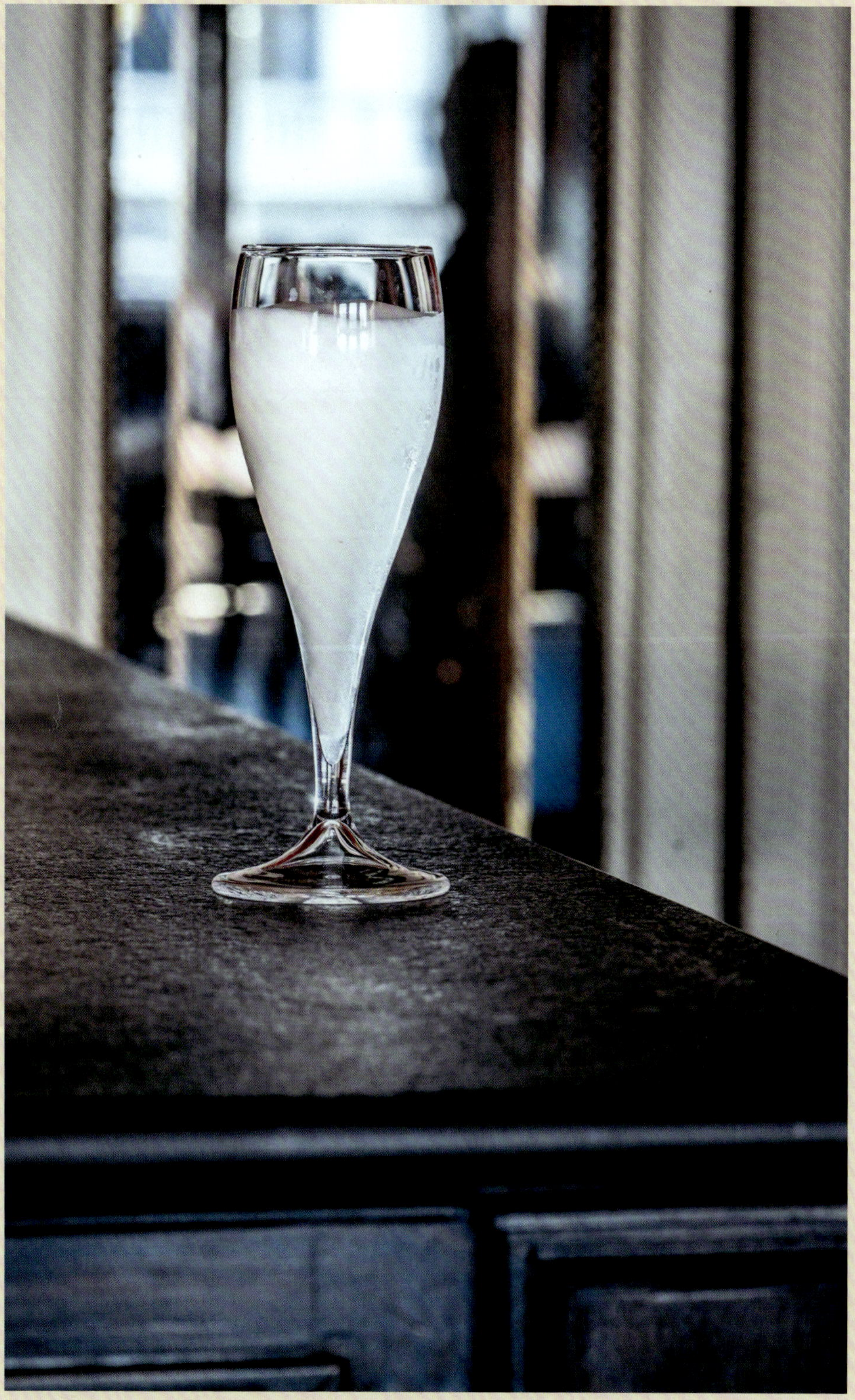

SPRITZ DEI MILLE

APERITIF

5 cl. (1¾ oz) orange juice
2 cl. (¾ oz) Bitter Campari
8 cl. (2¾ oz) Prosecco
Garnish with a ½ slice of orange and a cherry

PREPARATION

Put the ingredients in the glass and stir gently.

Curious fact

This is my personal version of the Garibaldi, to which I add Prosecco. It is rather more alcoholic than the classic version, but you can vary the amount of spumante.

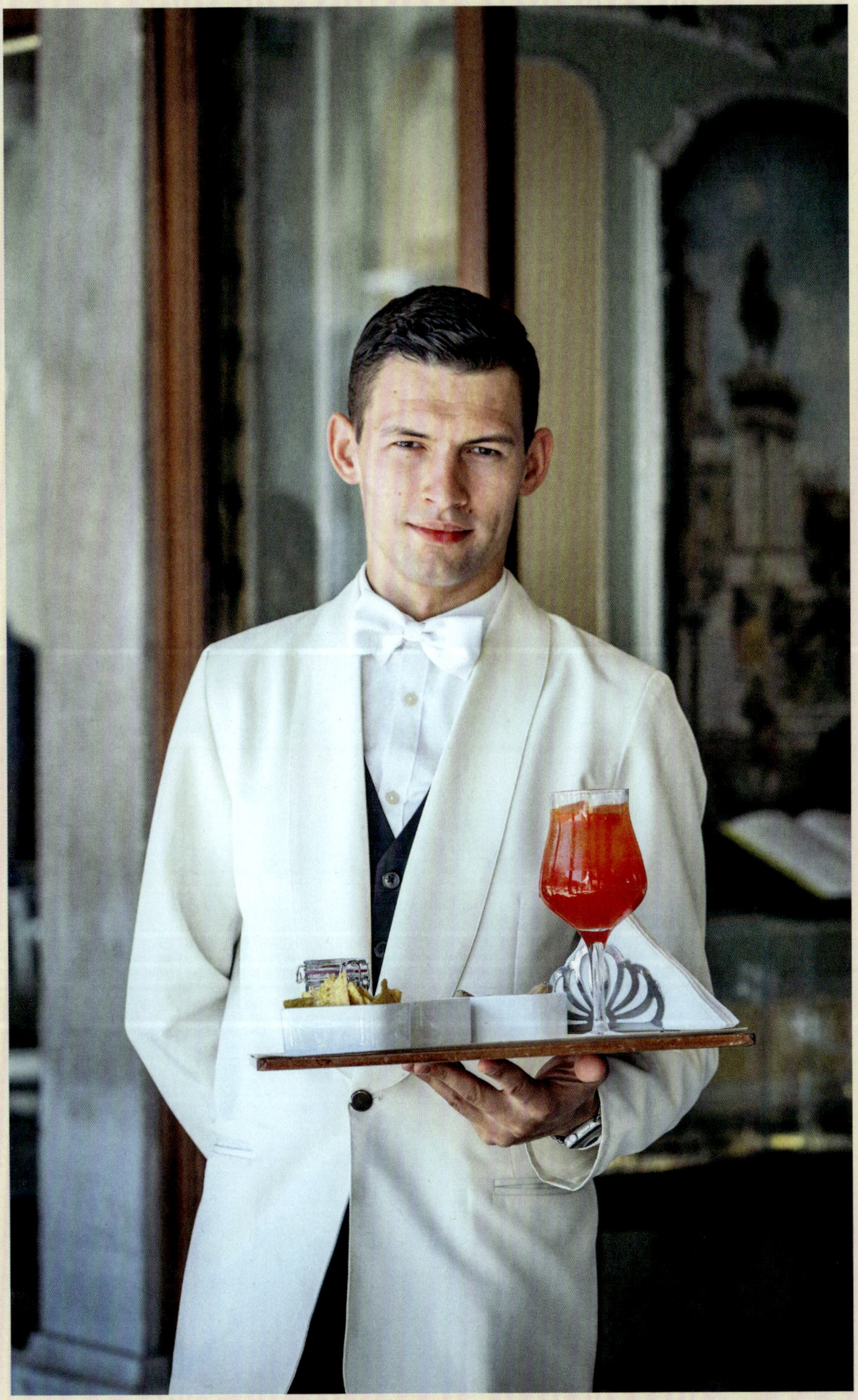

CASANOVA

APERITIF

5 cl. (1¾ oz) passion fruit juice
1 cl. (¼ oz) sugar syrup
1 cl. (¼ oz) Bitter Campari
8 cl. (2¾ oz) Prosecco
Garnish imaginatively

PREPARATION
Shake the first 3 ingredients,
pour into the glass, add the Prosecco.
Stir gently.

Curious fact
Passion fruit is always intriguing. It is used fresh because it is available all the year round, being an imported fruit. It arrives unripe and it is important to allow it to ripen fully until the skin wrinkles.

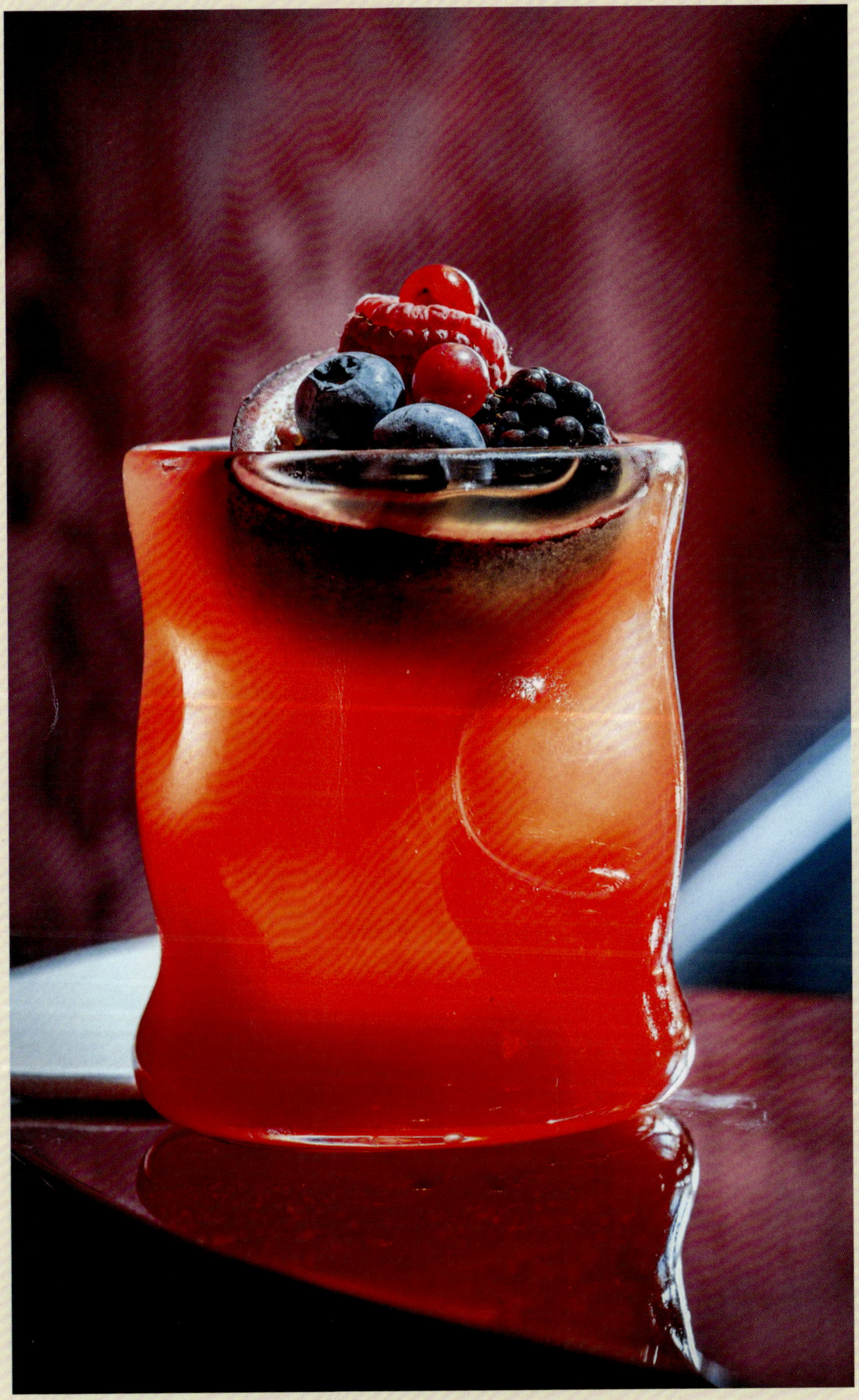

GOLDEN SPRITZ

APERITIF

7 cl. (2 2⁄4 oz) juice from Golden Delicious apples
2 cl. (3⁄4 oz) Vodka
7 cl. (2 2⁄4 oz) Prosecco
Garnish with apple slices

PREPARATION

Pour the ingredients straight into the glass.
Stir gently.

Curious fact

I often use apple because it is one of the fragrances characteristic of Prosecco's sensory profile. It does not alter the taste of the sparkling wine.

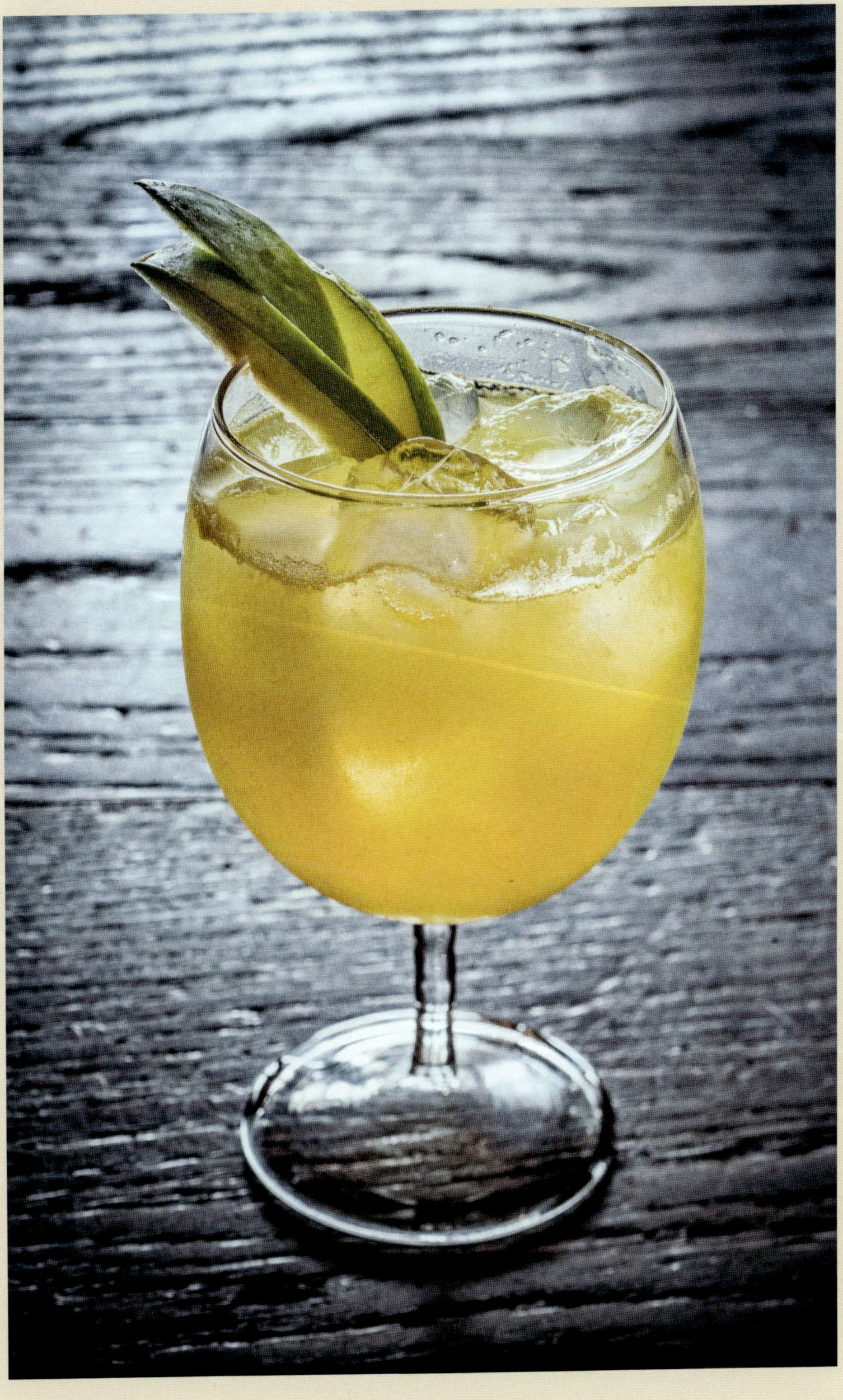

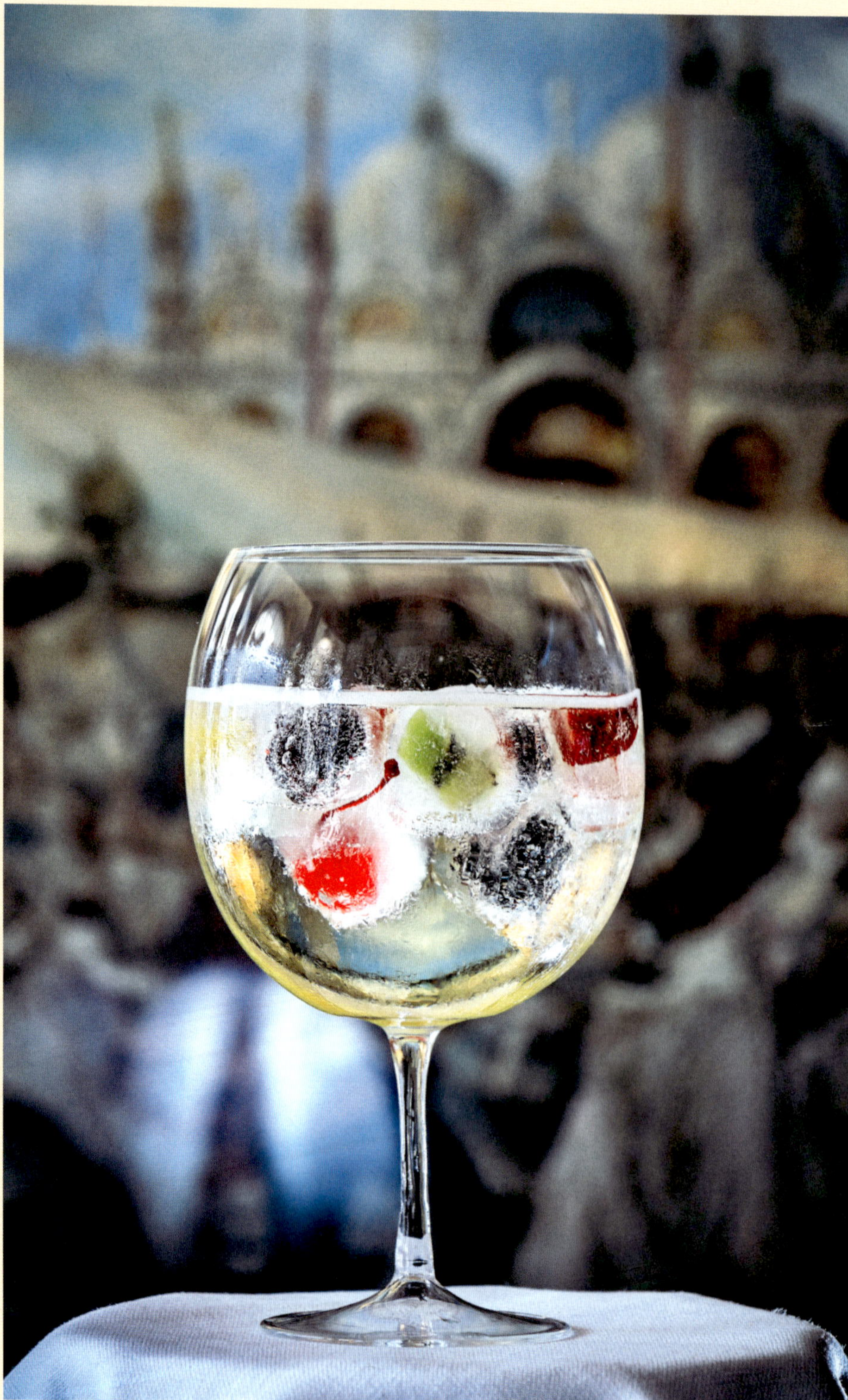

BELVEDERE

APERITIF

2 cl. (¾ oz) Triple Sec
3 cl. (1 oz) Vodka
10 cl. (3¾) Prosecco
Ice cubes with fruit

PREPARATION

Pour the ingredients straight into the glass, add the ice cubes with fruit.

Curious fact

This cocktail looks stunning, colored with ice cubes with fruit. Just use your fantasy and add any fruit: pineapple, kiwi, apples, pears, cherries, strawberries, blueberries, blackberries, bananas. Use a balloon-type glass, which is capacious.

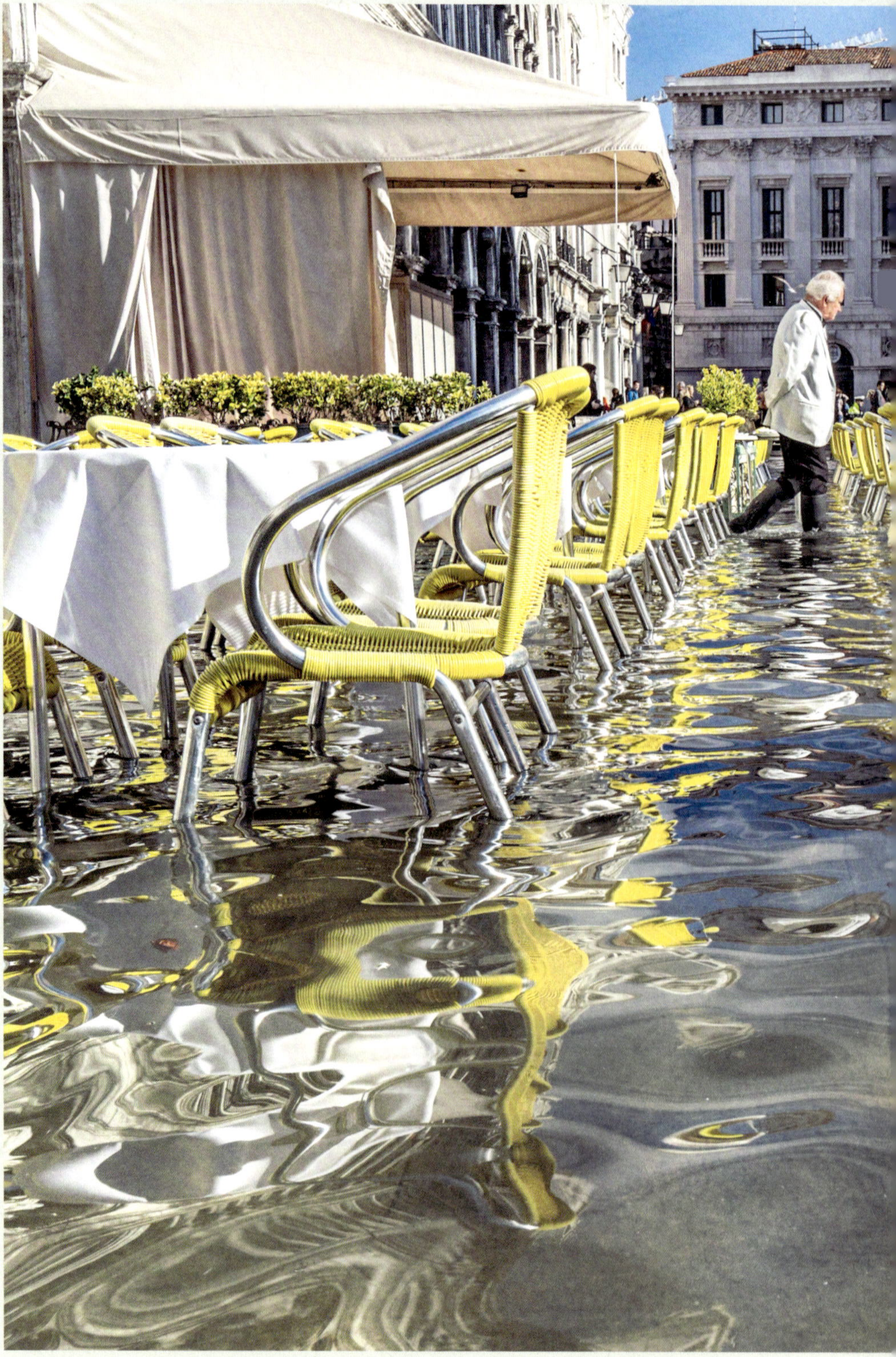

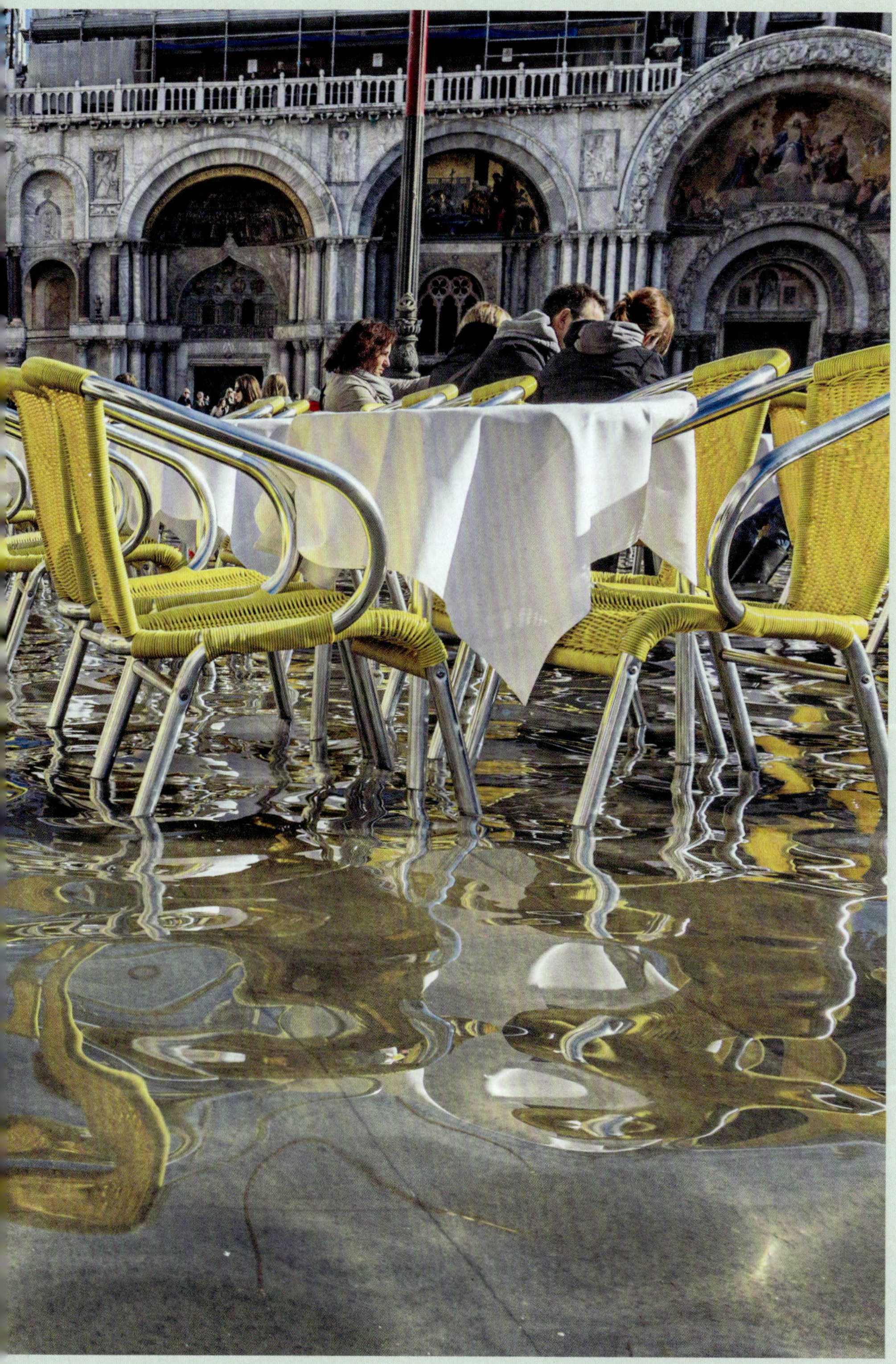

NEGRONI SBAGLIATO

APERITIF

3 cl. (1 oz) red Vermouth
3 cl. (1 oz) Bitter Campari
3 cl. (1 oz) Prosecco
Garnish with a ½ slice of orange

PREPARATION
Pour the ingredients straight into an old fashioned glass.

Curious fact
This cocktail owes its invention to an error. It happened at the Bar Basso in Milan back in the seventies. It seems the owner Mirko Stocchetto had popped out and a group of friends ordered a Negroni. In the barman's absence, the waiter mixed the aperitifs but instead of gin he used Prosecco. And his mistake proved a great hit!

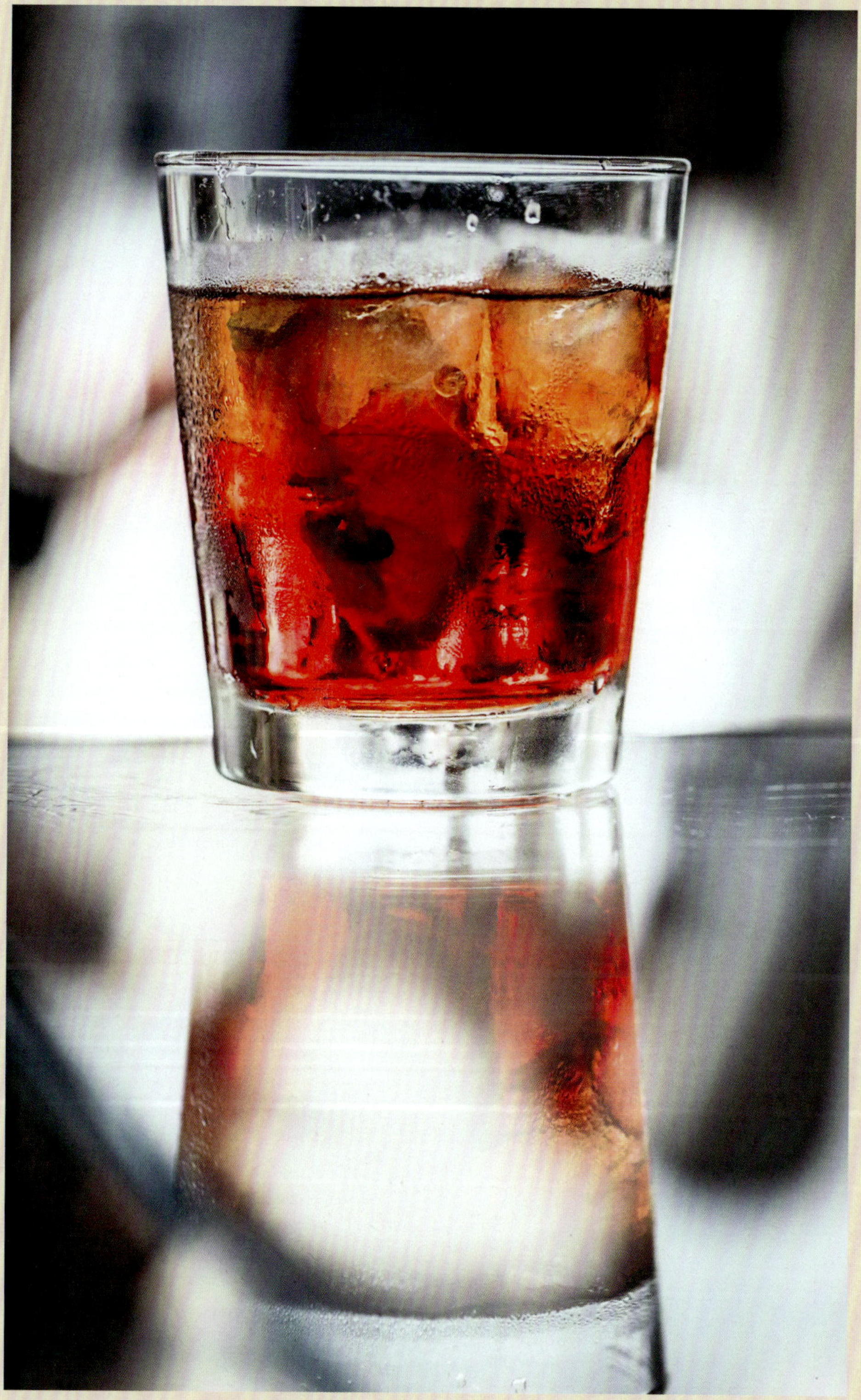

SOGNI DI UNA NOTTE D'ESTATE

LONG DRINK

4 cl. (1¼ oz) cranberry juice
4 cl. (1¼ oz) orange juice
1 cl. (¼ oz) peach liqueur
11 cl. (3¾ oz) Prosecco
Garnish with a slice of orange and a cherry

PREPARATION

Shake the first 3 ingredients, pour them in a tumbler, add the Prosecco and ice.

Curious fact

This is a personal variation of the Sex on the Beach cocktail, with Prosecco instead of vodka.

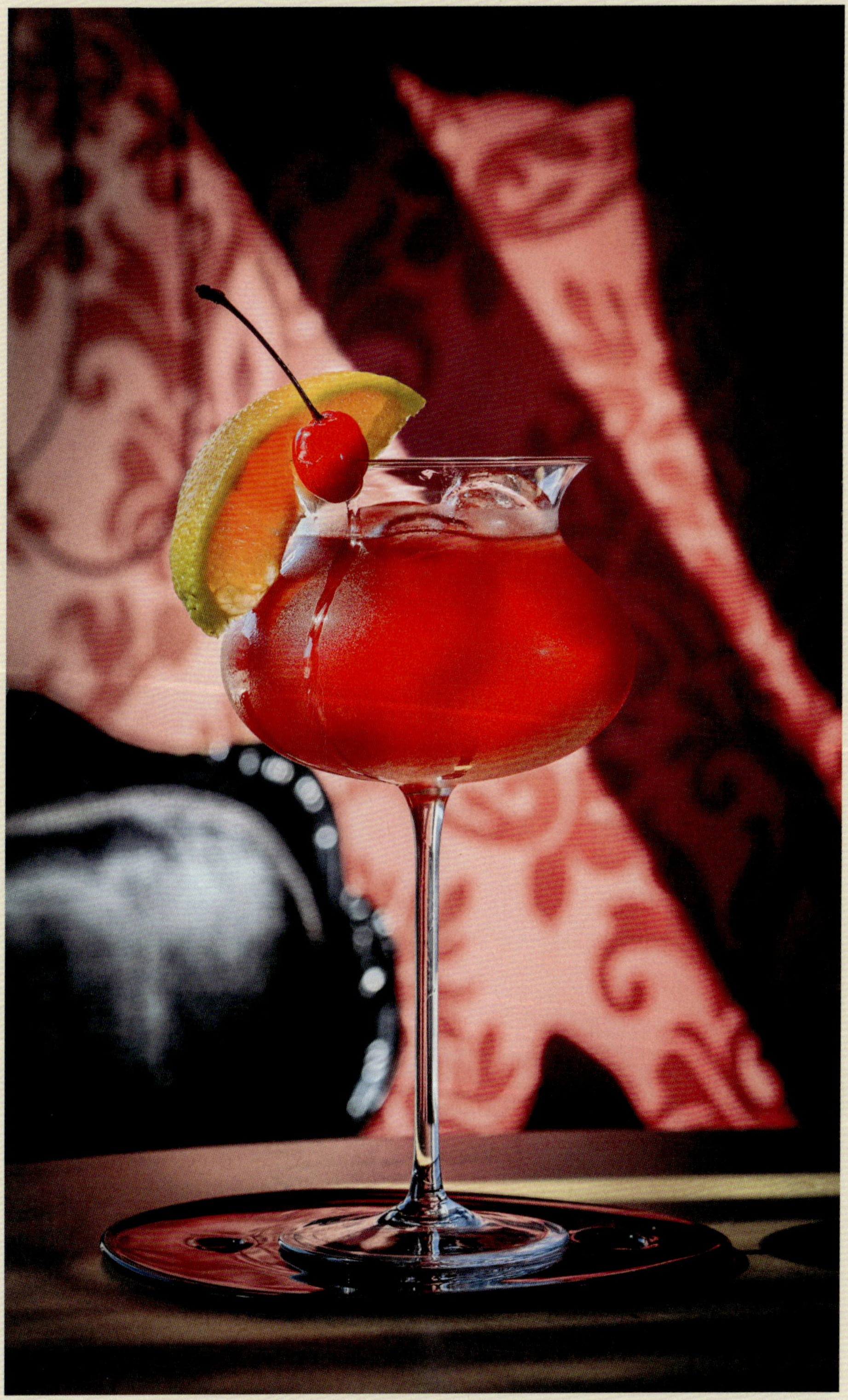

SPRITZ MORLACCO

APERITIF

2 cl. (¾ oz) Cherry Brandy
1 cl. (¼ oz) vodka
12 cl. (4 oz) Prosecco

PREPARATION

Pour the ingredients straight into the glass. Stir gently.

Curious fact

Luxardo Cherry Brandy is also called "Sangue Morlacco." Gabriele D'Annunzio invented the name when he occupied Fiume (Split) in 1919. After the battle, he was offered a glass of cherry brandy, which in poetic vein he metaphorically dubbed "sangue Morlacco." The Morlachs are a people of the Dalmatian hinterland.

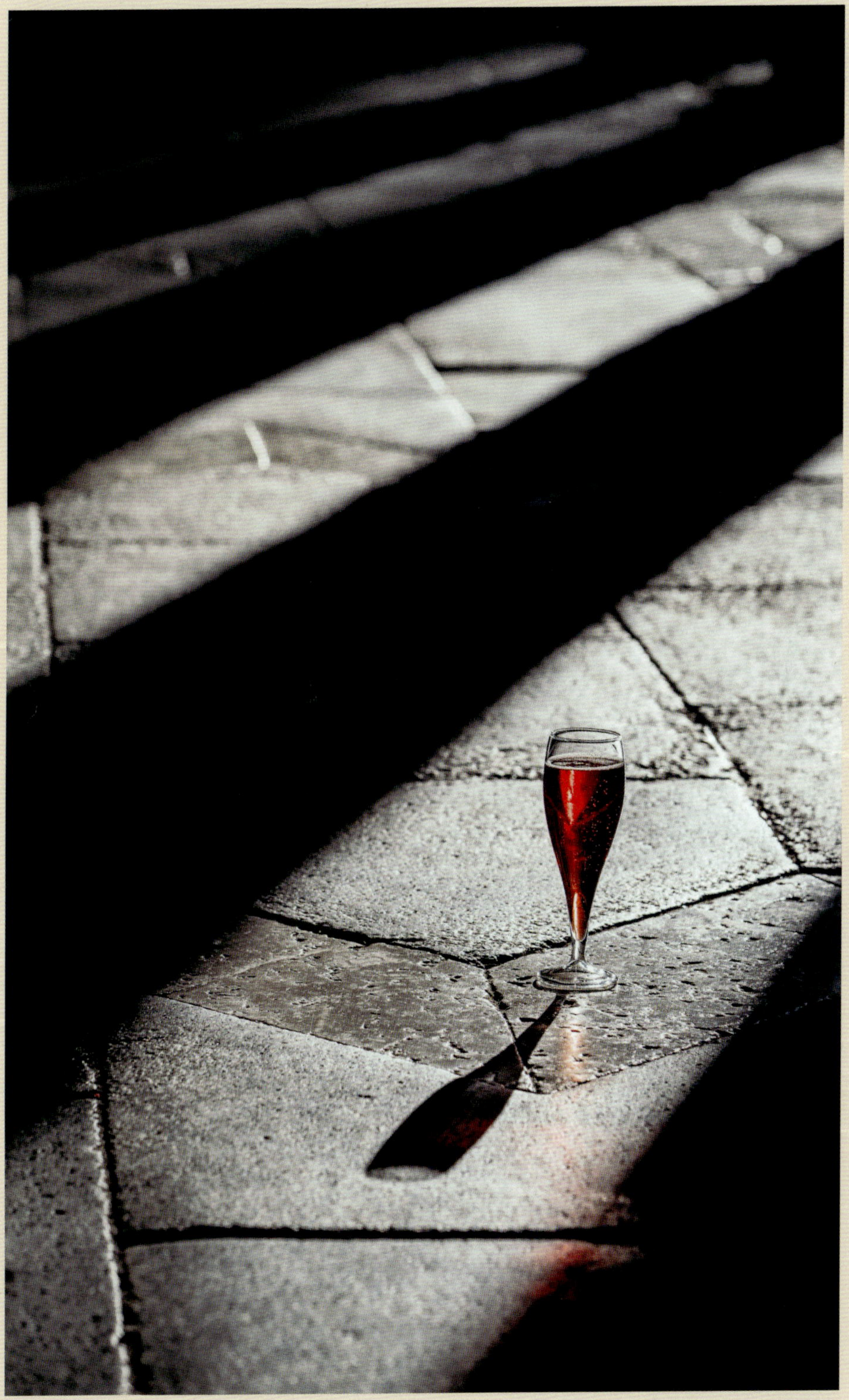

VENETIAN 17

AFTER MEALS

3 cl. (1 oz) Gin
1.5 cl. (2⁄4 oz) lime juice
1 cl. (¼ oz) sugar syrup
11 cl. (3¾ oz) Prosecco
Garnish with a slice of lime

PREPARATION

Pour the Prosecco into the glass.
Shake the first 3 ingredients and add them to the Prosecco.
Stir gently.

Curious fact

This is a personal variant of a French 75, with Prosecco instead of Champagne.

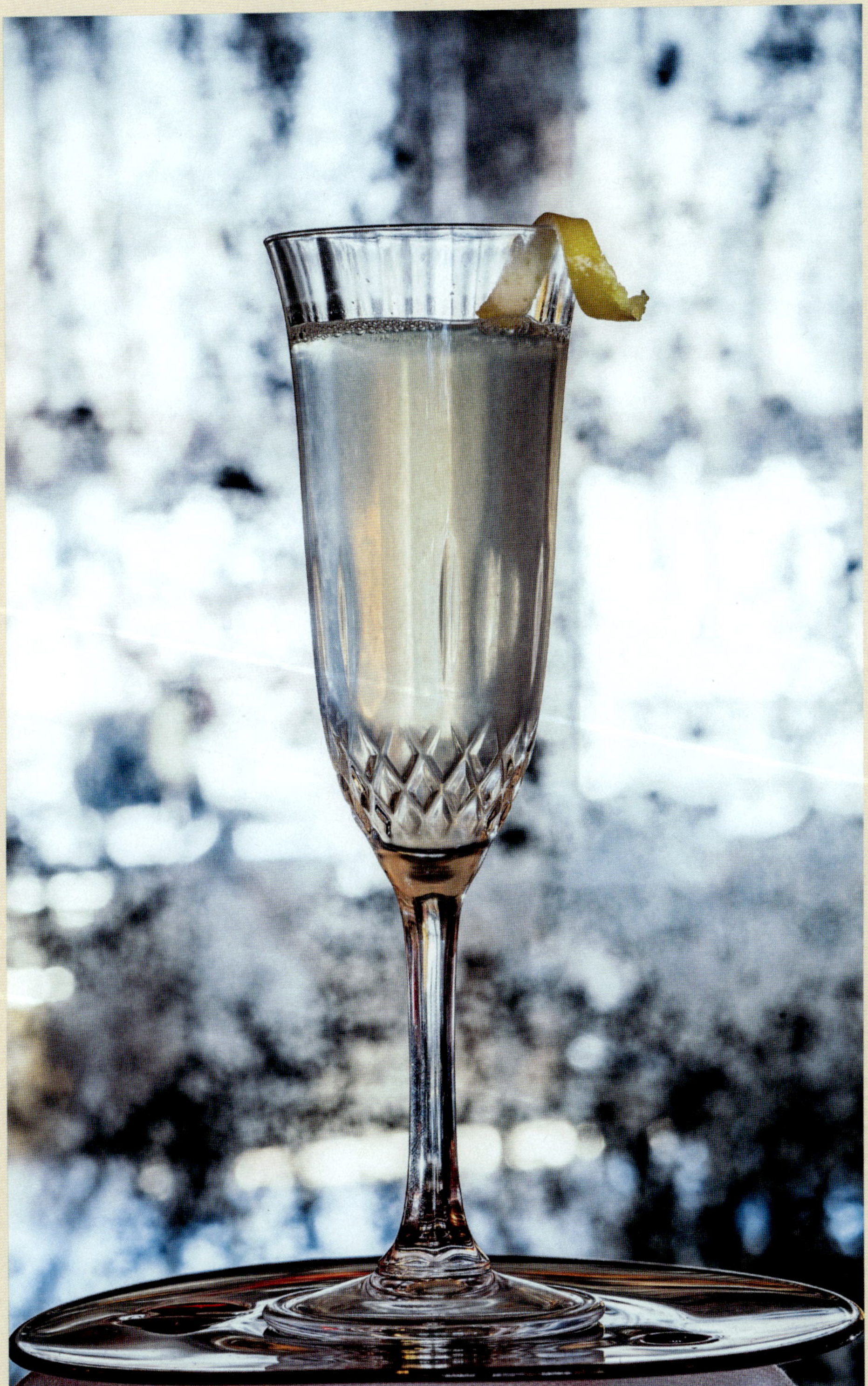

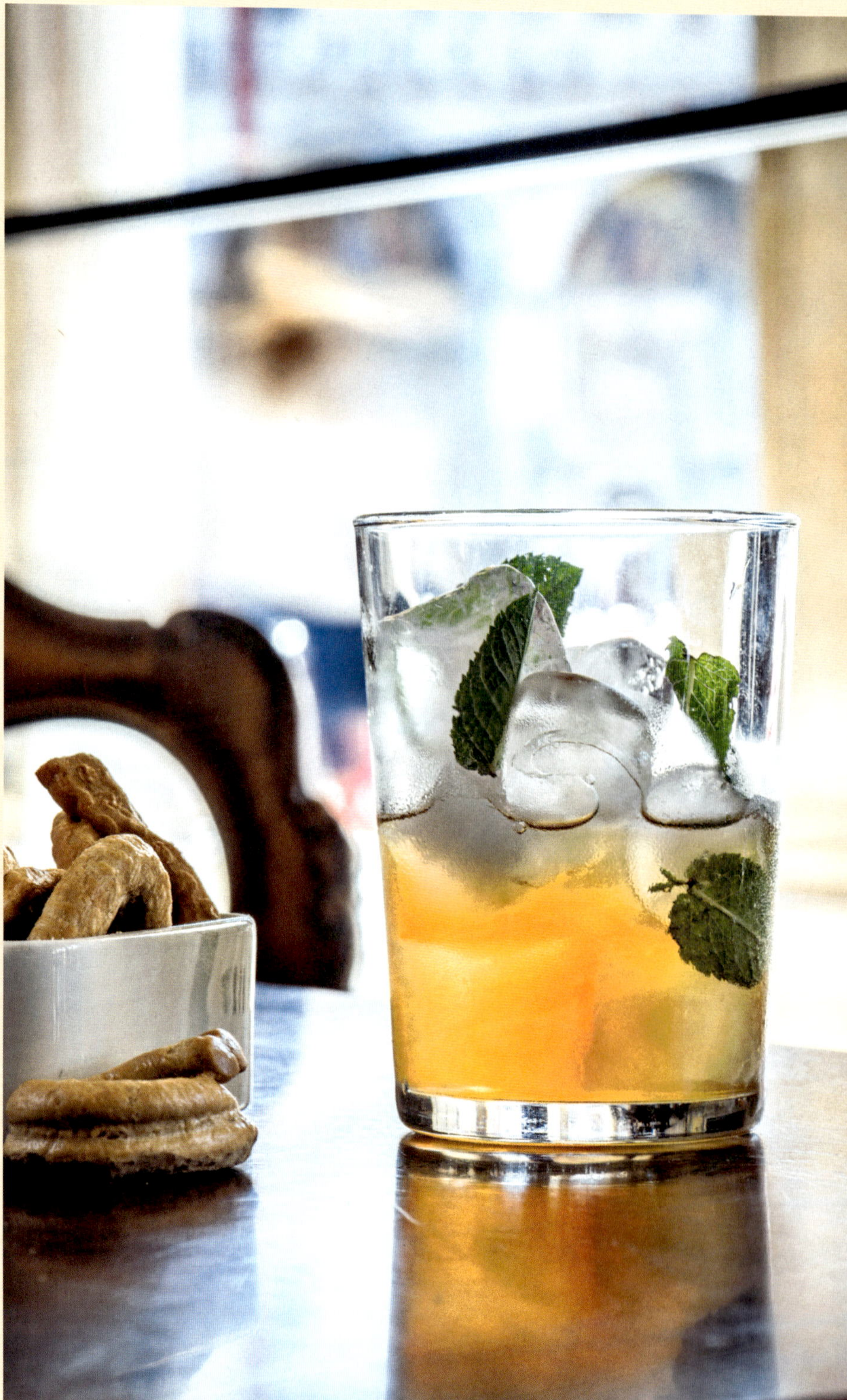

GUGLIELMO TELL

AFTER MEALS

3 cl. (1 oz) Calvados
3 cl. (1 oz) apple juice
0.5 cl. (2/4 oz) liquid sugar
3 mint leaves
12 cl. (4 oz) Prosecco
Garnish with a sprig of mint

PREPARATION

Put the first 4 ingredients in the glass and stir for a few seconds. Add the Prosecco, gently stir and fill the glass with ice.

LEONARDO CISOTTO

Leonardo Cisotto was born sixty years ago in the Bassa Padovana. His parents wanted him to go to university, but he felt no urge to study. So, as his uncle had a trattoria, he decided to go to hotel school. He alternated study and work. He enjoyed being with people. He completed the school and gained the diploma so longed-for (by his mother and father). Luck smiled on him and he gained work experience in a grand hotel in Venice, the Hotel Bauer. He worked as a waiter for six and a half hours a day, with occasional Saturdays and Sundays off. He earned more than many a father of a family who got up at five in the morning to do a ten-hour shift in a factory. Working as a waiter in the hotel, he would see the bartender talking to famous TV personalities. He was fascinated and decided that would be the work for him. They advised him to look for a job in Cortina and so he did. There he had his second stroke of luck. He met a bartender who took him under his wing, like a father, and passed on a passion for the work. Between ups and downs, he made his way in his chosen career. In 1996 he won the Italian bartenders' championship and was signed up by an important multinational that marketed aperitifs and sparkling wines. Moving between the Venice Film Festival, Twiga at Forte dei Marmi and Flavio Briatore's Billionaire nightclub, those were the roaring years. He even found time to teach school and hold classes. He would end his working career at the very top, as head bartender of Grancaffè Quadri in Venice.

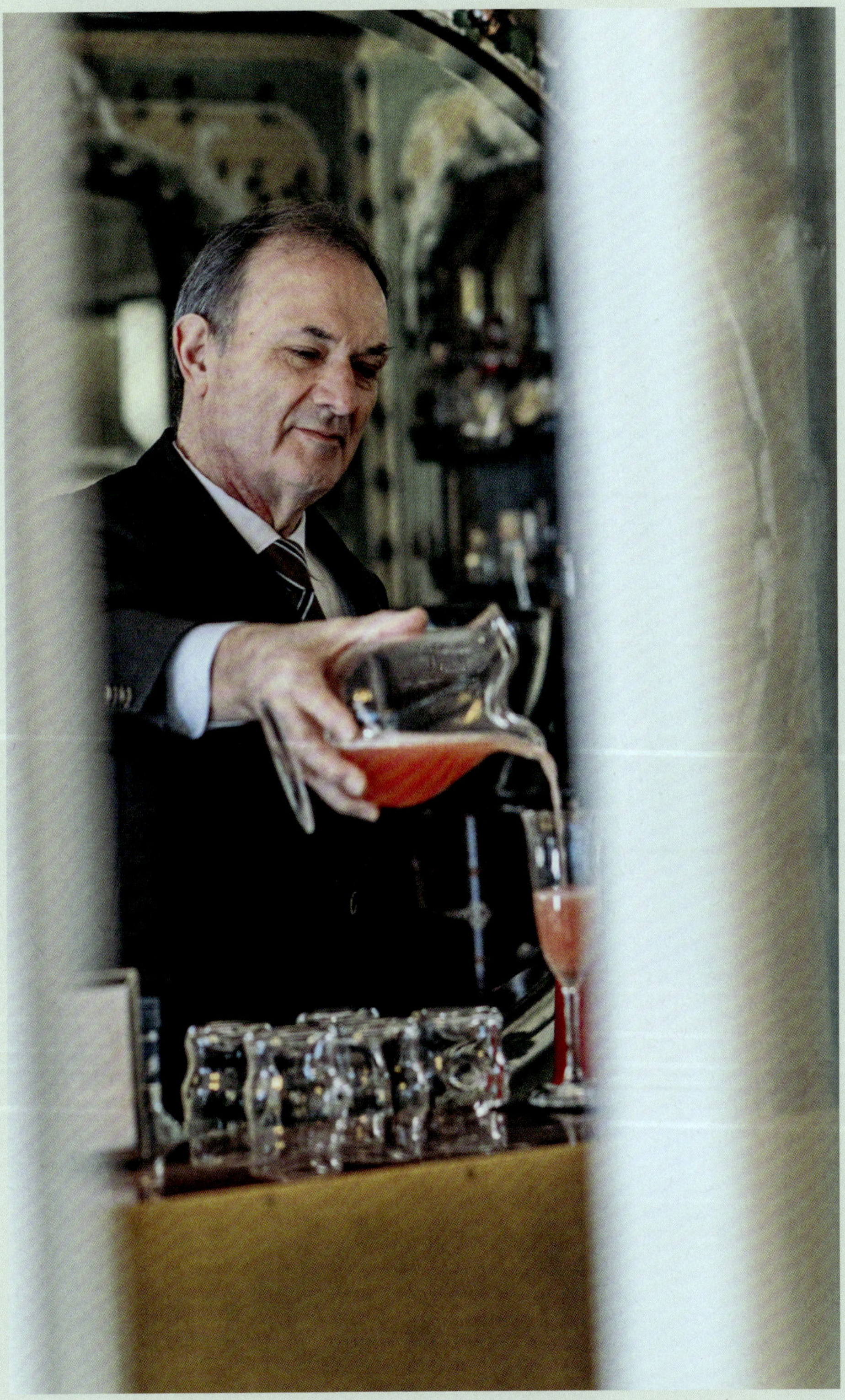

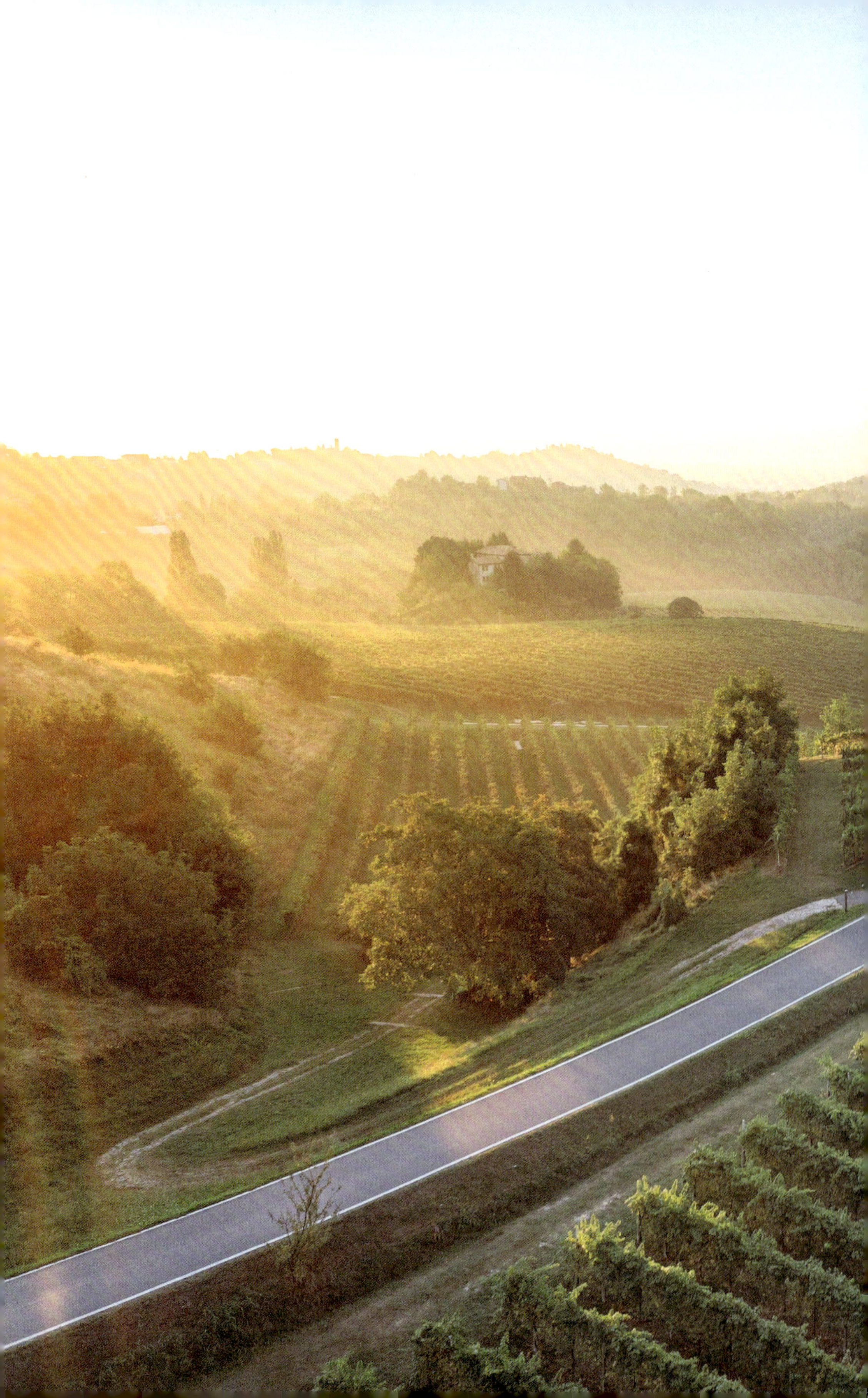

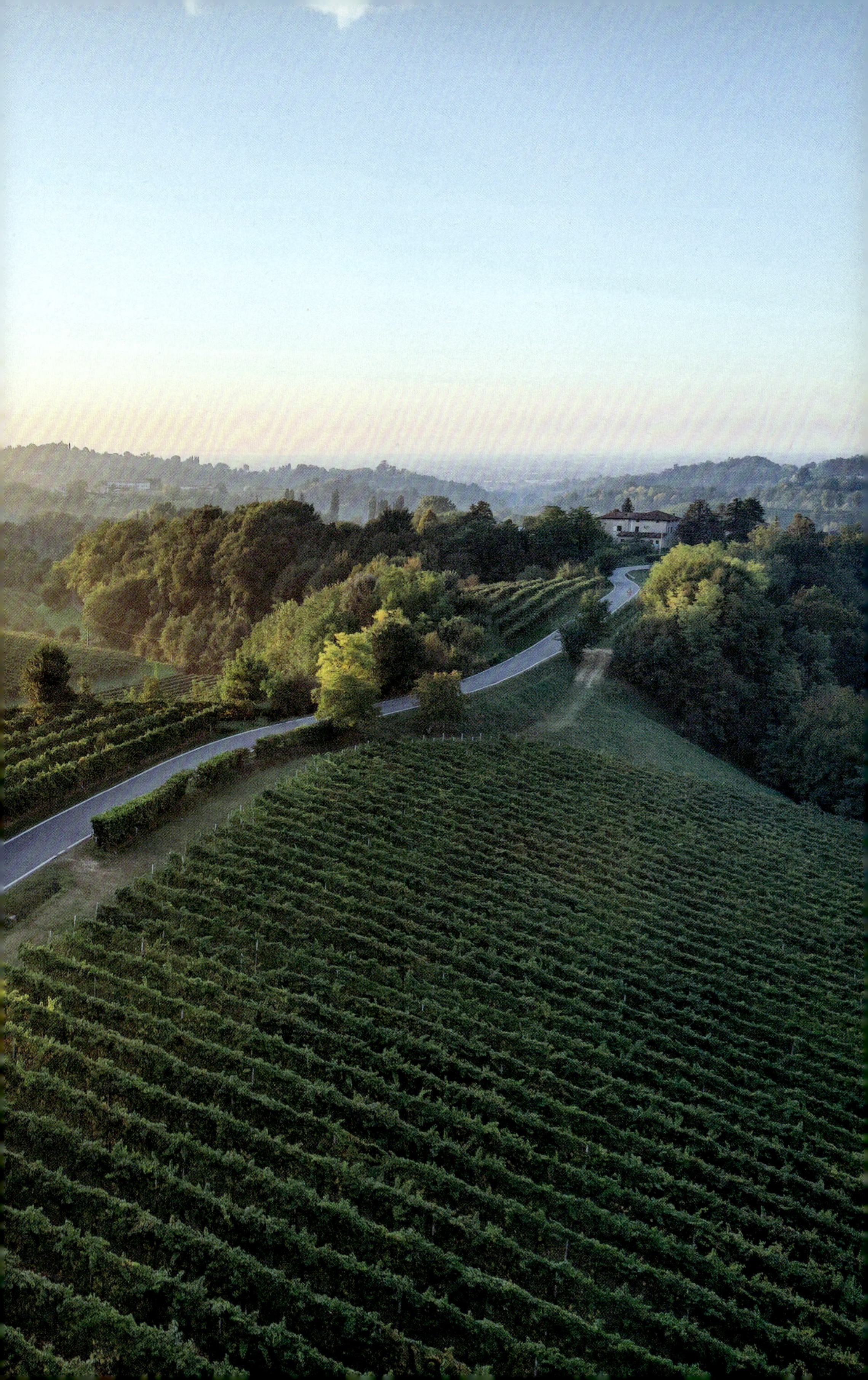

Text
Elisa Giraud
Translation
Richard Sadleir
Photo Editor
Giovanni Simeone
Illustration
Monica Parussolo
Design
What! Design
Layout
Jenny Biffis
Prepress
Fabio Mascanzoni

All images were taken by **Arcangelo Piai** except for:
Guido Baviera p. 24, Manfred Bortoli p. 76, p. 176-177, Matteo Caressale p. 120(1), p. 148, Stefano Cellai p. 68, Franco Cogoli p. 44(2), p. 67, p. 117(1). p. 121, Guido Cozzi p. 113, p. 114, Gabriele Croppi p. 112, Luca Da Ros p. 14-15, p. 20, p. 52-53, p. 61, p. 117 (1), Colin Dutton p. 17, p. 42, p. 44(1), p.50, p. 72, p. 78(2), p. 79, p. 81, p. 120(1), Olimpio Fantuz p. 2-3, p. 5, p. 26-27, p. 78(1), p. 84, Cesare Gerolimetto p. 82-83, Laurent Grandadam p. 120(1), Luca Gusso p. 36, Johanna Huber p. 6-7, Lisa Linder p. 16, p. 156, Guillem Lopez p. 140, Nicolò Miana p. 30, Joe Murador p. 149, Aldo Pavan p. 117(2), p. 157, Sandra Raccanello p. 78(1), p. 120(1), Stefano Renier p. 105, Anna Serrano p. 132-133, Giovanni Simeone p. 10-11, p. 29, p. 60, p. 93, p. 180, p 124

Photos available on **www.simephoto.com**

First Edition February 2018
ISBN: 978-88-99180-92-8

SIME BOOKS
www.simebooks.com

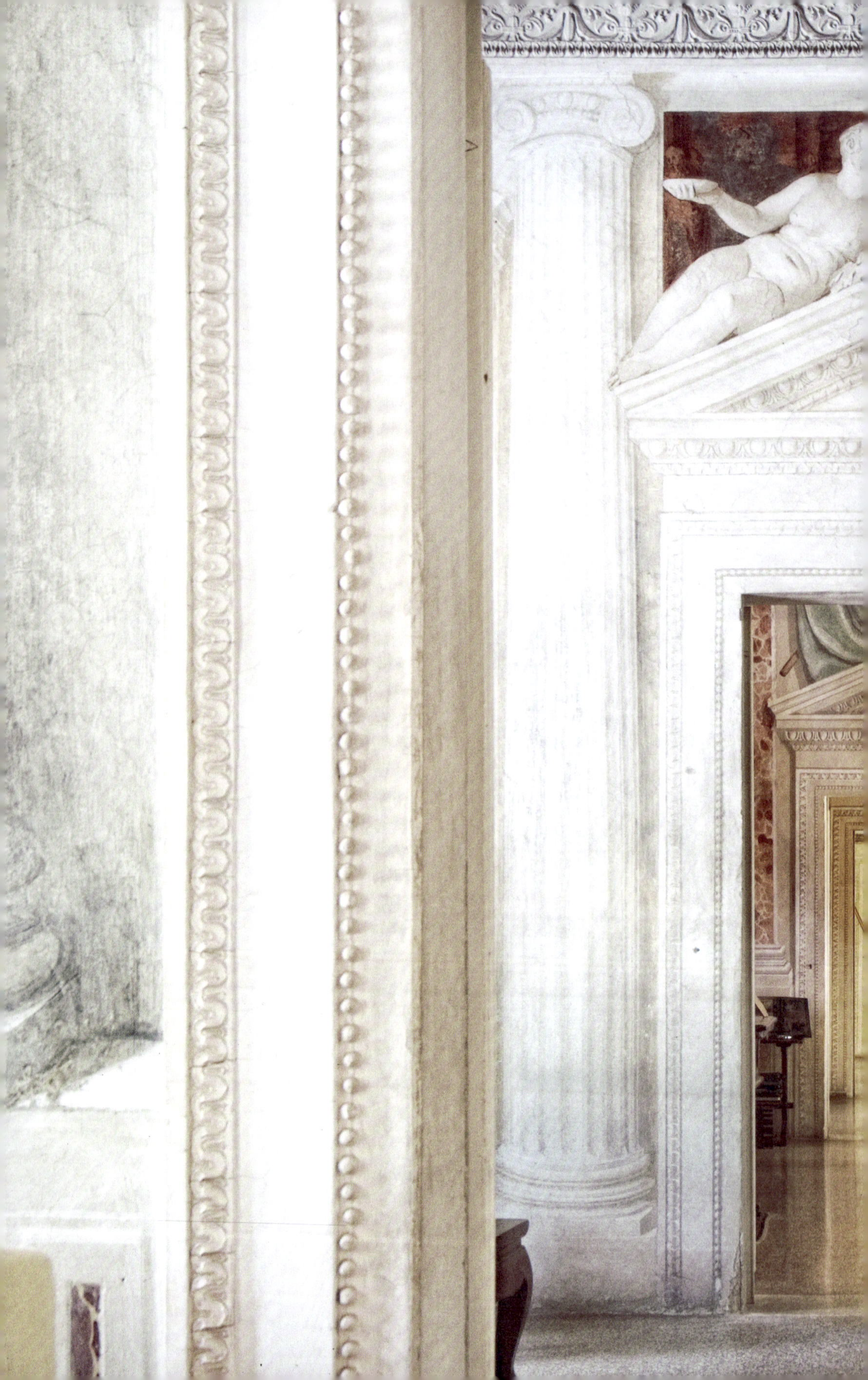